Transformative Education
Personal Construct Approaches
to Practice and Research

Transformative Education

Personal Construct Approaches to Practice and Research

MAUREEN L POPE AND PAMELA M DENICOLO

Department of Professional Education in Community Studies
University of Reading

W

WHURR PUBLISHERS

LONDON AND PHILADELPHIA

© 2001 Whurr Publishers
First published 2001 by
Whurr Publishers Ltd
19b Compton Terrace, London N1 2UN, England and
325 Chestnut Street, Philadelphia PA 1906, USA

British Library Cataloguing in Publication Data
A catalogue record for this book is available from the
British Library.

ISBN: 186156 201 2

Printed and bound by CPI Antony Rowe, Eastbourne

Contents

Foreword   ix
Prologue   xi
Acknowledgements   xix

Chapter 1   1

Alternative perspectives on education

Chapter 2   23

Personal construct psychology approaches in education

Chapter 3   47

Alternative constructions of educational research

Chapter 4   66

Practical considerations in the use of repertory grid techniques

Chapter 5   91

Beyond the grid

Chapter 6   121

Developing an appropriate climate

Chapter 7   132

The learner as personal scientist

Chapter 8   **157**

Teachers' perspectives

Chapter 9   **197**

Anticipation and transformation

References   **207**
Index   **219**

Dedication

To Adrian and Kathlyn, Marie-Anne and Paul, who have been a constant source of constructive revitalization.

Foreword

BY PROFESSOR MICHAEL KOMPF

Groucho Marx was once asked to review a book on comedy. He wrote: 'I was convulsed with laughter from the moment I picked up this book. I hope to read it some day.' I admire Marx's sentiment and have waited for years to find an opportunity to include his clever remark in such a place as the foreword to a book.

As Marx was 'convulsed with laughter' when he picked up a book on comedy, readers can sometimes be 'tickled with anticipation' when the opportunity arises to pick up the works of exceptional contributors to the theory and practice of teaching and learning. *Transformative Education: Personal Construct Approaches to Practice and Research* is such a book. Building on an impressive array of individual and joint projects, the dynamic collaboration of Maureen Pope and Pam Denicolo has taken a long-awaited further step in applying the principles of Personal Construct Psychology (PCP) to the heart of teaching and learning: the practical and theoretical thinking of teachers.

There is evidence of the influence of PCP in teachers' practices throughout the world, an accomplishment in no small part fostered by such luminaries as Pope and Denicolo. Exposure to PCP through its application to a variety of matters in education has created an increasing flow of students of the broader work of George Kelly and the overall PCP movement. Kelly would have acknowledged 'the person the learner is' as the foremost concern of the constructivist educator.

This work stands as an invitation for educators to understand PCP and use it as a valuable orientation for understanding aspects of learning and teaching. It serves double duty in that it also acts as an invitation for PCP adherents outside of the practice of education to see PCP as a theory in action and as a theory of action.

Pope and Denicolo approach this important task in much the same way as they each approach life: with simplicity, practicality and style. The book addresses the three issues of theory, technique and practice. From the beginning of the book the reader is taken on an exploration. Chapter 1 ('Alternative perspective on education') includes discussions of philosophy, professional development and the roles of learner and teacher. Chapter 2 ('Personal construct psychology approaches in education') introduces the principles of PCP as an aspect of constructivism, and deals with learner implications and the relativity of knowledge. Chapter 3 ('Alternative constructions of educational research') explores the foundations of PCP for interpretative research and examines the other possible worlds of meaning within research strategies and applications.

Next the reader is introduced to the practicalities of PCP. Chapter 4 ('Practical considerations in the use of repertory grid techniques') discusses its purpose, procedures and analyses in addition to suggestions and caveats. Chapter 5 ('Beyond the grid') shows the other side of PCP and includes reflection, narrative techniques, and examination of experiences and using other perspectives for interpretation. Some valuable caveats are presented in Chapter 6. The reader is brought into the PCP fold in Chapter 7 ('The learner as personal scientist') through the use of research examples drawn from, intra alia, science education, language learning and the needs of special children. Chapter 8 ('Teachers' perspectives') considers the teacher as learner, as constructivist negotiator and the potential for teacher transformations by examining appraisal and staff development. Chapter 9 ('Anticipation and transformation') brings this marvellous series of teachings full circle by encouraging the reader to consider alternative ways of operating within an educational framework, coping with constraints and initiating change.

This book is necessary for theorists, administrators, veteran practitioners, new teachers and graduate students and anyone else who wishes to take seriously the challenges in dealing with personal, professional and environmental changes in education throughout the world. As information technology creeps into educational systems, the responsibilities of teachers and learners to self, family and community will become more complex, intricate and puzzling. Applying the principles of PCP to the essence of learning and teaching can raise the levels of awareness that teachers bring to the classroom and enable them to take a more robust role in anticipating the future challenges in teaching and learning.

Professor Michael Kompf
Brock University, Canada
Chair of the International Study Association on Teachers and Teaching

Prologue

We have developed this book to meet the needs of educators across a range of sectors whose work involves them in developing their own knowledge and concepts and those of others. Our extensive experience of supporting teachers and learners to do this from within a framework of Personal Construct Psychology has encouraged us in this enterprise. We have drawn on this experience to produce a book which combines theory and practical guidance with suggestions and examples of applications of Personal Construct Psychology in educational settings.

The concept of 'transformation' appears in the title, and throughout the book, to acknowledge that the development of an alternative way of looking at practice and research can result in productive change which is intrinsic to the person instead of being imposed from without.

We argue that professionals and researchers have their own implicit theories of what constitutes effective education, training and practice. We begin in the book by examining various educational ideologies, each of which embody theories about the nature and development of the person. Any theory about teaching is inextricably linked to an underlying view or model of the nature of the learner. Each of these represent alternative views on education which may influence the lived experience of all those engaged in education and training, whatever their role in the process. As Personal Construct Psychologists we suggest that Personal Construct Psychology, developed from George Kelly's seminal work on Personal Construct Theory, provides a fruitful framework within which to explore education. In the book we share with you what we see are the implications of such an approach for practice in a range of learning environments. We also suggest that the approach has ramifications for research in and on practice. We have endeavoured to describe in detail a range of instruments that have been productively employed within interventions in such practice. Inevitably we have discussed the repertory grid technique, perhaps the most well-known technique emanating from Kelly's original work. However, we have also suggested a range of alternative techniques which are innovative methods consistent with a constructivist approach. Towards the end of the book the reader will find examples of applications of these approaches and techniques for the transformation of the knowledge and practice of learners and of teachers in a variety of educational contexts. We hope that these illustrative examples will stimulate readers to consider ways in which the approach and techniques may be implemented and adapted in their own professional contexts in order to address productively current problems and dilemmas relating to developments in education.

This is our interpretation of Personal Construct Psychology. It is drawn from our experience and our reading of the work of others. We have learnt a great deal from our students and colleagues and they have influenced what we have become as a result of our experiments with life.

In the book we draw attention to the role of biography as a research tool and as a technique that can be used in teaching and learning. We think it is proper, at this stage, to share with you some of the connecting threads in our own biographies that have salience for our construing of education, from the perspectives of learner and teacher. Readers will find in Chapter 5 some clues about how we explored our own memories using a technique called 'snakes' or 'rivers of life' to lift out those incidents which have special significance for who we have become as teachers who learn.

Maureen Pope

One of my first memories: I can still recollect many of my experiences at primary school and my favourite teacher. However, I shall begin with my experience in the Sixth Form which was probably one of the precursors of my interest in science education. I went to an all-girls school. Three of us wanted to do physics 'A' levels alongside chemistry and biology. There was only one problem – physics was not on the syllabus at that school. In those days, in Northern Ireland, it was deemed improper for three young ladies to attend the local boys' school so we were bussed 13 miles to a neighbouring town where there was a co-educational establishment offering physics 'A' level. All three of us found this a liberating experience and we were taught by a teacher who respected our enquiring minds. How we looked forward to those weekly trips. Things took a different turn when I went to university armed with three good 'A' levels in physics, chemistry and biology. It seemed to everyone, myself included, that reading for a Pure Science degree was my destiny. In my first year the students were faced with the fact that the chemistry nomenclature was changing. When I asked why this was the case, I was told 'Just learn it, you do not need to know why.' Disillusioned with this response I found myself drawn to psychology which was offered as a fourth, but incidental, subject. I was soon drawn to this subject and neglected my chemistry. I decided to withdraw. I had met my future husband, an Englishman and we decided to move to England. We soon had two young additions to the family, our son Adrian and our daughter Kathlyn, who have given us great joy over the years. However I was keen to resume work and contribute to something beyond the homefront.

After a period teaching in kindergarten I resumed university studies at Brunel University, this time studying – you guessed it – psychology. The psychology degree at Brunel was a four-year course and we had to spend up to six months working in an applied area of psychology. As I was interested in teaching I spent a term as a teaching assistant in a primary school. The conversations with the five year olds provided an insight into the stories they created to account for their experience. My next post was as an assistant psychologist at a 'subnormality' hospital. I was appalled at the constraints such an institution placed upon the development of the human potential of those in care. I realized, early on, that working in such an environment was not for me. The final placement was as a research assistant at the National Foundation for Educational Research. Now I found an activity which was to continue as a passion throughout my life!

On graduation, I was lucky enough to be awarded an ESRC quota award to continue my studies for a higher degree.

As an undergraduate I was introduced to Personal Construct Psychology although it was not until I studied for my PhD under the supervision of Laurie Thomas of the Centre for the Study of Human Learning at Brunel University that the full implications of this approach and its influence on my thinking became clear. As Beail (1985) noted, the Centre was one of the main institutions applying Personal Construct Theory and grid techniques in education. Pioneering work on the development of interactive computer packages for elicitation of repertory grids was carried out at that Centre. After a period of time researching and teaching within the Psychology department, in which the Centre for the Study of Human Learning was located, I obtained a post at the University of Surrey's Institute for Educational Development. I can remember the concerned expressed by the Head of the Psychology department at that time that I, as a good psychologist, was 'leaving the fold' and moving into education as an applied discipline rather than remaining closely tied to a psychology department. However, my move to Surrey was tinged with serendipity. Professor Lewis Elton, who led the Institute, had established regular courses on academic staff development. These were attended by lecturers from the UK and abroad. The constructivist approach to teaching and learning was welcomed at the Institute. I collaborated with John Gilbert researching teaching and learning in science education. We directed the Personal Construction of Knowledge Research Group whose work had a considerable impact on science education internationally. Pam Denicolo, a member of the group and one of my first postgraduate students, was to become a colleague and friend. Pam and I have published a number of books and articles together. We have also had the privilege of conducting workshops on teaching and learning, research methods, and Personal Construct Psychology in a wide range of institutions at home and world wide including South East Asia, Europe, Australia and America. We have shared many interesting adventures on these visits. In the early 1980s I became a founder member of the International Study Association on Teachers and Teaching (ISATT) and chaired the Association for some time. I am now a member of the Executive Panel. I have also acted as a convenor for the Guidance Panel of the European Personal Construct Association (EPCA). My work for these organizations has also had a profound impact on my research and thinking in the area of teaching and learning as conversations with many colleagues have inspired me to pursue new lines of enquiry.

Having spent 11 years at the University of Surrey it was time for change. I became Professor of Community Studies and Education and Head of the Department of Community Studies at the University of Reading. I was reunited once more with John Gilbert who had also become a professor at the University of Reading. John had established the Models in Science and Technology Research in Education (MISTRE) group. Although I retained an interest in science education and young people's conceptions in science, I had become more focused on teachers and teaching. The department I joined was engaged in the education of a wide range of professionals including community nurses, social workers, career guidance specialists, community and youth workers and counsellors. Inevitably this widened the scope of my teaching and research. Coming up to date, I have just completed a four-year term of office as Dean of the Faculty of Education and Community Studies. During this period of time I became acutely aware of the pressures facing teachers in schools. Many of my colleagues and students were wrestling the differences between their implicit theories of teaching and the requirements and constraints being imposed by government policies. Pam and I continued our PCP collaboration, but at a distance. However, a few years ago I was delighted that she was able to join the Department of Professional Education in Community Studies. We have established the Personal Construct Psychology in Education Research group which is designated centre of the University of Reading. There are a large number of doctoral students working in the

Centre and the Group has some 50 members including academic staff at the University of Reading and other institutions within the UK and a wide range of practitioners who are applying Personal Construct Psychology in their professional practice.

From this base, we hope to continue our explorations of alternative ways of construing and alternative ways of illuminating that construal.

Pam Denicolo

Since there are some aspects of my school days in Scotland that still impinge on my life, I reminisce about them here, particularly the teacher who encouraged my love of literature, instilled a joy of writing and taught me punctuation (much to the chagrin of some of my later students!). There were, of course, less happy memories but ones nonetheless of significance here. I will never forget the physics teacher who would tell any of the three girls in the class who had the temerity to study physics and to ask searching questions of him – 'away and do your knitting, girl!' He encouraged my stubborn and rebellious streak to such an extent that I made sure that my Physics, Chemistry , Biology and Maths Highers were as good as those in English, French and History!

Lacking any form of careers guidance (this was the olden days!), but encouraged to do something involving both science and people, I chose to embark on the first year of a medical/dentistry degree. It did not take me long to discover that I was not too keen on investigating people's bodies, besides which a handsome young Italian had come on the scene, so I married, withdrew from the course, and threw myself into domestication – and read every book in the local library. When the joy of growing up together with two lively toddlers began not to fill every corner of my mind, I discovered that the Open University was about to start up. Triggered back into academic action, I enrolled for a new degree and found myself proof-reading the courses as they came on stream. More out of habit than informed choice I started with the Science Foundation course but then moved to England. The obligatory second foundation course, in social sciences this time, coincided with my also studying for a teacher's certificate (I have never been able since to do anything other than pack my life with demands).

Of course, my children had started school by then and, thinking I might be bored during the day without them, volunteered me to their teachers to help with science lessons. I recall the fun of it all – the bricks, the planks, water and oil, weights and string, crystals and bugs; the wonderful questions the children asked; how we explored the possibilities in our meagre resources to find the answers; the whole sense of 'let's find out together'. It never occurred to me to tell them the answers, nor did they expect me to – after all I wasn't a teacher, I was a Mum.

What happened next was to influence my views on teaching and learning significantly. I applied for and gained a teaching post at the local technical college. How the sights, sounds and smells differed from the last image. I became a professional teacher rather than an amateur, my jeans were replaced by a white coat, eager children by sullen adolescents, relevant and interesting/interested questions by pages of detailed notes. A sense of fear of being asked a question to which I did not know the answer replaced the sense of adventure, and an abiding concern was what would I do if these big lads refused to co-operate. I was trying to fulfil the role imposed on me by the context and expectations of colleagues. But my confidence grew, the jeans came back, the sullen students metamorphosed into interesting people, succinct handouts replaced note-taking and we experimented not just with chemistry but with small group work instead of lectures. I learned to smile enigmatically when colleagues queried what could possibly cause gales of laughter, and whoops of delight, to emanate from a science lab – from their perspective but not mine, precision and objectivity precluded mirth and wonderment.

Thus began my drift away from science and into exploring through psychology how people learned. The last vestiges of science as a subject are to be found in my PhD, an investigation into the use of metaphor in chemistry teaching and learning. My OU first class honours degree helped me win an ESRC scholarship at Surrey University and I was able to indulge my abiding love of language and my growing passion for exploring people's ideas, rather than their bodies. At Surrey, I met Maureen, my supervisor, then mentor and now dear friend and co-author. Our first official foray together set the pattern for the coming years. At a time when qualitative research was undervalued as an approach, we presented a paper on constructivist approaches at a conference of fellow psychologists – and were overwhelmed not by their cynicism but by their interest.

Before I finished my PhD, serendipity found me again and I was appointed to a post in the Education department at Surrey. Years fled swiftly by as Maureen and I cultivated and refined our work as teachers of professionals and staff developers, travelling the world together and returning from each trip with a fund of funny stories about our adventures as well as a wealth of learning about new perspectives. As time went by, I became leader of the course for developing the teaching skills of professionals, the Director of the centre for staff development and the doctoral training course, eventually becoming the Director of the Professional Studies Unit. By that time Maureen had moved to Reading but we kept contact through the PCP research interest group which I had established to help my brood of research students share ideas and support.

A group of others interested in PCP approaches began to meet in London to develop a pan-European network and from this the European Personal Construct Association (EPCA) was born. Since then I have been its Treasurer, for six years, and its Convenor for four years while I joined Maureen in the International Study Association on Teachers and Teaching (ISATT), becoming the UK national representative and now being on its Executive Panel. The conferences and networks of both these groups, several of which we have organized, have been a continuous source of inspiration.

Another wave of serendipity found me taking up a post of Reader at Reading. My departmental work has a focus on developing research in professional education while I hold the faculty post of Director of Postgraduate Research. Maureen and I were able to conjoin our large entourages of doctoral students into one research group and they catalysed the development of the dynamic university research centre which is now our base for research and development activities.

Working across a department which includes community nursing, social work, youth and community, careers guidance and counselling within a Faculty of Education has enhanced my understanding of diverse professional perspectives, as has my long standing work with the educational division of the Royal Pharmaceutical Society. I was delighted recently to be made an honorary member of that society in recognition of my contribution to the profession's education and practice, though I suspect that my gain as a learner from it far outweighs theirs.

As we work and write together, exploring sensitive and exciting ideas with our research students and study groups, Maureen and I are inclined to forgive some of the members of our Centre for occasionally mixing our names up. Though we do not look alike (we have been known to style ourselves as Hinge and Bracket when running workshops), from reading both biographies, remarkable coincidences in life patterns emerge. One of them is that both see ourselves as in the process of growing up with both our children to whom this book is dedicated. We have a girl and a boy each, one being a lawyer and the other being inclined towards the arts, performing and craft. So it is not too surprising that we have some common constructs and can share sociality with others. Thus we have enjoyed crafting this book together.

Both

It can be seen from the above that our ideas are part of an enfolded impli-
cate order (Fransella, 1983). We have provided references within the book
to the ideas and the work of others where we are aware of drawing on
specific learning from our past. We apologize to those who have
contributed to our tacit learning (Polanyi, 1958) who go unreferenced but
not unacknowledged. They are certainly not unappreciated. We can,
though, direct readers to the papers, theses and books in the Fay Fransella
Collection and our own Resource Base at the University of Reading,
through which our travels through the literature can be emulated, or new
journeys undertaken.

Within the book the reader will note that we have drawn attention to
the importance of language and its relation to construing. We have been
careful to retain in quotations the authenticity of authors' language. While
we have, ourselves, adopted non-sexist language in our writing we have
not peppered quotations with the use of [*sic*] to draw attention to sexist
language. We recognize that many of the authors we quote were living in a
era when such political correctness was not part of the literary genre. We
hope our book will be enjoyed and that our ideas will be both explored
and challenged by those who engage with it. We can be contacted for
debate and help at:

The Centre for Personal Construct Psychology in Education
The Faculty of Education and Community Studies
The University of Reading.
Bulmershe Court
Earley
Reading RG6 1HY.

Acknowledgements

We have already acknowledged, although not by name, the many colleagues and students past and present who have shared their ideas and been part of our personal journey. However, the writing of the book is a very specific journey and a number of people have helped us to realize this task. We would like to take this opportunity to thank our colleague Jon Roberts for his punctilious help with proofreading early drafts and Pam Burnard and Hafdis Ingvarsdottir for their very helpful feedback at the draft stage. Brian Peters, who worked magic in helping us with the diagrams, deserves a special mention too. However, in particular we must thank Amanda Harvey our excellent secretary who typed and retyped various drafts with good humour and the utmost patience. Last but not least we want to thank our husbands Vince Denicolo and Michael Pope who had to forgo a great deal as the book increasingly impinged on the joys of family life.

CHAPTER 1

Alternative perspectives on education

'Tis education forms the common mind
Just as the twig is bent, the tree's inclined.

Alexander Pope, 1688–1744, *Moral Essays*, Epistle I.

Introduction – views from the chalk face

In common with many of our readers, our work context in education is in a constant state of flux and we with it. Our 'twigs' are being buffeted by many winds so that though we seem to have relative stability in a core of ideals and principles, it is the stability of running along a moving walkway – much about us and around us seems to change and develop moment by moment. As educators/researchers we work with other adults, some of whom are undertaking initial training courses though most are seasoned professionals engaging in developing their practice through courses, programmes of study or research. All of us together are subject to a turbulent life whether we seek to maintain stability, 'go with the flow' or to influence the course of events, to name but a few options.

It is difficult to identify any profession or occupation which is not heir to the knowledge explosion, or indeed to the obsolescence of some forms of knowledge within it, to the technological revolution and to modifications in both values and practices. The profession of teaching is no exception, with the additional problem that teachers must remain alert to changes in other professions as they prepare pupils or students for them. Thus, although we might try 'just to get on with our jobs', a life composed of rapid and continual change makes it imperative for us to engage in learning, for mere survival if not for personal growth. To set the scene, we begin this book with an historical overview of the main philosophical influences which have some bearing on our current practice in education.

Because we are defining education in a broad way, to encompass all sectors and to include teacher education as well as that found in

1

schools/colleges/universities, we will in our general discussion use simple terms for participants in the process. Thus 'learner' and 'teacher' will be used generically to subsume those with whom the individual reader might identify: student, pupil, mentee, lecturer, mentor, etc. Where we are referring to specific case studies or examples of practice we will try to honour the terminology used in that context.

Identifying potential participants in generally educative (or transformative) processes is an easier task than to define what we mean by 'transformative practice' or indeed what we intend to convey by the common word 'learning'. The former term we hope will be understood better by the end of the book, while the rest of this chapter will explore further a range of interpretations about learning so that we clarify our own view on this nebulous concept.

That view derives from our lifelong learning (a concept we will return to later in the chapter), beginning with our experiences as children in formal and informal educational settings which were then built on and modified by our training as psychologists and later by our experiences as educators and researchers. Much of our learning as adults has been influenced by the work of George Kelly and others who have espoused the Personal Construct Theory perspective and so it is those understandings which pervade this book.

This philosophical and theoretical perspective includes models of humankind and learning which fit more comfortably with our own experiences, and are proving more resilient to challenge, than those other models we were exposed to but held more tenuously in the past. Each person has a 'philosophical style' encompassing an implicit model of the learning process which impacts on behaviour as a learner or a teacher. These models are intellectual tools or devices which give coherence to our experiences, thoughts, feelings and actions, within the context we believe or know to exist. They also allow us to make predictions and to create experiences. Thus the models we adopt are exceedingly influential, as Eisner (1993: 5) noted:

> Humans do not simply have experience; they have a hand in its creation, and the quality of their creation depends on the way they employ their minds.

The next section discusses some of the more prevalent theories of education which have been adopted in Western society, by people with an education remit.

The theories underlying the practice of educational research are also intimately linked to general educational ideologies. These educational ideologies embody theories on the nature and development of the person.

As Bruner (1966) pointed out, instruction can be seen as an effort to assist or to shape growth, and any theory of instruction is in effect a theory of how growth and development are encouraged. Any theory about teaching is thus inextricably linked to an underlying view or model of the nature of the learner. A teacher may conceive of the nature of the learner as active or passive, meaning: seeking, impulse driven, fixed or constantly developing. Whichever model is adopted will influence the teacher's strategy and aims.

Much of the current debate on education revolves around fundamental differences in the models of learning held by the individuals concerned. Many educationalists argue that a major problem is that at any point in time educational issues tend to be dominated by one particular viewpoint or 'frame of reference' so that education becomes monolithic in structure (Joyce, 1972). Those involved in education often adopt rigidly opposing positions which militate against a more constructive and flexible approach. There is now a growing recognition that alternative models can co-exist and enrich rather than detract from development in education. Some educational researchers are seeking new approaches – recognizing that past educational research has been conducted on too narrow a base.

This chapter looks at some of the major themes inherent in differing educational ideologies and relates these to particular models of the nature of knowledge and psychological development. In Chapter 3 some of the current issues within the arena of education research are raised. It is suggested that alternative methodologies are needed if we are to adopt the perspective of the person in educational research. Aspects of Personal Construct Psychology which seem to have a direct bearing on current concerns in education are discussed in Chapter 2. Rather than the imposition of a monolithic approach to educational issues, a Kellyian framework allows for diversity of viewpoints and constructive alternatives in transforming professional practice through research and education.

Philosophical approaches which underpin education

Inevitably, any attempt to categorize perspectives on education will do an injustice to the great diversity of viewpoints on education held by particular individuals. Nevertheless, the following categorization represents one possible way of construing the alternative themes presented *within* differing perspectives on education. It is suggested that there are at least five major schools of thought in the development of Western educational ideology, each exhibiting a coherence based upon particular assumptions of psychological development and philosophies of the nature of knowledge. These assumptions identify what is of importance and what is problematic in the field as well as what its goals and standards should be. Together with political and economic constraints, they therefore largely determine pedagogic practice in schools and colleges and universities. They also provide educators with schemas for developing and analysing their own practice. Some of the major theoretical issues underlying each approach will be indicated in this chapter and the practical application of these theoretical stances within traditional education contexts will be discussed. These schools of thought may be termed:

(a) cultural transmission/instrumentalism;
(b) romanticism;
(c) progressivism;
(d) de-schooling;
(e) humanistic approaches.

Since cultural transmission is rooted in the classical academic tradition of Western education and is experiencing a resurgence of interest, though in a modified form as Instrumentalism, particularly in continuing and vocational education, we shall consider this first.

Cultural transmission/instrumentalism

Theorists of this persuasion would see the primary task of the educator as the transmission of information, rules or values collected in the past. The educator's job is the direct instruction of information and rules. For example, Robert Maynard Hutchins (1936: 66) wrote:

> Education implies teaching. Teaching implies knowledge. Knowledge is truth. The truth is everywhere the same. Hence, education should be everywhere the same.

In the classical tradition it was thought that by studying the great works of literature, philosophy, science and history, learners imbibe the 'truths' of their cultural heritage. Much of the basis of modern educational technology and behavioural modification approaches to education and skills training can be seen as variants of this cultural transmission approach. Knowledge and values are seen as located in the culture and are internalized by children imitating adult behaviour models or through explicit instruction and the use of such training strategies as reward and punishment. The criterion of successful education and training for such theorists is the learner's ability to incorporate the responses which have been taught so to respond appropriately to the demand of the system. The major objectives are literacy and mathematical skills which are seen as necessary for adjustment to technological society.

This philosophical approach is that absolute truth can be accumulated bit by bit, subject by subject. Knowledge is objective and can be measured by culturally shared test procedures. This approach is exemplified by the Black Paper, *Fight for Education*, edited by Cox and Dyson (1969). The learner is seen as naturally lazy and must be prodded into action by external incentives. Thus, they said:

> Exams make people work hard. Much opposition to them is based on the belief that people work better without reward and incentive, a naiveté; which is against all knowledge of human nature. (p. 56)

The view of absolute truth accumulating in fragments corresponds to the basic principles of philosophic realism. In the Realist's view the world exists independently of man and is governed by laws over which we have little control. Most scientific realists deny the existence of free will and argue that individual behaviour is determined by the impact of the physical and social environment on genetic structure. John Locke assumed that the mind of the individual at birth was a *tabula rasa*. For Locke the intellect was essentially passive and acquired its content and structure through the impact of sensation through the senses. The world we perceive is not a world that we have recreated mentally but is the world as it is. The epistemological position of the Realist is that true knowledge is knowledge that corresponds to the world as it is; facts are independent of what we think about them. The task of the educator would seem to be the instruction of a body of knowledge whose truth had been repeatedly confirmed.

The Lockean tradition is central to psychological theories of development which stress the passivity of the human mind. This emphasis is found in all types of associationism, behaviourism, stimulus-response psychology, contingency theories etc. One might suggest that the appropriate metaphor for the view of the person put forward by cultural transmission educational ideology, is that of the machine. The machine can be anything from the wax upon which the environment makes its mark (Locke) through to the computer. The environment is seen as 'input' whose information is more or less directly transmitted to and accumulated in the 'organism'. The resulting behaviour is the 'output'. Using this mechanistic metaphor, cognitive development can be seen as the result of guided learning and teaching, and behaviour is the result of an association between stimulus and response (Hull, 1943).

Skinner (1968) viewed teachers as architects and builders of learner behaviour. He defined learning as a change in the probability of response. He explained all human behaviour in terms of respondents and operant reinforcement. On the basis of his animal laboratory work he set out a detailed methodology for the timing and spacing of scheduled reinforcement. Through progressively changing the contingencies of reinforcement in the direction of the desired behaviour (as defined by the experimenter) learning is seen to occur. Educational change is evaluated from performances, not from changes in thoughts or feelings. Thus Skinner (1971: 15) stated:

> We can follow the path taken by physics and biology by turning directly to the relation between behaviour and the environment and neglecting ... states of mind ... we do not need to discover what personalities, states of mind, feelings... intentions – or other prerequisites of autonomous man really are in order to get on with a scientific analysis of behaviour.

This 'Black Box' or 'Empty Organism' approach with its emphasis on human behaviour being controlled by the environmental situation, flourished in the decades following the 1920s. Theorists holding to a cultural transmission educational or instrumentalist ideology find much support in the Realists' philosophy and the psychological theories put forward by the behaviourists, neo-behaviourists and contingency theorists. Although this dominant position has been challenged by three major contenders – the Romanticists, the Progressivists and the Humanistic school of thought – remnants of it can be found in the contemporary move towards Instrumentalism in Western society. It is asserted that an educated workforce is needed to respond to international competition. Competence-based courses in which particular behaviours indicate achievement of learning for assessment purposes illustrate the tenacity of this perspective.

Romanticism

The Romanticists stress that what comes from within the child is the most important aspect of development. Thus the pedagogical environment should be permissive enough to allow 'inner good' to unfold and 'inner bad' to come under control. The emphasis is on 'health' and 'growth' and working through aspects of emotional development which may not be allowed expression in the home. Rousseau's *Emile*, although written over 200 years ago, contains what many consider are the fundamental principles behind more humanistic modern educational ideas. Believing that people are born naturally good, Rousseau considered that by lifting social and pedagogical restraints, one would preserve natural goodness. Rousseau's 'negative education' was not to be an education of transmitted norms, but one based on the psychological principles of natural development of the child and a non-directive approach on behalf of the teacher.

The writings of G. S. Stanley-Hall in the early twentieth century suggested that before we let pedagogy loose on children we would have to overcome the fetishes of the alphabet and of the multiplication tables and must reflect that but a few generations ago the ancestors of most of us were illiterate. He maintained that there were many who ought not to be educated and that these would be 'better in mind, body and morals if they knew no school'. The type of school to which Stanley-Hall was referring was that in which the transmission of public knowledge was instilled without reference to the thoughts and feelings of children and the perceived relevance of such knowledge to them. This stress on emotions, thoughts and feelings can be seen to be part of a romantic philosophy which was prevalent in the nineteenth century and whose epistemology involved the discovery of the natural and inner self.

The Romanticists probably come closest to the Idealist school of philosophy which holds that ultimate reality is spiritual in nature rather than physical, mental rather than material. While not denying the existence of things in the 'Real World' the idealists believe that these are part of a more fundamental incorporeal reality, although individual idealists, e.g. Plato and Kant, disagreed as to the nature of the ultimate reality and the relation of the spiritual being to that reality.

Idealist educators instil a closer intimacy between the person and the spiritual elements of nature. However, within the idealist tradition, different philosophers have produced different theories of knowledge. Thus for Plato, since the material world is only a distorted copy of a more perfect reality, the impressions which come directly via the senses must be uncertain and incomplete. True knowledge for Plato was the result of the process of reasoning, since this process transcends the material world and can discern pure spiritual reality. More modern idealists in the Kantian tradition maintain that knowledge is the imposition of meaning and order on sense impressions. This latter view of knowledge is held by many Progressivists but the goals of the two philosophies are distinct. For Idealists their aim is communion with the ultimate reality, while the Progressivists, within the context of moral relativism, acknowledge no such ultimate goal.

Romantic ideology would seem to be supported by maturationist theories of psychological development, e.g. Freudian psychoanalytic theory and Gessellian maturational theory. While individual rates of development may be inborn, cognitive and emotional development is seen to depend on the unfolding of the biologically given although remaining vulnerable to fixation, as in the Freudian sense, or frustration by the environment.

Rousseau in *Emile* made a plea for recognition that: 'Childhood had its own ways of seeing, thinking and feeling; nothing is more foolish than to try to substitute our ways.' Accordingly we must 'hold childhood in reverence, watch him, study him constantly'. A similar idea was expressed by Freud (1913: 189) in 'The claims of psycho-analysis to the scientific interest – the educational interest', he said:

> Only someone who can feel his way into the minds of children can be capable of educating them and we grown up people cannot understand children because we no longer understand our childhood.

Although the tenets of this school of thought do seem to be most relevant to childhood education, the Romantic movement has left a legacy to those involved with post-compulsory education. In counterpoint to the mechanistic, 'personless' approach of the Cultural Transmission/Instrumentalist school, this perspective on learning and teaching emphasizes the imagination, emotions and their freely individualized expression which has had particular impact on the Arts. In addition, followers of the movement introduced the notion of using introspective autobiographical material as a means of gaining greater understanding of the other's perspective and advocated the development of a freely accepted 'contract' between learners and teachers.

Contract learning methods became very popular in the 1970s in recognition of the benefits of allowing learners to pursue their own specific interests and to take some responsibility for their own learning. Egan (1975) argued that, for adults to learn in an adult way with freedom granted to all participants, contracts or formal agreements about boundaries, expectations and commitments contributed to generating greater respect and valuing of each other between individuals. These ideas formed a basis from which the multiplicity of self-directed learning methods grew.

This philosophical approach has also contributed to interpretative forms of research by noting the rich resource provided by folklore, fairy tales, songs and legends for supplying insight into the perspectives of groups of people. Of particular note for constructivist approaches, the Romanticists are credited with drawing attention to the worldview that is implicit in particular language use. We will refer to this important concept while describing techniques and methods in the chapters which follow and will include further detail in Chapter 6.

While the Progressivists and Romanticists are in agreement in their rejection of the cultural transmission approach, Progressivism is based on a different set of theoretical assumptions, both psychological and philosophical.

Progressivism

John Dewey is usually cited as the founder of the Progressive School Movement. Two of his most quoted books are *Schools of Tomorrow* (1915) and *Experience and Education* (1938). Progressivism holds that education should nourish the person's natural interaction with a developing society or environment. Unlike Romanticists they do not assume that development is an unfolding of an innate pattern or that the educational aim is the creation of a conflict-free environment in order to foster healthy development. They see development as a progression through ordered sequential stages and their educational goal is the eventual attainment by the child of a higher level or stage of development in adulthood. In 1895 Dewey and McLellan said:

> Education is the work of supplying the condition, which will enable the Psychical functions as they successively arise to mature and pass into higher functions in the freest and fullest manner.

Thus the educational environment for the Progressivists should be one which actively stimulates development through the presentation of a milieu in which the organizing and developing force in the person's experience is the person's active thinking. Thinking is stimulated by cognitive conflict. Like the cultural transmission theorists, they emphasize knowledge as opposed to feelings and experience but they see the acquisition of knowledge as an act of change in the pattern of thinking brought about by experiential problem-solving situations. The Progressivists view morals, values and the nature of knowledge to be in constant change.

Progressivism in its pure form declares that education is always in the process of development. Education is not a preparation for living but it should be life itself. Like Rousseau, Dewey and his followers maintained that learning should be directly related to the interests of the person; motivation to learn should come from within the person rather than knowledge being externally imposed. The teacher is seen more as a guide or adviser in a process whereby the person reconstructs the subject matter in accordance with its perceived relevance to his own life. Learning should take place through problem solving rather than the inculcating of subject matter. Knowledge itself is seen as 'a tool for managing experience'. For knowledge to be significant one has to do something with it and hence it must be linked to experience. For the Progressivists, education is not limited to a recollection of information obtained from the teacher or a textbook, it involves 'perpetual grappling' with the subject matter. In this sense, grappling is not only the physical handling of material, but it involves the critical thinking process of reconstruction of previous ideas and discovery.

The teaching method upheld by Progressivism encourages learner–learner interaction as well as learner–teacher interaction. Teachers are interested in learners developing their own criteria regarding the quality and relevance of ideas. Thus the teachers' role of arbiter of what is acceptable is minimized. Their aim is not the transmission of 'nuggets', but rather the facilitation of the process of 'learning how to learn'.

The particular philosophy aligned with Progressivism is that of Pragmatism. It is mainly a twentieth-century philosophy which has grown out of the British empiricist tradition which maintains that we know only what our senses experience. A basic principle of Pragmatism is that the world is neither dependent on nor independent of human ideas about it. Reality is the interaction of the human being with the environment; it is the sum total of what we experience. The emphasis is on active people reaching out to make sense of their universe by engaging in the reconstruction and interpretation of their own experiences. Pragmatists agree that knowledge is produced by transaction between people and their environment and that truth is a property of knowledge but they disagree about what can be defined as truth. William James maintained that an idea is true if it has a favourable consequence for the person who holds it. On the other hand, Dewey insisted that an idea was true only if it had a satisfactory consequence when objectively and, if possible, scientifically tested. As constructivists we would suggest, that the core of universal ideas are redefined and reorganized as their implications are played out in experience and as they are confronted by their opposites in argument.

Psychological theories which support these ideas are those which discard the dichotomy between maturation and environmental determinism in learning. For example, Piaget claims that mature thought emerges through a process of development that is neither direct biological maturation nor direct environmental pressure, but a reorganization of psychological structures resulting from organism–environment interactions. Cognitions are seen as internally organized wholes or systems of internal relations through which events in the person's experience are organized. For Piaget the processes of 'accommodation' and 'assimilation' are not passive processes which can result from a programme of reinforcement. Such a programme would only change the person's behaviour and cognitive structure if it was assimilated by the person in terms of his/her present mode of thinking. For Piaget the teacher's role is to facilitate movement to the next stage of development by exposure to the next higher level of thought and by conflict requiring active application of current thoughts to problematic situations.

Jerome Bruner (1966) suggested that perception and conceptualization involve similar processes which include the categorization of data.

'Whereas perception involves categorization of data from sensory input, conceptualization is the process of grasping relationships or patterns within material to be learnt. He also pointed to the necessity for learners to relate new material to relevant ideas already established in their cognitive structures, for them to apprehend in what ways it is similar to and different from related concepts and to translate it into a personal frame of reference, consonant with each person's idiosyncratic experience. Bruner makes two points of particular value to the ideas we will present later in the book. He alerted teachers to the misconceptions which can arise when a person has miscoded or wrongly categorized something and therefore draws ill-founded inferences. An example might be that a child, in seeing similarities between a deep sea diver's suit and a space suit, assumes that the environmental conditions in which they are used are similar.

Secondly, he maintained that teachers should take note of the hierarchical organization of the cognitive structure of the learner when devising instruction. He suggests that content should be arranged so that learners are able to draw relationships which are both meaningful to themselves (since they are a result of their own activity) but will also share many links with the set of relationships that are commonly derived and which form the publicly accepted definition of the subject matter to be learnt. Thus he proposed that a teacher should not present subject matter in its final form but rather should require the learner to do some organization and discover relationships for him/herself. He saw teachers as guides who use a non-directive approach to encourage learners to take some responsibility for their own learning so that they might eventually become self-directed learners.

Both Bruner and Ausubel (1968) are concerned with the organization of information. They agree that the knowledge a person possesses is arranged hierarchically with the more inclusive ideas at the top and the exclusive/more specific ideas at the bottom levels (parallels with Kelly's notion of the hierarchically organized construct system can be drawn with this). When new material is presented to learners they have to 'assimilate it' into their own cognitive structures. Ausubel stresses that new information is not received passively without any distortion nor is the cognitive structure receiving it merely added to. The set of ideas already in the cognitive structure provide a framework through which the new information is analysed and given meaning while the learner's cognitive structure too will be modified in the process. He suggested that the more meaning can be attributed to new material, the more organization of it can occur and hence it is recalled more readily. It is his contention that teachers can help with this process by understanding what is currently meaningful to the learner and thence building new information on this. Rather than education, then, being mono-directional, this demands an interactive exchange of information between teachers and learners.

The 'symbolic interactionists' maintain that in a fundamental sense the 'self' is a product of a person's interaction with others. A person's self-concept develops in relation to reactions of other people to that person. They propose that we react to our 'selves' as we perceive others acting towards us (Cooley, 1964: 168–210). This view has been extended by G. H. Mead and role theorists who recognize that the self in a social structure is that which arises through communication. By anticipating the other's reaction to us and our reaction to the other's reaction, we are able to examine and evaluate several possible courses of action and choose a particular course. A person's behaviour is seen to be influenced by such interactions, not based upon the action of the other *per se* but on the meaning which the person assigns to the other's acts. Thus individual action and development are seen to be constructed in relation to the other, rather than simply determined by outside forces or evoked by internal impulses.

Whether the psychological theories are emphasizing cognitive development, as in the case of Piaget, Bruner or Ausubel, or social development, as in the case of role theorists, the emphasis is on interaction with the environment. These theories are in accordance with Progressivism which sees education as an interaction process rather than as a totally child-centred process as in the case of the Romanticists, or society-centred, promoting the discipline of social order, as seen by the Cultural Transmission theorists.

Although the originators of Progressivism couched their discussion in terms of children's learning, seeming to espouse a 'front end' conception of education, this is perhaps a reflection of the social mores in which they were working rather than an intellectual commitment *per se*. Certainly the roots of the approaches and methods which pervade late-twentieth-century post-compulsory education can be discerned in their work. Dewey (1916: 51) himself said:

> It is commonplace to say that education should not cease when one leaves school ... The inclination to learn from life itself and to make the condition of life such that all will learn in the process of living is the finest product of schooling.

He went on to say:

> Since life means growth, a living creature lives as truly and positively at one stage as at another, with the same intrinsic fullness and the same absolute claims. Hence education means the enterprise of supplying the conditions which ensure growth, or adequacy of life, irrespective of age.

The contemporary concepts of lifelong learning, experiential learning and continuing professional development are echoes of this 'common place' saying which have taken almost a century to become an accepted and required part of education provision, although some have benefited from the luxury of liberal adult education in the meantime.

De-schooling

The preceding three sets of philosophical and psychological assumptions and the one included in the section to follow (humanistic approaches), represent perhaps the main streams of development of Western educational ideology. However, for completeness it is necessary to mention another stream which emerged in the 1970s, namely de-schooling. Rousseau and Stanley-Hall both argued that the inculcation of knowledge could be harmful to the student. Ivan Illich (1971), who is perhaps one of the best known de-schoolers, pointed out that, in his opinion, most of the really important and useful things learnt are learned outside the classroom, i.e. from friends or from interested others. These things are seldom learnt from certificated teachers or under the process of compulsion. He recommended abolishing the school as a unit and reorganizing learning by bringing together, within a given area, those who want to teach and those who want to learn. Some schemes modelled along the lines which Illich suggested were established for a time in both the United States and in Great Britain. They were known as the 'school without walls'. Staff made arrangements with pupils to meet for sessions in informal venues with the programme chosen by the group in a common desire to learn.

Illich was not alone in his attack on education as we know it today, although few would go so far as total demolition of schools. Charles E. Silberman in *Crisis in the Classroom* (1971) claimed that the school has been given too much credit as an agent of social change. Silberman proposed an educational process in which the rights of children are observed and learning methods are varied. Children would be expected to work on their own, at their own pace and at work of their own choosing. An institution might offer children advantages which their locality may lack. The leaving age would be open-ended, since this would be a school for the whole community where children and adults of all ages might come and go as they please. Some prototypes of this type of school were established in the private sector of British education. A. S. Neill's Summerhill and Dartington Hall are examples of schools based on revolutionary philosophies of education.

This accent on rejection of imposed structure can be found in Everett Reimer's *School is Dead*; John Holt's *How Children Fail*; Paul Goodman's *Compulsory Miseducation* and Neil Postman and Charles Weingartner's

Teaching as a Subversive Activity. The majority of these theorists would acknowledge the attempts of Progressivists to initiate active enquiry on behalf of the learner but they felt that the pedagogy that has resulted still leaves a lot to be desired. Postman and Weingartner (1971: 59) made this point very forcibly in a chapter headed 'Pursuing relevance' in their book *Teaching as a Subversive Activity*. Thus they wrote:

> There is no way to help a learner to be disciplined, active and thoroughly engaged unless he perceives a problem to be a problem, or whatever is to be learned to be worth learning. It is sterile and ridiculous to attempt to release the enquiry power of students by initiating studies that hold no interest for them.

Much of the thought expressed in the above-mentioned works is reminiscent of existentialist philosophy. Existentialists reject the traditional view that philosophy should become detached. They say that philosophy should be reason informed by passion because it is in passion and in states of heightened feeling that ultimate realities are disclosed. They reject the notion of the 'Natural development of man'. In his book *Existentialism* Jean-Paul Sartre (1947: 18) said:

> Not only is man what he conceives himself to be, but he is also what he wills himself to be after this thrust towards existence. Man is nothing other than what he makes himself.

For the existentialists, people have responsibility for their own being. What they becomes is of their own choosing and their freedom is in their potential for action. Every person must act according to their strongest feelings and be prepared to take the consequences which will result from their actions. Knowledge is essentially phenomenological – a person's knowledge depends on his/her understanding of reality.

For the existentialist it is not sufficient that a body of knowledge from a textbook or given out by the teacher is accepted unquestioning by the student. The students must find their own truths for themselves. They must be able to incorporate them within their view of the world. In *Between Man and Man*, Martin Buber (1965) wrote about what he believed to be the tyranny of impersonal knowledge. For him teaching should be a true dialogue in which the teacher is not simply a mediator between the learner and the subject matter. Rather than become a means for the transmission of knowledge, teachers should offer knowledge, i.e. they must familiarize themselves fully with the subjects they teach so that this subject becomes part of their own inner experience which they can then present to the students as something issuing from themselves. Each teacher and learner can then meet as persons as the offered knowledge is not alienated from the teacher's real world of feeling. The learner must take responsibility for rejecting or accepting the teacher's interpretation of the subject matter. The aim of the teacher should be the establishment of an atmosphere of mutual trust in which the teacher sees the learner not as a category, a first former for instance, or in evaluative terms, e.g. as in 'bright' or 'dull', but as a person.

Many existentialists, Buber included, would maintain that as it now stands the school is a powerful reinforcer of alienation in modern society. Some psychologists share this concern with alienation and failure of real communication between people. They suggest that one of the many reasons why some youths become disaffected with education is because they perceive little relevance in it to their lived experience. There must be few of us who cannot remember at least one school subject that seemed abstract and irrelevant until we either found a use for it in adulthood or had the advantage of having a teacher who helped us 'make connections'. Psychologists who have these concerns regret the lack of emphasis on the person and individual 'views of the world' in some psychological theories of development – in particular those of the behaviourist and neo-behaviourist schools. They bring a Humanistic psychology approach to education which is particularly relevant to and has had much influence on contemporary education for adults returning to education in colleges and universities. This approach will be discussed further in the next section but first let us summarize some points worth noting from the ideology of de-schooling.

First, its proponents varied in their aims – on one hand we have Illich, who advocated total demolition, and on the other Postman, who aimed for a revolution within the system, thus allowing for relevant education which would facilitate the growth of 'strategies for survival' and ability to cope with the ever-changing facets of our society. Secondly, there is the agreement that the cultural transmission approach is inappropriate to the needs of the person and modern society. Thirdly, there is the acceptance of many of the Romanticist and Progressivist principles put forward, for example by Rousseau and John Dewey. However, there is a rejection of the biological model found in much of the writings of the Romanticists. While accepting the act of 'questioning' and 'learning by doing' approach of the Progressivists two main criticisms are put forward by the De-schoolers. One is the disproportionate emphasis on the structure of cognitive processes rather than on the meaning content. The other is that despite innovations within the educational system, the hierarchical power structure remains static. For the De-schooler 'relevant' education will only take place within a framework in which the power structure barriers are broken down between staff and students and between the school and community at large.

The humanistic approach

Sullivan, Laing, Bateson and Carl Rogers have all been influential in raising the interpersonal encounter as an important topic within psychology. The writings of Laing and Rogers in particular lay great stress on personal experience as the origin of action. Their views on personality, psychological development and methodological issues in psychology also bear a great resemblance to the thinking of existential philosophers. R. D. Laing was quite specific in his connections with the works of Heidegger, Jean-Paul Sartre, Merleau-Ponty, Friedrich Nietzsche and Søren Kierkegaard. Thus in his book *The Politics of Experience*, R. D. Laing (1967: 20) talked about personal experience:

> It is tempting and facile to regard 'persons' as only separate objects in space, who can be studied as other natural objects can be studied ... one will never find persons by studying persons as though they were only objects.

Carl Rogers in *On Becoming a Person* (1961), *Freedom to Learn* (1969) and *Freedom to Learn for the 80s* (1983) took up this perspective of the personal with specific reference to the learning situation. Rogers differentiated between two processes in learning: teacher-based (the traditional cultural transmission approach) and learner-based learning.

Learner-based learning is self-initiated, has a quality of personal involvement and is evaluated by learners in terms of whether or not it is meeting their needs. This significant learning is pervasive, i.e. it makes a difference in behaviour, attitudes and personality of the learner, and its essence is meaning. The knowledge/truth that evolves in self-discovered learning is 'private' knowledge – truth that has been personally appropriated and assimilated in experience. According to Rogers this 'personal' knowledge cannot be directly transmitted from the teacher to the student. This is not to say that the 'public knowledge' or facts, ideas, etc. that the teacher is trying to impart can never become personal knowledge. What Rogers contended is that the process is not one of direct impersonal association between the issues to be learnt (stimuli) and knowledge of them (response). If the public knowledge to be imparted is personally appropriated by learners and has significant influence on their behaviour and attitudes, then public knowledge becomes personal knowledge. While distinguishing between the two processes, Rogers made a value judgement that personal knowledge should be the aim of the educational process. For Rogers, personal knowledge is facilitated by a specific type of interpersonal encounter between the teacher and learner.

The encounter he advocated is similar to that found in the client-centred, non-directive therapeutic process that Rogers used in his psychotherapy. A main feature of this encounter is the quality of regard one for the other. The teacher needs to have regard for what the individual learner is, i.e. independent of her/his ability, interests, social class etc. Labels should be abandoned. Only within the context of unconditional acceptance may learners feel free to express their best and most creative aspects instead of merely regurgitating imposed knowledge. This type of interpersonal encounter does not necessitate sentimentality or laissez-faire attitudes within education, rather it encourages self-directed discipline with the learners setting limits rather than obeying imposed rules.

Reaction against the imposition of both rules and the dominant cultural perspective on knowledge and values pervades the writings of Paulo Freire, whose work based in literacy education in Brazil is now well known to adult educators since it has relevance for those working in the post-compulsory sectors of education. Like the Romanticists, he recognized that each language form contains a construction of reality so that the language of education used, in a didactic form, perpetuates a world view and subjugates the learner's self-identity. He referred to this as 'education for domestication' (Freire, 1973: 79). In common with others taking a Humantistic approach to education, he emphasized the need for an inter-active dialogue between the teacher and the learner and, like the Progressivists, he advocated experiential learning in which reflection on experience is facilitated as a means of *empowering* the learner.

The work of Schon has relevance for teachers engaged in developing their own practice as part of continuing professional development and for those who are involved in teacher education. He judged the power to make independent judgements and to exercise personal discretion and creativity in their work to be at the heart of professional practice and this can be achieved best, he asserted (1987: 300), by teachers and learners articulating their reflections on practice:

> When inquiry into learning remains private, it is also likely to remain tacit. Free of the need to make our ideas explicit to someone else, we are less likely to make them explicit to ourselves.

Mezirow's particular concern, too, is with emancipatory education and his work draws heavily on Habermas's theories of emancipatory learning. Mezirow (1990: xiv) defined emancipatory education as an organized effort to precipitate or to facilitate transformative learning in others, while he proposed that this involves *critical reflection*, that is, the assessment of the validity of the presuppositions of one's meaning perspectives and examination of their sources and consequences. From this latter definition and elsewhere in his writings (1981: 5) it is clear that challenging our presuppositions as teachers is essential if we are to be liberated:

> from libidinal, institutional or environmental forces which limit our options and rational control over our lives but have been taken for granted as beyond human control.

(Some reverberations of the concerns of de-schoolers can be detected in this.)

Continuing professional development (INSET) and lifelong learning

From the foregoing historical review of schools of thought influencing education in general, it is clear that current knowledge which informs education has not been accumulated by building on incremental 'nuggets of truth' but has been contributed to by the interaction of different ideas and ideals, perspectives which sometimes have much in common and sometimes take radically different stances. Practice within particular sectors of education has, at different points in recent history, been influenced by particular ideologies, sometimes leaving practitioners open to censure when learning outcomes fail to meet society's expectations, or those of a powerful hegemony within society. One example, in the 1990s, was the politically motivated denunciation of 'progressive teachers and teacher education' (though whether they or the original Progressivists would recognize it as such is debatable) who were failing to produce a workforce with the skills required by the technological society.

Dogmatism, political or philosophical, can be a major block to development in education. Much non-productive argument in education is due to the adoption of opposing dogmatic viewpoints which determine that this method or theory is correct, therefore all others are wrong. G. Kelly's meta-theory (see Chapter 2) recognizes all theories as temporary constructions which should be abandoned when another theory leads to a better prediction of events. His theory acknowledges the importance of the personal theories which we all erect to explain events in our experience and to predict future happenings. This recognition allows one to break down barriers in education and to recognize that for different people, with different purposes and faced with different circumstances to predict, alternative constructions regarding the nature of education, teaching and learning will evolve. Thus dogmatic ideologies could give way to a more flexible approach to education which recognizes the viability of these alternative constructions.

Flexible approaches to education are essential if teachers are to cope with the vicissitudes and profound social changes impinging on their work which already involves a complex array of skills, attitudes, attributes and intentions. Smyth (1995) provided a summary of trends which appear to be developing worldwide in relation to demands on teachers' skills, time and patience. These include:

- intensification of testing and measurement; focus on observable performance aspects;
- increase in needs for explicitness of practice;
- teaching competence defined against static, invariant standards derived from industry;
- reward on the basis of demonstration of achievement – oriented learning gains in students;
- demand, under the guise of accountability, that what they do enhances students' skills that contribute to international competitiveness;
- teachers and schools appraised and ranked, schools compared with each other through league tables;
- teachers marginalized as self-interested producers, with 'consumers', vaguely defined as parents and employers, favoured;
- teachers treated as not to be trusted and in need of surveillance through performance indicators.

Continuing professional development or INSET can provide a means for teachers to adapt to such a plethora of demands if this is based on axioms which promote professional growth rather than taking the form of continuous exhortations to fit some new, externally determined criteria. Smyth (1995: vii) recognized the contrast between imposed change and development that has personal meaning:

> The quality, range and flexibility of teachers' classroom work are closely tied up with their professional growth – with the way in which they develop as people and as professionals ... The ways they teach are grounded in their backgrounds, their biographies, in the kinds of teachers they have become. Their careers – their hopes and dreams, their opportunities and aspirations, or the frustration of these things – are also important for teachers' commitment, enthusiasm and morale. So too are relationships with their colleagues ...

What teachers think, believe and do at the classroom level is for Hargreaves (1994: ix) what shapes the kind of learning experienced by their learners since, he argued, all the restructuring changes that impinge on schools are of little value if they do not take the teacher into account:

> Teachers don't merely deliver the curriculum. They develop, define it and reinterpret it too.

Chin (1997: 129) confirmed that effective professional development derives from having opportunities to articulate, critique and understand personal beliefs about teaching and learning. Through such activities it is possible to establish frameworks of understanding so that the individual teacher might continue to monitor teaching effectiveness in an iterative process of professional development. Carlgren (1996: 27) emphasized another dimension in considering the importance of providing teachers with opportunities to articulate their ideas, that of opening them up to challenge and debate, not simply to facilitate elaboration but to consider their appropriateness and relevance:

> Sometimes the tacit knowledge of a professional group is equated with professionalism. However, the concept of tacit stupidity exists as well as the concept of tacit wisdom. Tacit knowledge is not gold in, and of, itself.

Loughran (1997: 6) expanded on the importance of teachers learning in the real world of the schools as well as from formal sessions in which they take the role of the taught in universities and colleges, though the purpose of the book in which this chapter is set is to develop the practice of teacher educators within such settings. While he acknowledged that, as in other contexts, the transmission mode might seem the easiest route in teacher education, he promoted the designing of experiences that reveal the inner nature of teaching and highlighted the importance of documenting the purpose, passion and pedagogy of the teacher educators themselves. The need for teacher educators to practise what they preach seemed obvious to him, as did the need for collaborative investigation of what it means to teach.

Ruddock (1992: 168) urged that higher education can make a distinctive contribution to teacher education by a commitment to the collaborative kind of action research which is both reflective and emancipatory. Teachers-as-researchers with whom we have collaborated agree with this principle. To illustrate their views we present some of the phrases they used in describing their research activities: 'creative; ownership of direction; transformative; requiring courage and vision; arduous; lonely; challenging; requiring passionate commitment'. Apparent contradictions abound in this list, yet they all agreed that these were pertinent descriptors of the process: it could not be transformative without being challenging, nor could they own the direction without it.

Other researchers concur with these views, especially the salience of ownership of the developmental process. For instance, Huberman (1989: 18) stated:

> these individuals are not passive, are not the puppets of sociological or maturational strings pulled from above. Human development is largely teleological; that is, human actors observe, study and plan the sequences they follow and, in doing so, are able to orientate and even determine the course of events in each succeeding phase [of professional life].

Exploring how teachers change, Hargreaves (1994: 3) warned that even well-intentioned strategies for change can be frustrated if they become 'squeezed into mechanistic models or suffocated through stifling supervision'. His contention was that strict adherence to bureaucratic procedures would turn collaborative cultures into contrived collegiality, not just undermining teachers' own desires in teaching:

> They threaten the very desire to teach itself. They take the heart out of teaching.

Our book is intended to help teachers to take heart in their teaching.

Teaching and learning and the development of understanding

In the previous section it became transparent that the roles of the learner and of the teacher are not just those of receiver and transmitter of information nor are they simply reciprocal, each responding to the other. In effective education the roles are also interchangeable. In striving to understand the perspective of the learner, the teacher becomes a learner and the learner teaches. Novice teachers begin by teaching in ways that match the ways in which they themselves learned but soon discover that the diversity of learners demands new or different approaches. Even experienced teachers occasionally discover that existing practices and approaches are unsatisfactory so that a need to explore alternative ways of being a teacher is required. In the chapters which follow we suggest ways in which this exploration can take place.

We will also describe ways in which teachers can choose to illuminate and develop their own understanding and gain insight into personal meaning, should they wish to do so, either alone or with others. We hold the view, like Schon (1987) quoted earlier, that we cannot comprehend our own misconceptions, or the limits on our understanding, unless we confront that understanding by first articulating it and then contemplating how it could be otherwise. Nor can we identify mismatches in understandings, whether they be between colleagues or between teachers and learners, whether they be knowledge or value based, without sharing those understandings or frames of reference with others and allowing them to share theirs with us. Without such identification, and without the means for each participant to become active, meaning seeking individuals, attempts to dispel them will be frustrated. In a previous work (Denicolo and Pope, 1990) in which we reported on a technique used to help professionals gain from an exploration of their personal perspectives on their professional development, we referred to the words of Dilthey (as translated by Rickman, 1976) who observed:

> Understanding of other people and their expressions is developed on the basis of experience and self-understanding and the constant interaction between them ... it is not a matter of logical construction or psychological dissection but of an epistemological analysis.

Though these words were written at the beginning of the twentieth century, they have special relevance in this chapter written a hundred years later. We have explored the epistemological positions taken by educationalists and reviewed the implications that they saw them as having for practice in their day, and that we might view them as having for our current practice. Readers might like to contemplate at this point which, if any, of the schools of explicated here comes closest to their own position and also to the implicit or explicit philosophy which pervades the culture of their work context.

As Candy (1990: 272–3) argued, knowledge of one's meaning perspective in itself is not sufficient to bring about a perspective transformation, the opportunity to experiment with alternatives is also required. Like others, including ourselves in our own pasts, Candy was disillusioned with much of traditional educational research which 'put words into respondents' mouths, or acted like 'conceptual straitjackets' or in which others interpreted the participants' (subjects') meaning for them.

However, just as at the beginning of this chapter we commented that any attempt to categorize perspectives in education would no doubt do injustice to the great diversity of viewpoints that do exist, it would be a gross generalization to suggest here that all previous educational research has been of the same genre. In educational research the issues to be raised and the methodologies adopted to pursue them have themselves undergone shifts in perspective which in many ways parallel the changes in viewpoints outlined in this chapter. Having established in the next chapter the value of a Personal Construct Psychology framework for understanding current issues in education, some of the problems with alternative research approaches are discussed in Chapter 3 as a prelude to introducing a research approach congruent with that theoretical framework.

CHAPTER 2

Personal construct psychology approaches in education

Personal Construct Theory has also been categorised by responsible scholars as an emotional theory, a learning theory, a psycho-analytic theory (Freudian, Adlerian, and Jungian – all three), a typically American theory, a Marxist theory, a Humanistic theory, a logical positivistic theory, Zen Buddhistic theory, a Thomistic theory, a Behaviouristic theory, an Apollonian theory, a pragmatistic theory, a reflective theory, and no theory at all. It has also been classified as nonsense which indeed, by its own admission, it will likely some day turn out to be. (Kelly 1970a: 10)

When discussing personal construct theory, Kelly took great delight in raising the ambiguity of categorized systems which sought to place his viewpoint within one framework or another. The various categories of cultural transmission, romanticism, progressivism and de-schooling which we elaborated in the previous chapter represent alternative ways of looking at education. At different times these approaches and their under-lining metaphors have had their heyday. We should not assume, however, that these categories have rigid boundaries nor indeed that there may not be alternative educational perspectives that will arise in due course.

In this chapter we seek not to categorize Kelly's work *but, instead, we will highlight areas we see as relevant to constructivist education.* This abstraction represents, of course, our own perspective and preoccupations. We do not intend to cover in detail Kelly's theory nor do we seek to encapsulate it in the proverbial nutshell. The reader is referred to the personal writings of George Kelly for a fuller appreciation of the implications of Personal Construct Psychology. Consideration here will be given to aspects of Kelly's work which relate to the educational process.

Kelly was a true radical whose education and interest spanned a range of disciplines. He first studied physics and mathematics and intended to complete an engineering course after graduation. His interest in social issues led him instead to study educational psychology in which he obtained a MA at the University of Kansas in 1927. After a period of teaching, he obtained a B Ed at the University of Edinburgh and a PhD in Psychology at Iowa University. Thus Kelly engaged with a number of disciplines. It is not surprising then that he advocated a multi-disciplinary approach to education rather than rigid subject boundaries. Kelly rarely wrote specifically on education. However, while studying at the University of Edinburgh he wrote a paper which was eventually published in 1979, in a book edited by Stringer and Bannister. The paper was entitled 'Social Inheritance' and in a foreword to the paper, Bannister suggested that: *the most significant aspect of this early essay is the argument running through it that education should be about personal meaning* (p. 3). It is this emphasis on personal meaning that harmonizes Kelly's perspective, and that of those who have drawn on his seminal writings, with contemporary approaches in education. In particular we will concern ourselves with issues such as the 'perspective of the personal', the focus on relevance and responsibility within the teaching and learning process and the epistemological issues surrounding relativity of knowledge. Underpinning all of these is Kelly's recognition and valuing of alternative perspectives.

Perspective of the personal

The current vogue for constructivism may mask Kelly's pioneering spirit which enthused many Personal Construct Psychologists to take his lead and explore the implications of his work. Bruner (1990: 163) when discussing the 'cognitive revolution' noted that Kelly's two volumes *The Psychology of Personal Constructs* appeared in 1955 'a year before the by-now-standard date for the "opening of the cognitive revolution"', and noted that when he reviewed the work, he 'hailed it as the first effort to construct a theory of personality from a theory of knowledge'. Bruner recognized that Kelly was in the forefront of those concerned with how people make sense of their worlds.

Britton (1976: 3) discussed his approach to teaching and drew heavily on Kelly's theory. For example in his discussion on the limitations of behaviour modification he said:

> there is in behaviour modification, that is to say, a method educators may use, ... no ethic for the educational process. For my part, therefore, I would go with George Kelly whose methods are themselves exponents of the philosophy that provide the ethic.

For many years writers on educational issues have argued that it is time that recognition be given to the perspectives of the people engaged in classroom interaction. Blumer (1966: 542), writing on educational research, suggested that:

> Since action is forged by the actor out of what he perceives, interprets and judges, one would have to ... take the role of the actor and see his world from his standpoint.

We took this to heart in naming one module of a course we ran for professional practitioners 'Education as if people matter'.

This 'perspective of the personal' is central to the work of George Kelly. It is implicit in the title of his theory – personal construct theory – and explicit in his writings. e.g. 'We start with a person. Organisms, lower animals and societies can wait' (Kelly, 1970a: 9). The fundamental postulate of personal construct theory is that 'a person's processes are psychologically channelised by the ways in which he anticipates events' (Kelly, 1955: 46). For Kelly a person's behaviour is not driven by instinct (as in psycho-analytic theory) nor is it determined by the schedules of reinforcement and associations between stimulus and response (as in Skinnerian and Behaviourist theories). These were the dominant models within American psychology in the 1950s when Kelly wrote his two volumes.

There have been many metaphors used in psychology, for example man: the telephone exchange, man: the hydraulic system, and man: the computer. Man: the scientist was Kelly's metaphor. He suggested that people and scientists are both engaged in a process of observation, interpretation, prediction and control. According to Kelly, each person erects a representational model of the world which enables him or her to chart a course of behaviour in relation to it. This model is subject to change over time since constructions of reality are constantly tested out and modified to allow better predictions in the future. Thus for Kelly the questioning and exploring, revising and replacing in the light of predictive failure which is symptomatic of scientific theorizing, is precisely what people do when attempting to anticipate events. The person can be seen as a scientist constantly experimenting with a personal experience. For Kelly a person is 'a form of motion' – thus he denies the necessity of 'carrot and stick' or 'impulse-driven' theories of motivation. People are inevitably and constantly attempting to make sense of their environment. A person's anticipation of future events, is 'both the push and pull of the psychology of Personal Constructs' (Kelly, 1955: 49). Kelly does not deny the importance of early experiences or present environmental circumstances, but he suggested that it was more important to know what and how people think about their present situation than to know what their early childhood experiences were or what environmental circumstances they now find themselves in. This stems from his fundamental postulate; central to this was the view that people are constantly engaged in testing their anticipation and their understanding of their worlds.

Clandinin (1986: 166) used the term image in a similar way to our reading of personal constructs in her concern with the development of teachers:

> Images as components of personal practical knowledge, are the coalescence of a person's personal, private and professional experience. Image is a way of organising and reorganising past experience, within reflection and as the image finds expression in practice and as a perspective from which new experience is taken. Image is a personal, meta-level, organising concept in personal practical knowledge that embodies a person's experience; finds expression in practice; and is the perspective from which new experiences is taken.

The 'Progressivist' movement in education emphasized the activity of the person struggling to impose meaning on his or her experiences and rejects the notion of a passive receiver of knowledge. The following quotation from Berman and Roderick (1973: 3), writing about the school context, indicated some assumptions about curriculum which appear to us to be compatible with Kelly's viewpoint:

> Curriculum has long been thought of as that which is taught to somebody else ... The view of these writers is that curriculum must put the person at the centre of what is learned. Curriculum development and subsequent research on the curriculum will then see the person as the meaning maker and plan curricula experiences which enable the child to consider, contemplate, and expand his meanings. Critical to curriculum development, then is the ascertaining of what is happening to the individual child as he interacts with persons, materials, time and space within the context of the school and the classroom.

This emphasis on the person as the meaning-maker is central to Kelly's position. In order to understand a person's behaviour it is necessary to know how he or she construes his or her particular situation. Kelly argues that persons differ from each other in their construction of events (individuality corollary). The structural analysis of the education system which was prevalent in the late 1970s had limitations. A major assumption of this approach is that the structural variables of a school are directly related to aspects of its pupils' success. Research on the pros and cons of particular structural aspects of schools, e.g. streamed versus unstreamed, produced contradictory findings. A Kellyian viewpoint would reject social determinism – as Kelly said, 'Societies can wait'. Kelly would not presume that the members undergoing a similar education system or belonging to particular groups would *necessarily* share the same system of construing. However, he did admit the possibility of shared areas of personal meaning and this was made explicit in his commonality corollary:

> To the extent that one person employs a construction of experience which is similar to that employed by another, his processes are psychologically similar to those of the other person. (Kelly, 1970a: 20)

Nevertheless, while acknowledging that we might share some constructs with others, it is Kelly's stress on the personal nature of meaning and the elevation of the person to the central focus of inquiry that aligns him with much of contemporary theorizing on education.

Beattie (1995: 146) emphasized the importance of construction and reconstruction within an educational process and the personal nature of these events:

> In the telling and retelling of our stories we change, we learn, we grow, giving up the stories of ourselves that we hold when we can replace them with richer and more significant versions most suited to our current environment and to the environments and to the future we foresee.

Relevance and responsibility

In the section on De-schooling in Chapter 1, we drew attention to the viewpoints of theorists, such as Postman and Weingartner (1971) and Rogers (1969), who argued that it is important that we realize that significant learning will only take place if the learner perceives personal relevance in the matter being learned. Personal construct theorists Thomas and Harri-Augstein (1985: xxiv) argued that if learning is to be an enriching experience, the meanings that emerge must be personally 'significant in some part of the person's life. The viability of these meanings depends on how richly the individual incorporates them into personal experience.'

Berman and Roderick (1973: 8) held a similar viewpoint. In their discussion on curriculum development, cited earlier, they made the distinction between public knowledge, i.e. that which exists in books, films, museums etc. and personal knowledge. They suggested that it is only, however, 'when knowledge has meaning for the person so that he or she can take an idea and turn it to see its many facets that real learning has taken place'.

Kelly recognized learning as a personal exploration and saw the teacher's role as helping to design and implement each child's own undertakings:

> To be a fully accredited participant in the experimental enterprise she must gain some sense of what is being seen through the child's eyes. (Kelly, 1970b: 262)

What is relevant to the person is of importance and, for education to be a joint venture between the teacher and learner, it would be beneficial if each has some awareness of the other's personal constructs. Kelly's (1955: 95) sociality corollary states: 'to the extent that one person construes the construction process of another he may play a role in a social process involving the other person'.

The perspective of the student as well as that of the teacher is important, although traditionally learning has been defined mainly from the latter's perspective. For the existentialist the ultimate responsibility for learning rests with the student – people have responsibility for their own being. The existentialist rejects the notion of unquestioning acceptance by the student. The responsibility lies with students to incorporate public knowledge within their own view of the world. Knowledge should be part of a person's inner experience and is therefore emotional as well as intellectual. This point was stressed by Kelly in that, for him, the distinction usually made between cognition and affect was inappropriate. He eschewed the dualism of body and mind and used the term *construing* by which he meant 'placing an interpretation which subsumes thoughts and emotion' (Kelly, 1955: 50).

Central to Kelly's theory is the notion that people may construe their environment in an infinite number of different ways depending on their imagination and the courageousness of their experimentation. People are not stimulus-bound but they may well be bound by their construal of the world.

Rose (1983) discussed the way we choose to engage with our experiences. We can either live our lives according to plans pre-determined by others or we can construct our own and choose to tell and retell our stories. As Rose (1983: 17) put it, 'all living is a creative act of greater or lesser authenticity, hindered or helped by the fictions to which we submit ourselves'.

'Man is nothing other than what he makes himself' is a tenet of existentialism which also applies to Personal Construct Psychology. Kelly was perhaps somewhat reluctant to accept the label 'existentialist'. However, in his dislike of labels, his view of construing as having an emotional as well as cognitive base, his accent on freedom and responsibility of the individual and on the relevance of events to the individual, he highlights areas of concern which are also of importance to contemporary education.

Relativity of knowledge

Kelly described his epistemological position as that of Constructive Alternativism:

Constructive Alternativism holds that man understands himself, his surroundings and his potentialities by devising constructions to place upon them and then testing the tentative utility of these constructions against such ad interim criteria as the successful prediction and control of events. (Kelly, 1966: 1)

While Kelly did not deny the existence of reality, he maintained that it is presumptuous to claim that a person's constructions of reality are convergent with it:

The fact that my only approach to reality is through offering some responsible construction of it does not discourage me from postulating that it is there. The open question for man is not whether reality exists or not but what he can make of it. (Kelly, 1969a: 25)

This echoes the philosophy of Pragmatism we discussed in Chapter 1.

For Kelly events are subject to 'as great a variety of constructions as our wits would enable us to contrive' (1970a: 1). He rejected an absolutist view of truth and contrasted his position with that of Accumulative Fragmentalism – the notion that knowledge is a growing collection of substantiated facts or 'nuggets of truth'. His philosophical position is opposed to that of the Realist. Even the most highly developed scientific knowledge can be seen to be subject to human reconstruction.

For Kelly the construction of reality is an active, creative, rational, emotional and pragmatic affair. 'Man: the scientist' evolves a set of constructions which is put to the test and may ultimately be discarded in favour of a new set of constructions if the former fails to adequately anticipate events. Kelly pointed out that all theories are hypotheses devised by people which may fit all the known facts at any particular time but may eventually be found wanting in some unforeseeable respect and be eventually replaced by a 'better theory'. An example from physics is the reappraisal of Newton's theory by Einstein. However, Einstein's theory is unlikely to be the ultimate truth and Einstein himself regarded his theory as defective and spent much of his life trying to find a better one.

Bell and Gilbert (1996:46) suggested that:

Kelly's great contribution to constructivism is his assertion that there are no pre-determined limits on constructs in terms of the nature and range of their application. The limit to their creation is only set by the imagination of the individual concerned and by the constructs being continually tested, for their predictive and explanatory adequacy in physical and social contexts; those that prove successful will be retained used again and used in a wider range of contexts, whilst those that do not will be modified or abandoned.

In putting forward his theory, Kelly suggested that, as a theory, it would be subject to revision since it is itself an example of a human construct and so can be seen as an hypothesis waiting to be put to the test (Kelly, 1970a: 10). This view of theory, science and knowledge was echoed in the writings of Karl Popper (1963). He saw science and knowledge as progressing through a series of 'conjectures and refutations'. Kuhn (1970) analysed the progress of science and suggested that growth of knowledge occurs when the dominant paradigm of the day is challenged by the revolutionaries who step outside the limits of present theory and engage in what Kuhn calls 'extraordinary science'. Kuhn suggested that professional scientists are educated in the 'normal' scientific mode which involves solving problems within the limits of the theory the scientist has been taught. The theory itself is not questioned. If problems are not solved the theory is not invalidated, the scientist merely lacks ingenuity! Kelly would see this as a lack of courage in experimentation.

Popper (1970), in reply to Kuhn, suggested that normal science in Kuhn's sense does exist but it is the activity of the non-revolutionary, the none too critical professional, the student who accepts the dogma of the day. In discussing Popper's philosophy of science, Magee (1973: 68) argued that it could:

> scarcely be more undogmatic ... it holds that we never actually know – that our approach to any and every situation or problem needs to be always such as to accommodate not merely unforeseeable contributions but the permanent possibility of a radical transformation of the whole conceptual scheme. A great deal of disillusionment with science and reason which is so widespread in our age is based on precisely such mistaken notions of what science and reason are.

Kuhn and Popper, like Kelly, are both arguing for the relative nature of knowledge. In recent years this relativity of knowledge is acknowledged by constructivist educators, although it was recognized many years ago by Postman and Weingartner (1971: 100) who argued:

> We now know that each man creates his own unique world, that he, and he alone, generates whatever reality he can ever know ... the purposes and assumptions and therefore the perceptions of each man are uniquely his .. among other things, this means that no man can be absolutely certain of anything. The best anyone can ever do is say how something appears to him.

These words echo the view of knowledge put forward by Kelly and could be seen to be a re-statement of his fundamental postulate and individuality corollary.

Kelly recognized the subversive implications of his views. They pose a direct challenge, and possible threat, to teachers who see their role as passing on bodies of substantiated facts or 'absolute truths' without the necessity of presenting these as problematic or conjectural. The idea that all facts are subject to revision leaves the door open for the student to question the knowledge presented by the teacher.

More recently views on the sociology of knowledge emphasize a person's active construction of experience and offer a clear challenge to the static, analytic conception of knowledge which has failed to empower individuals in their pursuit of personal meaning. Many have drawn on the social phenomenology of Schutz (1967). Schutz suggested that action is mediated by a complex interrelational process within the constituted biography of the individual. Reality is interpreted in terms of the provinces of meaning which make up the individual's 'stock of knowledge', which is his/her *Lebensfelt*. This stock of knowledge seems similar to Kelly's view of a construct system. It is continually changing through the processes of constitution and accommodation in the same way as validation and invalidation lead to elaboration and reorganization in a person's construct system. Schutz, however, emphasized that the individual's 'frame of reference' is a social product in that confirmation or disconfirmation of it is likely to come from his/her 'consociates' – those with whom the individual has most social contact – with whom he/she is jointly engaged in reality construction.

The writings of Schutz and Berger and Luckmann (1967) have had significant effect on assumptions regarding the sociology of education. As Esland (1971: 96) pointed out:

> if knowledge is dereified, it is, then, a much more negotiable commodity between teacher and pupil ... there is no reason to suppose that these will remain within the 'boundaries' of what are now heuristically labelled as 'subjects'. New configurations of knowledge are likely to emerge from the combinations of questions which arise in the learning situations ... the boundaries are only human constructs and can, therefore, be broken.

The similarities between this position and that of Kelly's is most apparent when we compare it with Kelly's view of the relativity of categorization – 'subjects' being a case in point – and his view of teaching and learning as a process of negotiation between the joint experimenters in the venture, i.e. the student and teacher.

The area of curriculum development has become a focus of attention in education. Issues such as the relativity of knowledge and the recognition of the importance of the learner's, as well as the teacher's, perspective have had a profound influence. Those advocating humanistic foundations of education suggest that we should recognize that learning is more than an intellectual exercise. Joyce proposed that the curriculum should become pluralistic and should represent many domains of possible development. Attention should be paid to the creative and performing arts, education for greater interpersonal sensitivity and affairs of international concern. A goal of curriculum planning should be: 'To create environments which enable individuals to actualise themselves on their own terms – emotionally, intellectually, and socially' (Joyce, 1972: 169). Constructivists have advocated such an approach.

Change is occurring so rapidly that we can no longer foresee the information that would be necessary for a student to have in order to be successful in the future. It is for this reason education curricula should include helping students to deal with change – the teaching of strategies for survival. It is of vital importance that the teacher act as a facilitator of discussion, a resource for finding information and a stimulator of problem-solving. As we said at the beginning of this book, we live in an increasingly complex and uncertain world marked by accelerating technological and social change. As constructivists we suggest that educational procedures developed during an era of relative stability and certainty are no longer able to provide the students with the skills they need to exist effectively in contemporary society. Jordon (1973: 87) commented:

> How to learn is in itself something that has to be learned, though is rarely 'taught' in traditional schools ... the development of learning competence enables the child to become an active determiner of his own destiny and gives him the fundamental power of extending and releasing all other potentialities.

Educationalists have often been slow to rise to this challenge. Many argue that external constraints posed by government agencies and examining bodies militate against such an approach. However, other educationalists do support a move from an analysis of the curriculum content and sequence as a main focus towards an attempt to understand the student's current experiences of concepts in the classroom and how these might change. As Driver (1982: 75) suggested, 'we may need to pay as much attention to the learner's current ideas and how they change as we do to the structure of knowledge taught'. Driver's work has been informed by Personal Construct Psychology. Bell and Gilbert (1996: 156) warned us that there can be threats to the development of constructivist approach in teaching and learning. They noted that:

> for example, in the United Kingdom, the new curricula are couched in terms of content to be learnt and the amount of content is high. The teachers are required to 'deliver' that content, a term which implies a process of passing over something tangible. This trend is against the professional judgement of teachers, fails to recognise the active agency of students in their own learning, and is in favour of a commodity-production view of knowledge. Assessment policies ... are often in tension with constructivist views of learning ...

This notion of agency is central to the work of Thomas and Harri-Augstein who have applied tenets of Personal Construct Psychology within the wider field of learning. They have encouraged learners, teachers and managers in industry to recognize their potential through being able to become self-organized as learners. By self-organization Thomas and Harri-Augstein refer to a process by which learners are encouraged to reflect on their own learning process, often with the help of a facilitator. They have pointed out the limitations inherent in previous versions of learning theory that were predicated on experiments in the laboratory. Thus they stated:

> Experimental psychologists constructing theories in their meaning-isolated laboratories have largely ignored the simple truth that it is the meaning attributed to each event, not the event itself, which influences a person's reactions to it.
>
> It is their personal meaning which becomes the personal cause. Actions and subsequent events represent the 'effects' of this meaning, as it plays out in a given situation. The construction of personal experience is prior. This process is essentially conversational. An awareness of this process demands an awareness of a meta-conversation about learning. (Thomas and Harri-Augstein, 1985: 27–8)

Their book shares with the reader the various technologies they have invented which can 'represent personal meaning in ways which enable reflection, review and effective transformation of the quality of human experience and performance'. Learning-to-learn becomes a central task for the learner and the facilitation of this meta-cognition, part of the role of the teacher.

Kelly's epistemological position and the role of a teacher

So far in this examination of Kelly's basic ideas regarding knowledge and its implications for constructivist education we have stressed the relativity of knowledge and its personal nature. Lest the reader assume that this indicates that Kelly took a solipsistic view of personal construing it is important to note that, while Kelly advocated the position that events are subject to interpretation limited only by our creativity, he did acknowledge the existence of an external reality we are striving to map effectively. This is evident in the following:

> We presume that the world is really existing and that man is gradually coming to understand it. (Kelly, 1955: 6)

> Some of the alternative ways of construing are better than others. (Kelly, 1955: 45)

Since we all approach 'reality' with our existing constructions our appreciation of the external world is always represented or constructed in the light of our current theorizing and could well be improved upon by further experimentation.

Nystedt and Magnusson (1982: 34) noted the contribution Kelly's theory makes to the 'mainstream of constructivism in psychology' and neatly summed up the tenets of constructivism which permeate Kelly's writing:

> It is fundamental to the constructivist's view that the environment can never be directly known but that conception determines perception. We know reality only by acting upon it. This means that knowledge is neither a copy nor a mirror of reality, but the forms and content of knowledge are constructed by the one who experiences it. The active interaction between the individual and the environment is mediated by the cognitive structures of the individual. What we learn in interaction with the environment is dependent upon our own structuring of those experiences. Thus according to this view, man does not merely respond to the environment, he construes it.

This epistemological position has implications for how the teacher helps the student to actively construe experiences. In viewing our constructions of reality as potentially open to reconstruction, Kelly's stance as a therapist and as an educator was to encourage clients/learners to articulate their world views and to recognize these world views as current hypotheses potentially open to invalidation. In this way he hoped the clients/learners would put themselves in the position of opening their minds to potential alternatives which might serve his/her cause better. Her saw his concern as 'finding better ways to help a person reconstrue his life so that he need not be the victim of his past' (Kelly, 1955: 23).

He noted that people may be very resistant to accepting invalidation of personal construction (*hostility*). They may be reticent to experiment with alternative models. Their constructions may have been designated the status of 'the world as it really is' and thus not be amenable to contradiction. The pursuit of conceptual change and liberation from personal 'prisons' though potentially possible, may lead to anxiety. The very recognition that our personal construct system does not have the 'range of convenience' to accommodate events with which one is confronted is Kelly's description of *anxiety*. This point is of importance for educationalists who are concerned with development and conceptual change.

Conceptual development and change

Against the backcloth of Kelly's epistemology his theory is elegantly developed in terms of a fundamental postulate and eleven corollaries. We will now draw attention to some of these and suggest implications for the role of the teacher in facilitating conceptual development. To reiterate, the fundamental postulate states: 'A person's processes are psychologically channellized by ways in which he anticipates events.' Kelly had taken as his root metaphor 'man: the scientist'. He invited us to entertain the possibility that looking at people as if they were scientists – i.e. the view their scientist-like aspect – might illuminate human behaviour.

Just as the experimental scientist may design his/her experiments round rival hypotheses, so each of us can be seen as designing our daily explorations of life around rival hypotheses which form part of our system of constructs or 'world view'. People can be seen as scientists, constantly experimenting with their definitions of existence.

Kelly saw the scientist as engaged in the *anticipation* of events with the view to the prediction and control of events. The scientist imposes meaning on events in the hope that his/her predictions will be fruitful and useful. It is the invalidation of our anticipation that encourages reorganization of our psychological processes, i.e. conceptual development and change.

> Successive revelation of events invites the person to place new constructions upon them whenever something unexpected happens ... The constructions one places on events are working hypotheses which are about to be put to the test of experience. As one's anticipations are successively revised in the light of the unfolding sequence of events a construction system undergoes progressive evolution. (Kelly, 1955: 72)

For Kelly, the person with a capacity to anticipate events successfully has built a 'coherent' construct system and, if he/she keeps an open frame on the world, conceptual and personal growth is viable. Viable but not necessarily easy – his clients were evidence that people's attempts at changing their construing/anticipation of events was often a traumatic affair.

Kelly's fundamental postulate stated his belief that a person's behaviour in the present is determined by the way he/she is anticipating some future event. This anticipation necessitates the use of the person's constructs. Kelly likened the *personal construct* to an hypothesis which is erected to account for present experience and to forecast events (theory building) and also to assess the accuracy of previous forecasts after the events have occurred, thereby testing and validating or invalidating their predictive efficiency (theory testing).

Constructs do not exist in isolation but are hierarchically grouped; some having subordinate and others having superordinate positions within the system. This is the implication of Kelly's Organization Corollary which states that 'each person characteristically evolves, for his convenience in anticipating events, a construction system embracing ordinal relationships between constructs'. This corollary has profound implications for the development of one of Kelly's tools for investigating construing – the Repertory Grid (see Chapter 4). It also explains why some constructs are relatively amenable to change while others are clung to tightly.

Fundamental to Kelly's view was that motion is an inevitable aspect of human functioning and his use of the term *evolves* in his Organization Corollary was to stress his view that this organization is not a static entity but that constructs are potentially in a constant state of motion and therefore open to change, though some are more open than others.

A key assumption within Kelly's personal construct theory was his Individuality Corollary: 'Persons differ from each other in their construction of events.'

This central theme runs throughout his theory as he lays great stress on the uniqueness of each person's construct system. For Kelly, it is presumptuous to assume that another person will have the same idea as oneself or others who have ostensibly experienced the same set of events. Constructs can differ in their focus, range, permeability, their position within an ordinal hierarchical framework and the strength of their relationships with other parts of the system. These formal aspects of the nature of constructs will affect the content and structure of a person's system such that, seen as a whole, each one of us is likely to have a unique system. The essence of Kelly's clinical work was to help people to articulate at least a part of their individual constructions. He saw effective teaching as requiring a similar process.

This articulation is important on two counts:

1. It allows the clinician/teacher to have some understanding of the personal models the client/learner is currently using to impose meaning on the world.
2. The process of articulation may help the client/learner to clarify thoughts, recognize the significance of the power of these thoughts and reflect on potential avenues for change.

For Kelly the first was vital if the encounter was to be fully effective. This is indicated in his Sociality Corollary which we discussed earlier.

What Kelly intended to convey by this corollary was that, unless we have some understanding of another person's set of personal constructs about the domain within which we wish to converse, and that person has some understanding of our constructs, the process of communication between us will be inadequate. What is important is not that we share the same constructs but that we have some empathy with regard to each other's point of view. As a direct consequence of his Sociality Corollary Kelly recognized that learning is a personal exploration and that the teacher must come to some understanding of the experiments, lines of enquiry and personal strategies used by the learner. He saw the teacher's role as helping:

> to design and implement each child's own undertakings, as well as to assist in interpreting the outcomes and in devising more cogent behavioural inquiries. But usually she has to begin, as any apprentice begins, by implementing what others have designed; in this case, what her children have initiated. (Kelly, 1970b: 262)

Kelly's Sociality Corollary implies the need to come to some understanding of the current conceptualization of the child. His individuality and organization corollaries alert us to the need to assume that these conceptions are part of what will be an idiosyncratic construct system of personal meaning organized within a hierarchical network. In order that we address notions of conceptual change at least two more of Kelly's corollaries need to be introduced – namely Fragmentation and Modulation.

The nature of the relationship between constructs within a person conceptual system was seen by Kelly as one where incompatibilities and inconsistencies between constructs have been minimized while retaining maximum potential for elaboration of the system. That is, each of the clusters of constructs (and there are many) represent coherent domains of meaning that a person uses to explain and explore certain issues or experiences. He argued that the ways in which a person's systems can change are not random or *ad hoc* but are themselves part of a regulated system of change. Each system (or domain of meaning) is part of a person's overall system which not only binds the subsystems together, within overarching superordinate constructs, but which also regulates the processes of change within the domains. Whether or not a person will change his or her constructs depends on the *permeability* of constructs. The success or otherwise of predictions entailed by the constructs and the extent of change will depend on the nature of the inter-relationships between constructs and their position within the person's repertoire. Thus the Modulation and Fragmentation Corollaries are intimately linked to the Organization Corollary.

The Modulation Corollary states: 'The variation in a person's construction system is limited by the permeability of the constructs within whose range of convenience the variants lie.'

The construction system being referred to here is the whole-person system. Kelly has a particular meaning for the term *permeability*, by which he means a degree of openness to change and the potential to countenance new features. He said: 'What is meant by permeability is not a construct's plasticity, or its amenability to change within itself, but its capacity to be used as a referent for novel events and to accept anew subordinate constructions within its range of convenience' (Kelly, 1970a: 19).

If some parts of a person's system are *impermeable* then those parts will be resistant to change since those constructs will 'reject elements on the basis of their newness'. Resistance to change can also be the result of what Kelly referred to as 'hostility'.

Kelly's notion of 'range of convenience' also bears comment. Both a construct and a system of constructs is seen as having a limited sphere of applicability. Certain features or events can be ruled out of consideration by a construct on the basis that, for them it is an inappropriate or inadequate way of being viewed. The system is neutral towards them – they lie outside its range of convenience.

Kelly saw conceptual development as an evolutionary process which involved the progressive differentiation of conceptual structures (groups of constructs) into independently organized substructures and the hierarchic integration of these substructures at progressively higher levels of abstraction. The functional differentiation of structures enhances the 'range of convenience' of an individual's construct system. However, hierarchic integration of these differing substructures is necessary for the integrity of a person's construct system. Having a meta-theory which provides a linkage between a number of mini-theories can allow the individual to make a wider range of cross references than is possible within a very differentiated system.

The Fragmentation Corollary suggests that a person might use successive subsystems that are inconsistent. Thus, it says: 'A person may successively employ a variety of construction subsystems which are inferentially incompatible with each other.'

Clearly some individuals can tolerate a greater number of inconsistencies in their construct systems than can other people, though this tolerance is itself a function of the permeability of the overall, superordinate system. We both might view some people as 'good' though each of us might have different tolerances of aspects of their behaviour viewed as 'incompatible with good', for instance.

While adequate cognitive functioning requires integration through the deployment of superordinate constructs, differentiation, inconsistency or *fragmentation* can have its merits. Kelly (1955) suggested that one implication of his Fragmentation Corollary is that the constructive alternativist can test out new hypotheses without having just to discard the old hypotheses/constructs. Constructs are hypotheses and we can hold on to constructs which are incompatible – Kelly saw this as a feature of human thought which was especially noted in children:

> The nice thing about hypotheses is that you don't have to believe them. This, I think, is a key to the genius of scientific method. It permits you to be inconsistent with what you know long enough to see what will happen. Children do that. What is wonderful about the language of hypothesis is its refreshing ability to free the scientist from the entangling consistencies of adulthood. For a few precious moments he can think again like a child, and, like a child, learn from his experience. (Kelly, 1970b: 258).

Kelly clearly valued the child's, at times inconsistent, theorizing as scientific while the adult's tightly ordered constructs could limit their theorizing, thus stunting the development of new knowledge. However, he saw limits to incompatibility of constructs – we can tolerate some incompatibility but not too much. The amount that can be tolerated is determined by the permeability of superordinating constructs. Fragmentation and Modulation corollaries give a picture of a person using a variety of differing subsystems to make sense of what is happening. These are distinctive, semi-independent and are subsumed at some point by a unifying thread, some superordinate construct.

In this section we have highlighted some fundamental tenets of Kelly's theory that would underlie a Personal Construct Psychologist's view of conceptual development and change.

Science education as a discipline example

A Kellyan approach to teaching would suggest that, as a matter of policy, differences between the learner's personal meanings, those of the teacher and the formal concepts of the 'received view' of the subject should be dealt with within an open forum where the differences are valued for what they are, i.e. constructive alternative ways of seeing.

As teachers we may see ourselves as in the business of encouraging conceptual change. In science education there has been a growth in what is being called 'conceptual change teaching' based upon the premise that the instructional act starts with the learner's 'naive' conceptions being articulated and then 'experiments' devised so that these can be challenged and (hopefully) the 'accepted' view of science will prevail, given the 'failure' of their personal models to hold up to the challenge of experimentation. *Up to a point* this may seem to be an implication of some of Kelly's notions *but* Kelly had much more cognisance of the location of a particular domain of sense making within the overall construct system. The particular domain under experimentation may be more or less linked with other domains, may be more or less permeable and its position with respect to core constructs may be of vital importance to the person. The perceived consequence of change may engender anxiety, fear, or feelings of threat. What is difficult for a teacher to gauge is the *perceived consequence* and the degree of stress that 'conceptual change instruction' of the type referred to above, will induce. This is not to suggest that we do not engage in the *encouragement* of conceptual change. However, we should remember that the goggles through which others view their worlds may not be easily altered. There are some constructs which Kelly referred to as 'core constructs' which are fundamental and central to the maintenance of a person's 'sense of self'.

The notion that people have core constructs permeated Kelly's Fixed Role Therapy, which was a model of the process of encouraging conceptual change. We too must recognize that by encouraging students to articulate their personal meanings they are portraying something of their *selves*. As such, the climate has to be one in which this disclosure is valued. In putting forward the 'accepted' view of a concept we need to stress the conjectural nature of this current view. Fixed Role Therapy begins with the client 'painting a portrait' of him/herself – either through a written or spoken 'self-characterization sketch' or the completion of a repertory grid. These techniques are discussed in later chapters. In Fixed Role Methods, once the person's view of himself/herself, or some domain of the world under scrutiny, is exposed a negotiation may take place between client/student and clinician/teacher. The person is encouraged to see his/her point of view (range of constructs) as current hypotheses and as such potentially open to change.

It is recognized that the client would not be able to cope with a concurrent series of experiments with the negation of *all* his/her constructs and so one of the person's current hypotheses is selected. It is likely that, at first, this construct would not be a core construct that entailed a large number of other central tenets. The person is encouraged to construct an alternative hypothesis to the construct selected and then go away and *behave as if* this construct was one he/she believed in. In this way the person puts him/herself into a position where an alternative *may* be validated. However, as indicated earlier in this chapter, there could be prolonged resistance to change. The role of the clinician is to *support* the client during the unsettling period of experimentation with new ideas *and* at times to suggest alternative hypotheses for exploration. As Kelly (1969b) pointed out, this strategy had much in common with how he tutored his research students. We would suggest the process is one which sensitive teachers could use in schools or in other educational contexts.

The outcome of strategies such as Fixed Role Methods could be diverse. Some students might hold on to their current hypotheses and temporarily adopt another perspective (fragmentation). Others may choose to see their model as being invalidated and replace it with one proffered by a peer or the 'accepted' view supplied by the teacher. Yet another course of action may be that the students hold resolutely to their original models and reject others given (however, they may have a better *understanding* of the other perspectives). The process of interchange of personal models could also result in a person discarding his/her previous model, rejecting all of the other models put forward by members of the group and erecting an alternative model which goes beyond any of the models. The latter type of change is essential in scientific *progress*.

Whatever the outcome, it will be determined by the personal construction of the individual. This is *not* to say that issues such as the social power of the originators of alternative models, pressure towards group conformity, feelings of personal worth held by the person etc. will not be factors linked to the outcome. These issues will be *construed* by the individual in relation to his/her analysis of the adequacy of the prediction of the model within the particular domain. The expediency of changing one's viewpoint will be gauged and the outcome will be an integration of a number of issues such as range of convenience, modulation and permeability and the avoidance of excessive fragmentation of structure. For Kelly construing is an emotional *and* cognitive event and the personal construct system is *in toto* an holistic entity. Change in any part will have greater or lesser implications for other parts of the total system.

However, unless the learner's views are articulated the teacher cannot devise a strategy whereby the learner's model can be put to the test. Kelly noted that change in construing will only take place if the person experiments with his/her way of seeing things, construes the implications of these experiments and sees that it would result in an elaboration of his/her constructs system, if he/she were to adopt an alternative way of seeing things. For a Kellyan, teaching it should be based upon a rigorous consideration of alternative theories – *those of the students, the teacher* and '*received wisdom*'. The ethos of the social context within which such a consideration should take place would be one where the alternatives are treated in an equitable manner. There should be sufficient support for students as they try to articulate their concepts of science so that they are encouraged to talk about their ideas. As Sutton (1981) pointed out, talking about your ideas is one of the most powerful provocations to sorting out what you understand. Talking about ideas and listening to the conflicting opinions of others and the putting of these ideas to the test would represent an approach to teaching which is consistent with Kelly's model of 'man-the-scientist'.

The following extract from Bell and Gilbert draws attention to the work of White who summarized the implications of constructivist research on teaching and learning in science. These writers support the view that, in the learning of science, the nature of the learners prior understanding of concepts (constructs) is important. Although focused on science teaching the following summary is a useful one in drawing out the implications of a constructivist approach for conceptual development in any discipline domain:

- people construct their own interpretations of communications and experiences;
- personal interpretation is determined largely by existing beliefs, which are prior constructions;
- interpretation is often influenced, although not necessarily determined, by the interpretations expressed by others – parents, teachers, peers, texts, and other media;
- students at all levels enter the classroom already holding beliefs relevant to the topic to be studied;
- the extent of beliefs and the intensity with which they are held varies from topic to topic;
- in any given class, there will be a range of beliefs among the students;
- students' beliefs about scientific principles and natural phenomena often differ from the scientists' established beliefs;
- where students' views differ from those of the scientists, they are less economical in interpreting or predicting outcomes of an extended range of events;
- a person can hold beliefs that contradict each other, applying one belief in one context, another belief in another context;
- people often interpret events in a manner that supports a belief, and so avoid confronting discomforting instances. That is, they see what they believe;
- people might alter their memory of an event that contradicts a belief so that their recollection is consistent with what they believe;
- beliefs resist change but students can exchange an alternative conception for the scientists' conception;
- changes of belief, or resolution of contradictions, are usually slow and require repeated experiences that favour the final accepted interpretations; and
- teaching that encourages resolution of (the contradiction between) alternative conceptions with the scientists' view will include elucidation of the students' beliefs, discussion of the beliefs and their implica-

tions, and the design and execution of events that test the accuracy of the beliefs. (Bell and Gilbert, 1996: 4)

The professional development of the teacher as constructivist

The teacher of 1985 is a constructivist who continually builds, elaborates and tests his or her personal theory of the world ... we have begun to move away from those cybernetically elegant, internally consistent but mechanical metaphors that guided our earlier work. (Clark, 1986: 9)

Mahoney (1988:2), discussing constructivist theories, noted that three basic features exist in psychological constructivism – proactive cognition, morphogenic nuclear structure and self-organizing development. She maintained that: 'psychological constructivism refers to a family of theories that share the assertion that human knowledge and experience entail the (pro) active participation of the individual'.

Morphogenic nuclear structure implies a form-generating, centre-based, structural organization – a deep structure or nuclear core of an individual system which influences peripheral aspects. This core is less accessible and amenable to change – as Kelly (1955:82) noted 'core constructs are those which govern a person's maintenance processes – that is, those by which he maintains his identity and existence'.

Professional development strategies which do not invite challenge of a person's implicit theories may be seen as comfortable but may not lead to any reappraisal of current theory or practice.

Within pre- and in-service professional development teachers are being encouraged to rethink the 'metaphors they live by' (Lakoff and Johnson, 1980). The reflective practitioner (Schon, 1983) needs to reflect critically on the meaning of his/her thoughts and actions as a route to the enhancement of professional practice. Constructive alternativism is a view about knowledge and action which supports this recognition that, if practices are to change, the teachers need to examine some of 'their fundamental beliefs'. Teachers may find consideration of their current constructs threatening, especially if they deduce that change is needed. Threatening and revolutionary this may be but some teacher educators see this as empowering the teachers to make education a positive experience for learner and teacher.

Ben-Peretz (1984: 106) advocated participation in 'action research', e.g. in curriculum planning 'as a process of teacher development'. In discussing the investigation of teacher thinking within the framework of personal construct theory, Ben-Peretz argued that assisting teachers to become aware of their construing patterns should be planned as part of a teacher's professional training and development.

Denicolo and Pope (1990) emphasized an emancipatory approach to staff development and suggest a number of assumptions which are shared by Personal Construct Psychologists and those advocating action research as a form of staff development. These assumptions are discussed in detail in Chapter 3.

It has been assumed that learning and professional development are enhanced by reflection on and in practice. However, we reiterate that it does not follow that this process is easy. Kelly warned of the potential hostility and resistance to change of the individual whose core constructs might be threatened by the consideration of an alternative model which would require too much adaptation of the system. The teacher educator/action researcher needs to be aware of the extreme sensitivity of the reflective material which can be evoked using certain techniques. They must be prepared to give time and support during periods of deconstruction and reconstruction which may occur when an individual is confronted with an image or action which he/she wishes to change. This is a fundamental requirement within constructivist approaches to professional teacher education.

Clark (1995: 124) alluded to the fact that for many the phase 'professional development of teachers' contains:

> a great deal of negative baggage: it implies a process done to teachers; that teachers need to be forced into developing; that teachers have deficits in knowledge and skills that can be fixed by training; and that teachers are pretty much alike.

As personal constructivists we reject such an approach to professional development.

Diamond (1985) has used a staff development approach based on fixed role therapy and has conducted research on the constructs of pre- and in-service teachers regarding their role. He argued that teachers would give up a viewpoint, even if it were an integral part of them, providing that they had become aware of the more personally meaningful implications of an alternative. He gave examples of comments made by pre-service teachers who had taken part in the research using techniques based on Repertory Grids and commentary on outcome. One was from a student teacher, Mitzi, who wrote:

> Everyone was looking for something different and went about adjusting to their particular perceived environments in different ways. However, the grid seemed

to help most of us. To compare the three 'snapshots' of my year in Dip Ed has been a much appreciated reflective experience for me. I came to terms with how, as a person, I felt about the prospect of teaching as a chosen career, what fears and anxieties I had in relation to teaching, as well as my perceptions of students. I came to see both what and how I saw. (Diamond, 1985: 34)

As Diamond (1985: 34) said, 'if teachers can be helped to "open their eyes", they can see how to choose and fashion their own version of reality'.

Olson (1992:78) explained some of the potential difficulties of such a process:

Changing practice isn't merely a technical process – it involves considering what the change signifies. That entailed dialogue – a conversation between the old and the new. Some of those who hold a technocentric view of change, say that such dialogue is futile because innovations involve technical matters that practitioners cannot understand. This is a fake idea.

We have had the privilege of working closely with practising teachers from many professional sectors. We explored Personal Construct Psychology together and they considered the utility of the ideas within their own personal and professional contexts. The following comments reflect how some of these teachers saw the implications of Personal Construct Psychology:

An environment which is conducive to student inquiry and exploration requires a supportive accepting instructor who is willing to acknowledge his students' theories and at the same time make his theories known to them.

I think PCP could have a great impact in this area as teachers examine their own constructs towards students who have disabilities. If the teacher's perceptions of the disabled child are negative, then the mainstream experience would be a negative one for the child.

It is not an easy task this process of being a 'scientist' and the ways are very uncharted and of times uncertain. The process seems to require a great deal of emotional energy.

Since my recent introduction to PCP, I am not sure I want to 'play the game' safely, and less sure that I want to 'play the game' at all.

The challenge of Personal Construct Psychology for educators

We hope that in Chapter 2 we have shared with you our construing of the significance of Personal Construct Psychology for education. At the end of an earlier book Pope and Keen (1981: 163) it was suggested that:

> it is our belief that individuals and groups working in an educational setting will have evolved a particular construction of education within which they operate and that many different views on what education is and should be can and do co-exist. It seems to us that problems arise when an individual or group operates with one set of assumptions to others without any acknowledgement or understanding of an alternative framework or set of assumptions which the other values.
>
> We would suggest that each of us must, from time to time, review how we are construing education and the extent to which we understand the position of others with whom we interact. This seems to us to be a central message of Kelly's work and one which we feel is relevant to those who wish for an effective and democratic educational process.

We will pursue these notions further in ensuing chapters.

We all need to recognize that we are continually construing our world through constructive goggles. From time to time we may need to visit an 'optician' or take steps to *alter our own eyes* to paraphrase Diamond (1985). As teachers and researchers we need to examine our own goggles if we are to expect our learners to adopt such a stance in their conceptual development.

Concomitant with the awareness of the need to extend our approach to teaching and learning to incorporate notion and relevance and responsibility, of relativity of knowledge and to provide a medium through which personal strategies can be evolved, there is a growing emphasis on the need to reappraise educational research methodology which we discuss in the next chapter.

CHAPTER 3

Alternative constructions of educational research

Limitations of early research

> There is a growing body of opinion that the technology of psychometrics is largely irrelevant to education; from the application of psychometric techniques of analysis to the construction of tests. (Biggs, 1976: 280)

Professionals in the public and private sector have a duty to develop their own knowledge and practice and they frequently have a role in training and acting as mentor to others. In spite of Knowles (1978) indicating that adult learners are a neglected species, the foundation for much adult education has only superficially been enhanced in recent years by research that has focused on the adult learner. Nevertheless, Goodlad (1984: 9) did emphasize that education for the professions 'must involve some conscious attention not only to the technical component of the professional's service ... but also to the fundamentally moral issue of who is controlling what knowledge for whose benefit'.

On the following page he went on to question whether it was possible that professional education in the 1980s was beginning to shift from a focus on: *control* (by which institutions dominate individuals) to *facilitation* (in which individuals plan the form, pacing and detail of their learning, aided rather than constrained by institutions).

In this chapter we will argue that such a shift is congruent with that taking place in research in other domains of education research. While Knowles noted that it is misguided to assume that what is educationally relevant to the young is equally so for the mature, we suggest that it is inappropriate to transpose unquestioningly into educational environments the approaches and methods of research from other disciplines. To do so not only ignores contextual factors but neglects the complexity of the process.

Biggs (1976), in our opening quotation, agreed with Snow (1974) who had pinpointed the source of the problem as the fact that educational researchers have been obsessed for years by 'systematic' research designs borrowed from agricultural research. In the last analysis it is the people within a particular educational context who will determine the outcome of education within it.

Many researchers began to criticize previous educational research which focused solely on learner performance measured by test grades. In a complex of factors determining a learner's achievement, it must surely be recognized that the teacher's attitudes and expectations are of paramount importance.

There were numerous pen and paper tests of teachers' values and attitudes but these were criticized in that:

- They put the teacher in a test position which is at once a distorting influence. If people believe that they are being judged as good or bad on the basis of their responses it is easy for them to present a desirable picture of themselves.
- They tend to produce only global measures of such things as permissive teacher attitudes and may be limited indicators of actual classroom behaviour.

There was growing dissatisfaction with research into teaching which was based on inventories and attitude scales which use the experimenter's criteria, often without reference to the particular situation in which they are applied. This is a particular problem when research results and principles derived from the compulsory education contexts are applied in adult and professional learning situations. What is deemed effective in one context may be inappropriate in another.

Morrison and MacIntyre (1973) commented on the extensive diversity of criteria used to judge teacher effectiveness. Examples of such criteria are teachers' knowledge of educational psychology, teachers' knowledge of methods of curriculum construction, teachers' knowledge of subject matter, teachers' intelligence, teachers' values, and teachers' emotional and social adjustment. They suggested that research into teaching neglected the fascinating diversity of personal goals that teachers, learners and others within the education learning situation may hold. These criteria may be at odds with those of the experimenter who enters as a stranger in the situation, and who is often seen as an agent of a controlling authority. In the social memory of many work arenas the vision of the 'time and motion' expert, examining overt behaviour without regard to meaning, still persists.

Hamilton and Delamont (1974) noted that systematic observation schedules such as Flanders Interaction Categories tend to focus on surface aspects of interaction and neglect underlying features which may have more meaning. The Flanders system was also criticized heavily by Adelman and Walker (1975: 220) who maintained:

> We do not consider that interaction analysis provides information appropriate or adequate for any but the most limited of educational ideologies. The system is virtually unusable in informal contexts.

In more recent years attempts have been made to devise observation schedules which attempt to capture a more naturalistic appraisal of events in the learning environments, so that attributed meaning to actions and individual difference in achieving the same aim can be explored further. For instance, there was a growing emphasis on developing new forms of interaction analysis and on micro-teaching sessions in which personal feedback on practice was given to the learner-teacher. This was welcomed by educationalists as an attempt to bring the locus of inquiry to where it can have most effect. Wragg (1974: 193) hoped that such techniques would accelerate the move towards self-directed learning, both for teachers and learners. But he warned:

> To expect that the introduction of micro-teaching, interaction analysis, role playing or simulation will of themselves vastly improve the quality of teaching both within the institution and of the students being trained, would be akin to hoping that birthday toys would make an unhappy child contented, irrespective of the relationships within his family.

As Wragg pointed out, the student teacher's perceptions of the original lesson and their interpretation of the credibility of sources of feedback will determine how they teach after a micro-teaching session. Similarly, feedback on practical skills in any profession will be filtered through the expectations and value systems of the novice. There is, then, a growing emphasis on the person – a particular teacher or a particular learner's opinions, attributes or decisions. These have become a prime focus of interest for those advocating professional education built on humanistic foundations.

Reidford (1972) raised the dilemma facing those wishing to adopt a humanist approach to educational research. The major preoccupation of educational researchers in the 1970s was the testing of hypotheses which were highly likely to be confirmed. As Reidford pointed out, few educational research journals were interested in publishing studies whose results indicate that the hypothesis investigated has not been confirmed.

In education research the tendency was towards the adoption of research strategies in which prediction and control are paramount. The aim of such research has been to discover 'laws' which can be generalized to other populations. Bakan (1967: 46) discussed the need to reconstruct psychological investigation. He argued that mastery, via prediction and control and studied ignorance of the meanings of the subject's protocol language, meant that the mystery of the psyche is not entered. He commented that 'the mystery-mastery complex is the neurotic core of contemporary psychological research enterprise'.

If the aim of research is to discover laws, it assumes an unchanging nature in those who are to be controlled. The scientist–subject distinction endows the scientist with autonomy, rationality etc. while denying the same processes in the 'naive subject'. Such an approach inhibits understanding. In our opinion researchers should be more open-minded about the areas they investigate and the methodologies they use. Good research into the unknown cannot be well designed in the usual 'controlling' sense of the term.

Tight control of variables in traditional approaches to learning experiments resulted in a tendency to trivialize the nature of learning and this may not be of much help to the teacher who is dealing with more complex learning issues. Earlier approaches to the study of learning had limited horizons and we need now to consider complex human learning in more natural settings. This necessitates alternative research strategies.

The disruption of the scientist–subject distinction provides an alternative framework for research. In discussing his 'conversational model' Mair (1970: 182), a personal construct psychologist, suggested that:

> As psychologists we seem to have an alarming tendency to transform important human characteristics into problems, weakness and sources of error. This largely seems due to a continuing, if often blurred, adherence to a view of science quite inappropriate to the subject matter we seek to understand.

Educational research has largely based itself on a notion that, if a sufficient number of relevant facts are assembled, the laws governing these facts will reveal themselves. Here we provide a summary of some of the views that have dominated educational research. Positivism is characterized as a striving for principles or generalizations, the production of a set of 'law-like' accounts that will enable prediction and control. In contrast, phenomenology is aimed at understanding a particular individual's perspective using methodologies that focus on the language and interaction of participants.

It is perhaps not surprising that the positivist paradigm has been the dominant mode of research in education since it is predicated on the cultural transmission view of education we discussed in Chapter 1, which has dominated Western educational thought. We indicated in that chapter that there are alternate views on education and these viewpoints may benefit from the invention of alternate research methodologies.

New directions

The 'perspective of the personal' now adopted by many educators, raises issues and problems which cannot adequately be tackled by the traditional empirical mode of inquiry. The traditional approach has been questioned by teachers and this has been well documented by Stenhouse (1975), Deforges and McNamara (1979), Elliott and Whitehead (1980). Jones (1989: 51) was forceful in his criticism of research which adopted a positivist stance:

> Much research related to education had the cutting edge of a sponge; for a long time I have questioned the honesty of much that I read about in some of the academic journals. Don't get me wrong, I'm not suggesting that their authors were anything but sincere and well intentioned. What I am trying to say is that their research did not speak the truth to me. These works seemed more concerned with statistics than sensitivities; rats rather than brats; research rather than the researched.

Jones, along with many other educators, recognized the potential of applying a personal construct approach to education and this has had a significant impact on educational research today. Biggs (1976) maintained that the honeymoon between psychology and education was over. We would suggest that the marriage between a psychology based on the idea of absolute truth and education is finished. However, we argue that psychology based on personal construct theory offers a positive relationship – one in which the views of those actually involved in the educational process are paramount and not subordinate to the elegance of experimental design.

George Kelly would have agreed with Biggs regarding the limitations of psychometric approaches. He contrasted his philosophical position with that of the psychometrican:

> There are two ways in which one can look at psychological measurement ... fix the position of the subject with respect to certain dimensions ... [or] concern himself with the subject's freedom of movement....the resources which can be mobilised ... from the point of view of personal construct theory the latter represents the more enlightened approach. (Kelly, 1955: 203)

Olson, who has been influenced by Kelly's writings, suggested that if one is concerned to engage in a process of improvement of teaching then the focus cannot only be on the teacher's behaviour:

Comprehension of what another person is doing cannot be had through mere
examination of the particulars of their behaviour ... we have to understand their
behaviour as pointers towards the purposes which they serve and in terms of
these purposes. The meaning of what people do lies in the purposes served by
these actions, which are not meaningful in themselves but indicators of the
purposes they serve which give them meaning. In themselves they mean
nothing. (Olson, 1992: 55)

We share Olson's view. Much of contemporary educational research is not
so much striving for the disclosure of the 'effective teacher' but for an
explanation and understanding of teaching processes and the teacher's
subjective experience. It is the teacher's subjective related knowledge
which has implications for what happens in the learning context. As
Halkes and Olson (1984: 1) said 'instead of reducing the complexities of
the teaching/learning situations into a few manageable research variables,
one tries to find out how teachers cope with these complexities'.

Emphasis has shifted to educational research being of a value to practitioners and to the participants within the research. This has necessitated a
change of relationship between teachers and researchers. Clark (1986: 4)
noted, the goal of research has become that of:

portraying and understanding good teaching in all of its irreducible complexity
and difficulty. Quality portraiture maybe of more practical and inspirational
value than reductionistic analysis and technical prescriptiveness.

Methods of enquiry have developed beyond the technology of micro-
teaching to include a wide range of approaches which try 'to make visible
the formally hidden world of teaching' (Clark, 1995: 56). He suggested
that these alternative methods of enquiry offer 'interesting possibilities ...
if an important goal of continuing education is to equip teachers to be
reflective, analytic and constructively critical of their own teaching' (Clark,
1995: 57).

The current focus is now on trying to understand and interpret the
ways in which teachers make sense of, adjust to and create educational
environments within their professional contexts. This shift in educational
research thinking has not been easy. Eisner (1988: 18) noted 'the research
language that has dominated educational enquiry has been one that has
attempted to bifurcate the knower and the known'. This point was also
emphasized by Elbaz (1990: 20–1), speaking of traditional education
environments, who suggested that:

teachers concerned come to be spoken of in a detached and a dispassionate
way: coping with the lively business of the classroom becomes *classroom*

management'. Caring for the welfare and development of each child becomes 'individualised instruction' and virtually every aspect of teaching has been similarly subjected to some form of labelling that empties the teaching act of any personal significance.

With the emphasis on personal knowledge in emergent curricula, objectivist/positivist research methods are limited. Such research methodologies are congruent with principles inherent in reactive curricular frameworks. If one recognizes the role of the emerging objectives of the learner in relation to the curriculum, one must entertain studies that are predicated on a conceptual framework that suggests a carefully delineated in-depth study of what happens to individuals in terms of processes as they interact with the components of their environment. Rather than consider participants in learning environments as actors to be viewed from the perspective of an outside detached observer, what is needed is a methodology which allows the person to elaborate on his or her personal meaning of events.

These concerns were central to Kelly's views on research and led to the development of his repertory grid and self-characterization techniques. These techniques and a range of other approaches will be discussed in detail in later chapters. Kelly was quite clear in his antagonism towards a psychology which sees a person as reactive, a mere input-output system, rather than constructivist:

> A psychology that pins its anticipations on the repetitions of events it calls 'stimuli', or on the concatenations of events it calls 'reinforcements', can scarcely hope to survive as man's audacities multiply. (Kelly, 1969a: 31)

If one adopts a construct theory approach to research, one rejects the assumption that 'laws of nature' will eventually evolve after a collection of an enormous amount of data. As Bannister and Fransella (1971: 190) pointed out:

> Construct theory does not argue simply that it would be very difficult to fathom the nature of man in practice – most psychologists would admit that. It argues that it is a meaningless ideal, since the nature of individual men and of mankind is evolving and therefore can never finally be explained by any theory.

This clearly sets a personal construct theory approach to research in opposition to those who hold that, through large sample, i.e. nomothetic studies, one will determine the 'nature of the beast'. It does, however, lend itself to support the methodology of the individual case. Kelly's viewpoint is also clearly in line with arguments put forward by contemporary researchers who argue against a rigid subject/experimenter boundary. Kelly saw research as a co-operative enterprise.

Kelly acknowledged that many of his views were similar to those who put forward a plea for a humanistic approach to psychology. However he suggested that much of what passed for humanism was 'backward-wishing' rather than 'forward-seeking'. He suggested that it would be a mistake for those who wished to depart from the dehumanizing tradition of psychological research to abandon technology. He suggested that humanistic psychology should devise appropriate technologies to realize its objectives: 'humanistic psychology needs a technology through which to express its humane intentions' (Kelly, 1969b: 135). This statement is, we feel, of great significance for research. There has been a tendency to divide psychology into 'hard' and 'soft' psychology, hard psychology implying rigid experimental procedures requiring rigorous statistics for the analysis of the data. Soft psychology, on the other hand, recognizing the individuality of the person, often adopts the extreme position of rejecting any systematic attempt to explore this individuality. Kelly's theory and methodology offers a bridge between these divisions which are in themselves arbitrary. Hudson (1968: 84) noted the attractiveness of work such as that of Kelly in this respect: 'It frees the experimenter from the rival hegemonies of the billiard ball and putty.'

In Chapter 1 we discussed the relationships between particular assumptions of psychological development and philosophies about the nature of knowledge and suggested that these assumptions play a part in determining teaching practice in the workplace, schools and in colleges. In addition, these assumptions provide a framework for various perspectives on educational research. Clark (1995: 48) advocates a 'thoughtful' approach to teaching and proposes that educational research can be seen as 'research in the service of teaching'. Although discussing the education of children, his words have salience for much education that takes place within a professional context. He suggested that:

> when we look at teaching from the child's point of view the buzzing confusion of researcher's claims and counter claims fall silent. Looking at the faces of particular flesh and blood children, in their need and vulnerability, in their optimism and eagerness, we begin to become humble. For these children, all children, are subjects, not objects. They are not empty vessels to be filled, not animals to be trained, not computers to be programmed, not barbarians to be subdued, disciplined and civilised. All these metaphors and more have been acted out with gravely demoralising effects, on many generations of school children.

The work of George Kelly offers both a theory and a methodology based on an epistemological position which would place emphasis within education on personal relevance and endeavour, relativity of knowledge, expansion of the curriculum and the extension of the objectives of educational research, supporting Clark's call for 'thoughtful' teaching and research.

It is Kelly's philosophy of constructive alternativism that we feel is of greatest interest for the educationalist. If one adopts this philosophy one can provide an adaptive educational system which assumes many ways of succeeding and multiple goals from which to choose. In such an educational system individual learning styles are important while educational research is predicated on the individual's perspective. Constructive alternativism invites innovation and rejects dogma. As Allport (1955: 18) suggested: 'Dogmatism makes for scientific anaemia.' Rather than be bound by the 'tyranny of fact' and tradition, a personal construct approach to 'education, research and transformative practice' would suggest a forward thrust towards recognition of constructive alternatives.

Constructive alternativism and qualitative research

The philosophy and theory which underpins PCP is congruent with many current approaches in educational research, particularly in what is often labelled qualitative research, which has now 'come of age' (Taylor and Bogdan, 1998: vii).

Although we prefer the term 'interpretative', the term 'qualitative' has been used as an umbrella term for a variety of approaches sharing basic ontological, epistemological and methodological assumptions. We have argued elsewhere that the terms qualitative versus quantitative would be best kept for the type of data collected during the research rather than used as the label for the paradigms (Gilbert and Pope, 1984). Crotty (1998: 15) said that 'every beginner researcher learns at once that all research is divided into two parts – and these are "qualitative" and "quantitative", respectively'. He also suggested that this division is inappropriate. The division is one of epistemology. He noted that:

> what would seem to be problematic is any attempt to be at once objectivist and constructionist (or subjectivist). On the face of it, to say that there is objective meaning and in the same breathe to say that there is no objective meaning certainly does appear contradictory.

We agree with Crotty's sentiments that we need to be consistently objectivist or consistently constructionist (or subjectivist). For our part we will try to be consistently constructivist. However, since qualitative research is a term still extensively used within educational research, we will continue to use it, though carefully, within this book. Qualitative-interpretative research is predicated on the principle that one engages with participants (not subjects). Our participants are active meaning-seeking individuals, whose views of the world are valued. This represents our ethic for research and our approach has been influenced by a range of constructivist perspectives, particularly that of Personal Construct Psychology (PCP).

There are many aspects of PCP that could be used in support of current educational research practice. The reader may have found others that he or she deemed to be important. Here we restrict ourselves to aspects that we feel have particular relevance for the contemporary push towards a constructivist underpinning of qualitative research.

Figure 3.1 represents an abridged version of a diagram which appeared in Pope and Denicolo (1986). In that paper we drew attention to the constellation of ideas or metaphysical commitments surrounding two opposing conceptions of research and the dilemmas faced at that time by researchers wishing to adopt a qualitative approach to educational research.

We argued that a fundamental difference between researchers was often the model of the person who was the focus of investigation in the study. The model in Figure 3.1 was juxtaposed with an alternative, the model of the *person as a machine* as a metaphor underpinning much of quantitative educational research with its emphasis on reductionism through control of variables and nomothetic large scale studies. We will use the framework in Figure 3.1 to structure our discussions in this section of the chapter.

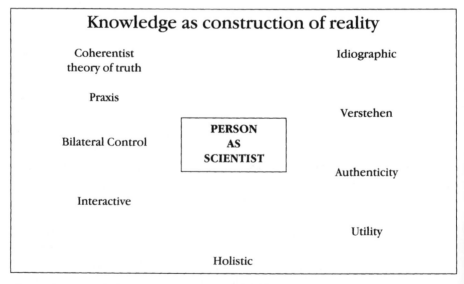

Figure 3.1. Knowledge as construction of reality (after Pope and Denicolo, 1986).

For this model we draw on Kelly's root metaphor *Man: the Scientist* as a pivotal theme. Person: the scientist and scientist: the person are both engaged in the process of observation, interpretation, prediction and control. For Kelly the questioning and exploring, revising and replacing in the light of predictive failure, which is symptomatic of scientific theorizing, is precisely what a person does in his/her attempts to anticipate events. Just as the experimental scientist may design his/her experiments around rival hypotheses, so each of us can be seen as designing our daily explorations of life around rival hypotheses which form part of our system of constructs or 'world view'. People can be seen as scientists constantly experimenting with their definitions of existence.

It is the 'world view' or personal constructs that qualitative researchers are seeking when they engage in research aimed at articulating the personal meanings of those who are participants in the research. It is recognized that differing actors in a situation may erect alternative perspectives and it is often the qualitative researcher's task to illuminate the rich diversity of meanings that participants have in relation to events or situations in their lives. *These alternative frameworks become the focus of research.*

Kelly's epistemological position was that *knowledge evolves as a construction of reality.* To reiterate what we said in the previous chapter, Kelly maintained that it was presumptuous to claim that a person's construction of reality is convergent with it:

> The fact that my only approach to reality is through offering some responsible construction of it does not discourage me from postulating that it is there. The open question for man is not whether reality exists or not but what he can make of it. (Kelly, 1969a: 29)

Since we all approach 'reality' with our existing constructions, our appreciation of the external world is always represented or constructed in the light of our current theorizing but that this may be subject to change can be a liberating thought. 'No-one needs to paint himself into a corner; no-one needs to be completely hemmed in by circumstances; no-one needs to be a victim of his biography' (Kelly, 1955: 15).

This is one of the ways Kelly wrote about his core metaphysical commitment. His notion of 'constructive alternativism' is fundamental to an appreciation of his theory. This epistemological position was a superordinate core construct of Kelly's construct system and, as such, permeates his writing. A major message is that our 'ways of seeing' reality can be likened to temporary goggles we wear to create a window on the world. Like goggles, they are subject to change. We can alter the clarity with which we inspect the world – however, in order to change our goggles we must recognize that we are wearing them!

Lakatos (1970: 104) in relation to this, noted an important demarcation between passivist and activist theories of knowledge:

> Passivists hold that true knowledge is nature's imprint on a perfectly inert mind: mental activity can only result in bias and distortion ... 'activists' hold that we cannot read the book of nature without mental activity, without interpreting it in the light of our expectations or theories. *Conservative 'activists'* hold that we are born with our basic expectations; with them we turn the world into 'our world' but must then live forever in the prison of our world ... but *revolutionary 'activists'* believe that conceptual frameworks can be developed and also replaced by new *better* ones; it is *we* who create our 'prisons' and we can also critically demolish them. (original emphasis)

Passivist views of knowledge were rejected by Kelly, which he labelled accumulative fragmentalism. He would also have rejected a conservative activist position such as that described by Lakatos, since it implies that the 'limiting cages' or 'goggles' of our constructions are permanent limitations. A Kellyan philosophy is akin to Lakatos's description of a revolutionary activist's views. Rather than see our constructions of reality as 'prisons', Kelly would see them as dynamic frames which could limit our creativity if we do not recognize the part we play in their construction.

There is much in Kelly's writing that is reminiscent of Goodman's (1984) philosophy. His constructivist philosophy is pluralistic and pragmatic. There are also shades of Von Glasersfeld's (1984: 24) 'radical constructivism'. Von Glasersfeld used the term 'radical' to emphasis his vehement rejection of the concept of reality:

> It is radical because it breaks with convention and develops a theory of knowledge in which knowledge does not reflect on an 'objective' and logical reality, but exclusively an ordering and organisation of a world constituted by our experience. The radical constructivist has relinquished 'metaphysical realism' once and for all.

Both Goodman's philosophy and that adopted by psychologist Von Glasersfeld have had a considerable influence in contemporary qualitative research. Such constructivist views can clearly be identified in research in mathematics and science education (for example see Novak, 1987; Driver and Oldham, 1986).

Lincoln and Guba (1985), in discussing the conduct of naturalistic enquiry, note similarities between the epistemological base of their approach and that of personal constructivism. It is interesting to note that Lincoln (1992: 381) now equates the constructivist and naturalist positions as models in scientific enquiry which are fundamentally different from positivist approaches in their epistemological underpinnings:

For the constructivist or naturalist, knowledge is composed of those constructions about which there is some consensus (or at least some movement towards consensus) amongst those competent to deal with the substance of the construction. It is the most sophisticated and informed construction available, but it is construction subject to reconstruction, with the addition of new data input, new claims, new concerns, new issues, or new circumstances.

Compare this with the following quotation from Kelly (1955: 72):

Successive revelations of events invite the person to place new constructions upon them, when ever something unexpected happens ... The constructions one places on events are *working hypotheses* which are about to be put to the test of experience. As one's anticipations are successively revised in the light of the unfolding sequence of events, a construction system undergoes progressive evolution. (our emphasis)

The researcher as personal constructivist recognizes the need to see the results of their enquiries as working hypotheses, potentially subject to reconstruction.

Lincoln and Guba (1985: 123) suggested that the classic idea of generalization be replaced by the notion of a working hypothesis – 'any generalisation is a working hypothesis, not a conclusion'. In constructivist work it is important that caveats with respect to generalizability are given and readers are invited to assess the goodness of fit between the context described in the research and the particular circumstances they may inhabit.

Kelly suggested that in personal construing an individual will weigh up alternatives and choose a path which he/she thinks offers the best possibility for elaboration of his/her construct system (choice corollary). An important criterion was that of *utility* or usefulness of the outcome for the person's everyday exploration. This criterion of utility is also important for qualitative researchers. They are concerned to engage in research that will help individuals or groups to consider alternatives and, as a result of reflection, engender emancipatory *praxis*.

Kelly was critical of the over-reliance on psychometric methods in research. He emphasized that knowing that there was a correlational link between two variables did not help him to decide what approach should be taken with an individual client within the clinic. Kelly questioned the utility of such research in that such approaches did not lead to emancipatory praxis. Thus he suggested that there should be more emphasis on *idiographic* studies in research. This is a fundamental stance adopted by qualitative/interpretative education researchers today. Cohen and Manion (1989: 38) noted that 'the interpretative paradigm, in contrast to its normative counterpart, is characterised by *concerns for the individual*'.

Guba and Lincoln (1994) have begun to use the term 'constructivism' in a similar sense to naturalistic enquiry when they discuss essential aspects of interpretative or qualitative paradigms. Personal Construct Psychologists place a high premium on research which allows insight and understanding of the views of participants within the study. We highlighted this (Pope and Denicolo, 1986: 164) when we drew attention to the role of *Verstehen* in Personal Construct Psychology research.

Schwandt (1994: 118) has similarly highlighted common points between constructivism and interpretativism as follows:

> Proponents of these persuasions share the goal of understanding the complex world of lived experience from the point of view of those who live it. This goal is variously spoken of as an abiding concern for the life world, for the emic point of view, for understanding meaning, for grasping the actor's definition of the situation, for *verstehen*. (Our emphasis)

Traditionally, educational researchers have concerned themselves with concepts of reliability and validity when judging instruments used and the significance or statistical credibility of research findings. With his belief that constructions are potentially open to change, concepts such as reliability were problematic for Kelly. He is quoted in Fransella and Bannister (1977: 8) as suggesting that reliability as a characteristic of a test is a measure of its insensitivity to change. Thus they say:

> the idea of a static mind is a contradiction in terms. We should look to the grid not to repeat the same results but to see, when it shows change, what is this signifying. In short, reliability is perhaps best seen as merely one aspect of validity.

Lincoln and Guba (1985: 222) also proposed that a demonstration of validity is often sufficient to establish reliability. These authors prefer to substitute other terms when considering naturalistic, or what they now term constructivist, research. The credibility or trustworthiness of data to those intimate with the situation/context is deemed to be important. Qualitative research has its own type of rigour. Aspects that are most important are the extent to which the researcher fully articulates the research protocol, gives copious verbatim evidence for interpretation and shows a concern for *authenticity*. They have now extended their concept of authenticity to identify *ontological authenticity* which emphasizes the function of the personal constructions; *educative authenticity* which refers to the sociality in understanding the researcher obtains within the research; *catalytic authenticity* – the extent to which the research promotes action; and *tactical authenticity* where the research empowers action (Guba and Lincoln, 1989).

Concern for authenticity has implications for procedure in that it is helpful if an iterative stance is taken within the research and the researcher takes interpretations of data back to the participants for authentication. This is certainly an approach that we have advocated where the situation allows it. This necessitates an *interactive approach* where there is *bilateral control* of the process between both researcher and participant. It is an essential characteristic of action research which we will discuss later. What is clear is that the *qualitative educational researcher as constructivist will employ the art of the skilled conversationalist* (Pope and Denicolo, 1993).

In discussing his notion of a personal construct, Kelly argued that a construct had *both* intellectual and emotional aspects. He rejected the idea of splitting human functioning into intelligence, emotion, motivation etc. as was the norm in traditional psychology text books. He preferred a *holistic* stance. This holistic position is fundamental within qualitative research and is a guiding principle in the conversations held and the style of engagement to be pursued.

Reason and Rowan (1981) discussed the concept of collaborative enquiry as one of the 'new paradigm' research approaches within the social sciences. Unlike traditional research, in which the roles of the researcher and the subject are mutually exclusive, in cooperative enquiry there is bilateral initiative and control. For Reason and Rowan, ideally there should be full reciprocity; certainly there needs to be full consensus reached on all decisions, derived from free and informed debate, with respect to the research process. More recently, in discussing social constructions of reality, Guba and Lincoln (1994: 111) emphasized the hermeneutical and dialectical approach required if one adopts a methodological stance of constructivism.

> The variable and personal nature of social constructions suggests that individual constructions can be elicited and refined only through interaction between and among investigator and respondent. These varying constructions are interpreted using conventional hermeneutical techniques and are compared and contrasted through a dialectical interchange.

Personal Construct Psychology would support those in educational research who recognize the importance of incorporating, within their methodology, the views of all those involved in the particular educational issues with which they are concerned. Kelly (1969b: 132) made an explicit statement to this effect. He would tell his students that they:

> should not overlook what their subjects have to contribute, for psychological research, as I see it, is a cooperative enterprise in which the subject joins the

psychologist in making an enquiry. I am very sceptical of any piece of human
research in which the subject's questions and contributions have not been
elicited or have been ignored in the final analysis of results.

Action research models particularly emphasize the participatory nature of
research and the importance of researchers and participants engaging in a
collaborative journey of enquiry (Carr and Kemmis, 1986; Whyte, 1991;
Elliott, 1995; Fals-Borda and Rachman, 1991). Many of these authors have
based some of their assumptions on the work of Jürgen Habermas (1971).
Others have drawn inspiration from the work of Schon's (1983) model of
the reflective practitioner, or Kolb and Fry's (1975) learning cycles. Figure
3.2 compares Kelly's personal scientist model with that of Kolb *et al.*'s
learning cycle.

Figure 3.3 represents Kemmis and McTaggart's (1982) action research
spiral. One purpose of action research is that the participants may come
to a good understanding of their context and, in so doing, develop strategies for solving problems of their own identification. This highlights a

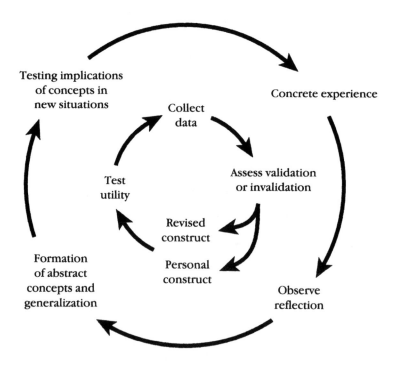

Figure 3.2. Kelly's personal scientist model (inner circle: Kelly, 1955) compared with
Kolb and Fry's learning cycle (outer circle Kolb and Fry, 1975).

parallel between Kelly, who saw the personal experiments of individuals as being a continuous process of forming a hypothesis (construct), testing it and reflecting on the outcome with a possible reformulation of the construct system, and Kemmis, who sees action research as critical education science with an ongoing process of problem identification, plans and strategies, reflection on outcome and redefinition of the problem.

In educational research, action research approaches encourage teachers to ground their analysis of educational issues in the evidence they generate from reflection on their own context rather than borrow from, or rely on, the 'grand' theories from psychology, sociology, philosophy etc., particularly those positivistic theories suggesting 'true' statements expressed as nomothetic context-free generalizations. Authentic contextual relevance and the empowering of participants both in order to contribute fully to such research and to apply the ongoing research in a practical way are of paramount importance, hence the emphasis on *praxis* (Figure 3.1).

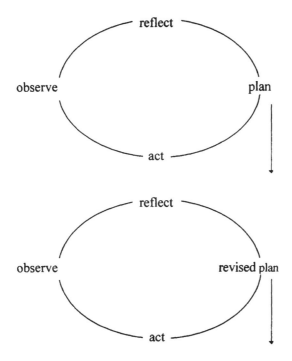

Figure 3.3. Kemmis and McTaggart's action research spiral.

In addition to the emphasis on collaborative participation, action researchers and Personal Construct Psychologists share the following core assumptions:

- the person is a responsible agent;
- growth may occur through reflection *on* and *in* action;
- understanding another's perspective requires empathy and a 'conversational' approach;
- the participant's and the researcher's account of events may differ and need to be negotiated;
- participants and researchers are engaged in cooperative enquiry;
- human beings are active, meaning seeking, potentially open to change and lifelong development and are capable of self-direction.

Action research is but one method within the qualitative paradigm. It does, however, embody the values identified in Figure 3.1.

We will now address the remaining notion within Figure 3.1, i.e. *a coherentist theory of truth*. This is inextricably linked with the view of knowledge as construction of reality. Educational researchers using a personal constructivist perspective would not be seeking to argue that their findings correspond to some absolute notion of truth. They would recognize the findings as having evolved from a rich interplay between participants and researchers and have reached a point where they feel that the findings best represent a coherent pattern within the data available. The results will often be presented with the caveat that readers should ascertain for themselves the extent to which their own context matches that which has been described in the research, with the entailed notion that results can be open to reconstruing. It is not unusual for a number of further questions to be raised at this point recognizing the heuristic value of the research in suggesting further constructive lines of enquiry.

Towards a story-telling metaphor

The coherentist theory of truth, together with the other metaphysical commitments which follow from Kelly's root metaphor person: the scientist, has been of considerable use in our own theorizing. More recently, alongside other Personal Construct Psychologists, we have explored the implications of an alternative metaphor, that of person-as-storyteller. Howard (1988: 270) suggested that the model of *human as storytellers* may assist in the evolution of Personal Construct Psychology as a *living, viable, intellectual enterprises*. Mair's (1988: 130) article 'Psychology as story telling' is an important text which has influenced our current work.

Mair advocated a psychology that shows more care for the 'stories we live and the stories we can tell'. We agree with Connelly and Clandinin (1990: 2) who pointed out that 'the main claim for the use of narrative in educational research is that humans are story telling organisms who, individually and socially, lead storied lives. Thus the study of narrative is the study of the ways humans experience the world.'

In our work we have noted an evolution in the techniques and metaphors that we have employed. In the next two chapters we will share the rich diversity of methods which we feel have been fruitful in our endeavour to allow authentic portrayal of the views of participants within our research. We will begin with the repertory grid since that is a technique most commonly associated with Kelly's Personal Construct theory. We will then move beyond the Grid to consider a range of biographical and autobiographical methods. The various techniques we will consider allow different stories to be told.

Both of us have engaged on research on teacher thinking. We recognize that much of teacher craft thinking is tacit – i.e. knowhow gained through experience and not carefully articulated. Constructivist tools endeavour to reveal something of this tacit knowledge. The telling of stories and reflection on information gleaned from repertory grids can make conscious for the teacher the images, core constructs and experiential metaphors that form part of the teachers' professional lore. It can be emancipatory in the sense that this telling of the story liberates an understanding of its power. By making the tacit articulate it can be critically appraised. We invite you to consider the utility of the various techniques we offer within the book. Yours will be a personal choice. We hope we will have provided a range of alternative routes that you will be encouraged to explore.

CHAPTER 4

Practical considerations in the use of repertory grid techniques

> The purpose of grids is to inform us about the way in which our system of personal constructs is evolving and its limitations and possibilities. It is a way of standing in the shoes of others, to see the world from their point of view, to understand their situation, their concerns. (Beail, 1985: 2)

Repertory grid techniques evolved from Kelly's personal construct theory (1955). Kelly's original technique was the role construct repertory test which he used to investigate the role relationships between patients and their families, friends etc. and for assessing the relationships between a patient's constructs about people. The repertory grid, however, is not a test but a methodology involving highly flexible techniques and variable application. Although in the past its main use has been to investigate constructs about people, denoted as elements in a grid, there is no theoretical reason why the elements of grids should not include inanimate objects or even abstract ideas. Indeed Bannister and Mair (1968) and Fransella and Bannister (1977) summarized many of the forms and applications of repertory grid techniques which have developed beyond Kelly's own approach. Examples in this book also bear witness to the variety of types of elements used in repertory grids at the present time.

The procedure has its theoretical roots in Kelly's definition of a construct: 'In its minimum context it is a way in which two elements are similar and contrast with the third' (Kelly, 1955: 61). The notion of contrast has been emphasized by Fransella and Bannister (1977: 5) who wrote:

> When we say that Bill Bloggs is honest, we are not saying that Bill Bloggs is honest, he is not a chrysanthemum or a battle-ship or the square root of minus one. We are saying that Bill Bloggs is honest, he is not a crook.

A construct is a dimension which may evolve when considering a particular set of elements (people, objects or events) but can usually be applied

66

to a further range of elements. The dimensionality of a construct allows one to extract matrices of inter-relationships between constructs and between elements.

For Kelly, constructs do not exist in isolation. Indeed his organization corollary made explicit his view that constructs are linked with each other in a more or less coherent and hierarchical manner. The organization of constructs at any particular moment in time exerts a limit beyond which it is impossible for a person to perceive, and thus the organization of the constructs has a controlling influence on behaviour. Kelly noted the importance of eliciting more than one construct or dimension. Thus he wrote:

> An event seen only in terms of its placement on one dimension is scarcely more than mere datum. And about all you can do with a datum is just let it sit on its own continuum. But as an event finds its place in terms of many dimensions of consideration, it develops psychological character and uniqueness. (Kelly 1969b: 118)

Many practitioners are now adopting the repertory grid as a means of entering the phenomenological world of an individual by exploring the nature and inter-relationships between various elements and constructs elicited by the method. However, since there is no such creature as 'The Grid', it is necessary to make certain methodological decisions *vis-à-vis* the format of a grid for any particular project. Five major considerations will be discussed at this point:

1. contract and purpose;
2. choice of elements;
3. construct elicitation;
4. going beyond the matrix;
5. methods of analysis and interpretation.

Contract and purpose

The repertory grid interview can be seen as a conversation (Thomas and Harri-Augstein 1985). Although the form of data collection and analysis of the grids has systematic and scientific aspects, grid elicitation requires a sensitive approach exploiting the art of conversation. At the outset of such a conversation it is essential to negotiate a contract with the participant in any intervention. It is the investigator's ethical responsibility to convey to the participants the aims of the intervention and the commitment sought from the participant. The repertory grid can be a powerful instrument to tap an individual's view of self and his/her world. If the investigator/

researcher is not prepared to support a participant should he or she be distressed through the revelation of these personal viewpoints within the conversation, the onus is on the investigator not to probe too far. A distinction may need to be made between research and/or professional development on the one hand and therapy on the other. In constructivist research or in professional development contexts, therapy is not the prime raison d'être for the research or intervention. In negotiating the contract, the purpose of the specific repertory grid should be discussed between the participant grid-maker and the researcher or staff developer, combined hereafter as 'investigator'. The repertory grid is not intended to explore all aspects of a person's construct system but is rather focused on a particular topic.

The definition of purpose is important, since personal constructions on a topic cannot be gathered if the participants do not know what the researcher is interested in, or do not have a focus for the conversation. Defining the purpose helps identify a suitable element set and focus for construing within the grid conversation.

The 'purpose' of the grid is a most important preliminary consideration before the process of eliciting elements can begin. Purpose has at least two aspects:

(a) What is the topic to be investigated?
(b) What is the intended use of the grid information?

The negotiation of these issues is a crucial aspect of any grid conversation and requires more care than is usually recognized by the new user.

What is the topic to be investigated?

Since the elements in a grid should be representative of the problem area to be explored, it is essential that adequate time is given to a discussion of this aspect of purpose. Even in situations where elements and constructs are provided rather than elicited this is an important consideration. The elements in a provided grid should be representative of what Kelly referred to as the 'universe of discourse' which is central to the problem area, and similarly, provided constructs should be dimensions which are appropriate to the particular purpose. The repertory grid is a procedure used to help gain an understanding of how an aspect is perceived by a person. Each investigation will be on a particular topic and must be focused on an area which represents to participants an area they are able to construe.

Take for example an organization interested in collecting information on the personal constructs used in appraisal. One could say to the person who is to complete the grid, 'the purpose of the exercise is to explore your ideas about people'. However, a free exploration of the person's views of people *in general* may not be what is required. If the purpose is to obtain the person's views of subordinates and others which he or she may have to appraise in the course of work, then this must be clearly understood and an appropriate set of elements elicited/provided which contain such people and omits others who are outside this remit, such as spouse or partner, mother-in-law, friend from the golf club, etc. Similarly, the constructs elicited could vary depending on the initial discussions of purpose. Once again, if the purpose is to allow the individual to express any of the constructs he might have about subordinates, this should be discussed. However, if the purpose is to explore the type of constructs the individuals bring to bear when they are appraising their subordinates from the *point of view of the adequacy of their performance in various activities at work*, then this more specific purpose should be conveyed. In this way constructs such as 'plays a good game of tennis/lousy on the tennis court' may well be excluded – unless of course the person truly felt such a construct was relevant when appraising his or her subordinates' activities at work!

The art of conversational elicitation of elements and constructs is to help participants to focus their attention on those aspects of their thoughts and feelings which are relevant to the purpose, without hinting at, implying or suggesting what those ideas and feelings might be. A clear negotiation and definition of purpose is therefore a very necessary first step and one which has an effect on the types of elements and constructs chosen, an issue which we discuss later.

What is the intended use of the grid information?

This second aspect of purpose also has an impact on the format and procedure of grid elicitation. Examples of different uses of the grid, although not mutually exclusive, could be:

(a) a conversation with one's self;
(b) gathering of information about an individual's views on a particular topic;
(c) a comparison of the viewpoints of two people in terms of either:
    – degree of agreement between them, or
    – the degree to which either can gauge the other's point of view;
(d) an exploration of the nature and sharing of construing within a group;
(e) a monitoring of changes in perspectives.

Each of these purposes calls for a slightly different approach. If, for example, the purpose of the grid exercise was for an individual to explore his or her own views about a particular topic area and these views were not necessarily to be transmitted to any other individual, it may not be necessary to have anyone eliciting the grid from this individual. For example, the RepGrid 2 (Shaw, 1993) computer program allows an individual to sit down at a computer terminal and go through a grid elicitation privately. A similar exercise can be followed using a paper and pencil format. In these instances, the individual can choose how explicit he or she wishes to be in naming the poles of his or her constructs and also the label identification of the elements. Any codes used will have personal meaning.

Since the object of this exercise is that the process of grid elicitation allows the individual an opportunity to explore his or her views and thus raise self-awareness, the information contained in the grid is for him or herself alone.

If, on the other hand, the purpose of the grid elicitation is to gather information and come to some understanding of the views of another individual, an interactive and conversational approach is necessary. The person eliciting the grid must ensure that, as far as is possible, the intended meaning of a construct or an element has been understood. Although a person may from time to time have some difficulty in articulating a particular construct, the individual should be encouraged to articulate as clear a description as possible in order that a person reading/learning the construct can gain a degree of understanding or, as in the case of (c) above, another person could attempt to use the same construct. This is also important when the individual is required to use the same construct and elements on different occasions over a period of time, as in (e) above. Similarly, if one takes the case of (d) above, when one wishes to explore how different people within a group view the same set of elements, it is important that time is set aside for a negotiation and full discussion of the elements set so that each member of the group can identify with each one. If, for example, one is interested in exploring the similarity and differences among a group of teachers in terms of how they view a specific set of techniques, one should not automatically assume that the labels given to these techniques as the set of elements are fully understood by each member of the group. For instance, not everyone agrees with the number which constitutes 'small' in small group teaching.

Similarly, if the group generates the set of elements one should endeavour to select from a pool of possible elements, the set which the majority of the group feel represent items which they can construe. Without endeavouring to ensure this common base, any judgements about similarities and differences in the constructs which individuals in the group may bring to bear on the set of elements could be inaccurate if not nonsensical. The intended use of the grid information is thus an aspect of 'purpose' which imposes some constraints on the grid technique which will be implemented . One can construe uses of the grid which have as their prime focus awareness raising as representing the Reflective Mode, and those occasions where the focus is primarily gaining information about a person as the Extractive Mode of grid application.

Choice of elements

When considering the use of repertory grid techniques, one of the first questions often raised is whether one should provide the elements and constructs for an individual or whether these should be elicited from each individual on a personal basis. In its original use as a clinical technique, personal elicitation of elements and constructs was the method adopted. Indeed purists would argue that Kelly's theoretical base for repertory grid techniques emphasizes individuality and that, by definition, constructs are personal. However, there has been an increasing tendency of late to detach the technique from its theoretical base and so the use of a standard form of repertory grid in which both the elements and the constructs are provided for the person, rather than elicited from the individual concerned, is becoming more widespread. Our own approach is, where possible, to use free elicitation of elements and constructs, though the negotiation of elements relevant to purpose has been particularly useful in group or comparative situations.

Whether or not one provides or elicits elements and/or constructs may well depend on the initial purpose and mode of application. For example, if one is exploring the nature and sharing of construing within a group, it is often the case that a common set of elements are selected and provided for each individual – this could be followed by either provision or elicitation of constructs or a combination of both. It should be emphasized, however, that if one decides to provide elements/constructs then adequate groundwork should be done in order to obtain what one hopes are representative elements and constructs. This would entail a series of discussions with the type of people to whom the standard grid will be provided, so that the items selected for elements may represent a range of events which can be construed by such people, and that the nature of the provided constructs is in line with the sort of dimensions which would, in the main, be used by them when considering the elements chosen.

Kelly insisted that in order to be useful and meaningful, each item should be representative of an individual's life experiences. In some cases provided labels may be identical with those normally used by the person in practice, but on the other hand, they may be far removed or incomprehensible to a particular person.

One should remember that whatever meanings words may have, they are assigned or ascribed to them by people. Thus when a person is provided with the investigator's labels on the construct poles, the meaning ascribed to those labels may not be isomorphic with the meaning the investigator assumes these labels hold. We will elaborate on this further in Chapter 6.

In summary, if one is forced through circumstances to use provided rather than elicited elements or constructs, one should be conscious of the need for extensive preliminary work to establish a reasonable selection of elements or constructs and the need for caution during the interpretation phase.

Whether elements are elicited or provided, it is important that they are representative of the area to be considered and that they span the range of items which are considered to be important in that area for the person or persons concerned.

A frequent question is 'how many elements should a repertory grid contain?' There is no fixed standard required. However, in practice, small numbers of elements may give rise to a grid which is devoid of sufficient detail or interest in terms of content, whereas construing large numbers of elements can be a very tedious exercise and thus should be avoided. In practice it has been the experience of the authors that between 8 and 15 elements provide a useful basis for the elicitation of an interesting grid within a reasonable timeframe.

During conversational elicitation of the elements, the investigator may have to offer some guidance on the nature of the elements to be included in the grid. It is important at this stage that the investigators refrain from imposing their own views about what the precise items should be. However, some discussion may be needed, perhaps especially with regard to the level at which the element item is pitched. For example, one may find that the elements which are initially suggested by a person are very abstract and they may have some difficulty in eliciting constructs with respect to elements of this kind. Initial suggestions in response to a request for element items representative of aspects of for example teaching, might be Tolerance, Patience or Interpersonal Relationships. This type of element may be difficult to construe especially on the first occasion one is completing a grid. Specific teaching events, teaching materials or techniques are more easily conceptualized and thus may be more suitable for initial grids.

Having decided on a type of element, it is also important to ensure that all the elements are at the same level of specificity within the type. For example, if one is considering activities at work, one could include chairing meetings, conducting selection interviews, marking examination scripts, and sharpening pencils. The last one represents a different level of specificity from those it follows, since it could be included in each, and this can pose difficulties when comparing and contrasting elements.

The concreteness of elements is also important. In investigations aimed at eliciting constructs about effectiveness in teaching, one might have as elements ineffective teacher, effective teacher, adequate teacher etc. However, it is important to ask the participant to think of an actual person that embodies such a role, rather than have them conjure up an abstract notion each time.

When considering the representativeness of the element set, it is important that it not only represents the universe of discourse under consideration, but also that it reflects a range of possibilities. For example, in considering teaching effectiveness, it would be important to have both effective and less effective teachers in the element set given the fact that the object is to compare and contrast in order to elicit constructs. All effective teachers would not easily lead to such comparisons. Kelly emphasized that we gain particular understanding from considering negative cases which illuminate particular aspects of positive cases.

It is generally suggested that the element set should be homogeneous. Lack of homogeneity can pose similar problems to a situation where there are different levels within the element set. Normally, the element set will consist of all people, all events, all situations etc. However, as we indicated earlier, there are no hard and fast rules regarding elements set selection. It has been our experience that, when considering significant others as an element set, one individual insisted on including the family cat! To the purist, this would not be seen as an homogeneous set. However, if people are anthropomorphic about their cat, then this is an important aspect of their personal construing. Similarly, if the elements are all individually named family members except for one denoted 'the aunts', we would encourage differentiation, perhaps naming one but noting that, for this person, aunts are seen collectively. The essential issue must be that the person is able to construe the element set and finds them relevant.

Construct elicitation

Having defined a list of representative elements, the next step is a process of construct elicitation. In practice, it is often useful to have each element written out on a separate card. This allows individuals to physically sort through the elements and to consider them in groups of three or more, depending on the process of elicitation adopted by the investigator. Kelly

(1955) describes six approaches to the elicitation of constructs. The Minimum Context Form or 'triadic method' is perhaps the most widely used, since it is closest to Kelly's theory about how constructs are actually formed. With the triadic method the participant is asked to consider first how two of the elements are alike and thereby different from the third.

When conversant with the procedure, participants may naturally move to the Full Context version whereby they can discern that there are two major groupings of the elements, one contrasting with the other.

As with element set selection, the investigator must decide whether to elicit or supply constructs. This issue has been debated widely in the literature (see for example Adams-Webber, 1970). We suggest that since it is the personal constructs one is interested in then, where possible, free elicitation of constructs should be adopted.

Depending on the purpose of the investigation, it is possible to consider that there may be at least four different types of constructs that may be central to the particular elicitation. These are sensory/perceptual, behavioural, inferential, and feelings/attitudinal. In a project aimed at identifying a professional's views of work effectiveness when appraising other colleagues then we would be more concerned with behavioural, inferential and feelings/attitudinal types of constructs than the sensory/perceptual. If the professional continued to offer constructs which are the sensory/perceptual kind, e.g. fat/thin, tall/short, swarthy complexion/pale complexion, the investigator is likely to encourage the grid maker to consider other types of constructs. This must be done with care, since these are obviously personal constructs of relevance to the individual. The fact that the individual offers such constructs is of interest to note and may be the starting point for further discussion.

The aim of the construct elicitation is to collect as many different constructs as the individual wishes to offer. Occasionally, the individual may repeat constructs when faced with different triads. These should be noted as part of the research record, but not included within the grid.

The investigator needs to be sensitive to situations where the participant needs help in 'splitting constructs'. In considering a group of three elements, the participant may, for example, offer that two of the elements are alike because two of them are *good company* and the other is *short-tempered*. On attempting to use these constructs for other people in the grid the person will have difficulty if some of the elements are deemed to be both *good company* and *short-tempered*. The person may realize this construct actually represents two dimensions and therefore can be encouraged to suggest two constructs, e.g. *good company* versus *boring* and *short-tempered* versus *even disposition*. The investigator needs to provide a facilitating climate in which this entailing of constructs can be fostered.

He/she needs to listen carefully to what the participant is offering by way of constructs. If the participants are not writing the constructs down themselves, and the investigator is transcribing what is said, it is important to retain the language utilized by each participant. The investigator needs to look carefully for signs indicating that the participant is struggling while completing the grid. In addition to the need to split, some other difficulties can arise; these are discussed next.

The individual may have no difficulty in naming the way in which a pair are similar (emergent pole) but may have difficulty in articulating the contrast or implicit pole. A climate needs to be created in which the participant is not threatened by pressure to complete the naming of the implicit pole, although through conversation they may eventually be able to find a form of words that encapsulates their thoughts/feelings. As with all forms of interviewing, grid elicitors must refrain from offering a suitable pole name! They may need to be content with a simple 'not' (the emergent description).

The triadic method can result in some of the elements not being able to be considered within a particular construct dimension. In this situation, the participant should be allowed to put a 'not applicable' in the relevant cell. This situation arises when the element is outside the range of convenience of the construct concerned. It is important that the participant does not feel compelled to fill in each cell with a rank or rating, if that procedure is used once a construct is identified.

The investigator needs to recognize that, as the grid conversation proceeds and the person fills in a number of constructs, there may be times when the person will want to change the labels given to the constructs as their ideas become clearer to themselves. They may then want to change the ratings given, having changed to a more focused or specific construct. Opportunities to change both the pole names and the ratings along constructs are important considerations. It is important to convey the freedom to make these changes. Participants may well be used to researchers/therapists using tests with assumptions of right or wrong answers. The participants may not wish to admit that they are having difficulty. The investigator in the contexts we are considering must provide a facilitating climate within which these opportunities are addressed.

Another aspect of the repertory grid that can pose a problem for some participants is the use of numbers within the grid. Kelly's original grids were done with ticks or crosses in which the person said whether an element could be best described by the tick end (emergent pole) or a cross end (implicit pole) of the dimension (see Figure 4.1).

✓	Mother	Father	Aunt Jane	Sara	Mr Grundy	Mrs Peabody	X
Good company	✓	X	X	✓	X	✓	Boring
Happy disposition	✓	X	✓	X	X	✓	Bad tempered
Etc.							

Figure 4.1. Repertory grid with ticks and crosses.

The advent of computer programs and the desire for more sophisticated interpretation of the richness of a person's construing has led to the use of rating or ranked grids. Pope and Keen (1981: 45-7) discussed the pros and cons of the tick-cross (dichotomous) approach and the rating and ranking scaling methods.

One important consideration when deciding to use dichotomous, ranking or rating forms of the grid is the population who will be asked to complete the grids. We prefer to use rating as opposed to ranked scales since, in practice, some individuals find the ranking form somewhat tedious, especially if there are a large number of elements to be ranked – they find it difficult to rank order large numbers and may be confused if tied ranks are allowed.

The advantage of rating elements between poles of a construct, as opposed to allocating them to one pole or another via the tick/cross method, lies in the detail of information shared. Participants are able to indicate the comparative degree to which elements match the description contained in each pole so that the poles represent boundaries on a continuum or spectrum (see Figure 4.2).

Three issues derive from this. The first relates to the nature of the boundaries, the identification of the poles. These should encompass the spread of descriptions that the participant would naturally use for that construct within the universe of discourse so that each element fits comfortably at or between the poles in relation to the other elements. (For those readers with a statistical frame, this is to ensure ordinal correctness of the data.)

The next issue concerns the rating scale itself. A frequently used scale is 1–5, where 1 represents the closest match to the elicited pole and 5 the closest match to the contrast pole. This scale provides more detail than the dichotomous approach, and allows for a midpoint score. (For those

	Mother	Father	Aunt Jane	Sara	Mr Grundy	Mrs Peabody	
Good company	1	4	5	2	5	3	Boring
Happy disposition	1	4	2	4	5	1	Bad tempered
Etc.							

Figure 4.2. Repertory grid using rating.

without computer help, a grid, using this scale with approximately nine elements and ten constructs, is just about within the realm of human practice to 'hand' analyse using least sum of differences methods (see Pope and Keen, 1981: 67–70). Obviously a scale of 1–7 provides more differentiation but as the scale increases so does the time and effort to rate each construct, so a balance must be struck between the value of detail accrued for each construct and the stamina of the participants.

Finally, the use of a numerical scale as a form of measurement requires some elaboration. Many researchers have been attracted to such forms of repertory grids because they have an air of both precision and research 'respectability' – the data seems to accrue the advantages of both qualitative and quantitative approaches to understanding human beings.

A note of caution is warranted here. A rating scale produces only ordinal information since the process contains no mechanism for ensuring that the intervals between, for example, ratings of 1 and 2 and 3 and 4, are the same within a construct dimension or between construct dimensions. Indeed, it is likely that the introduction of such a mechanism would be counter-productive to the quality of the elicitation – compare the issues (a)–(f) below. A simple example may illustrate this. In the universe of discourse of 'fruit I have eaten', and the construct 'soft-hard', strawberry may be rated 1, banana 2, pear 4, apple 5, but the difference in perceived texture between strawberry/banana and pear/apple may not be exactly the same, although they are in the right order. The numbers are, therefore, 'soft' and this imposes limits on the kinds of statistical operations which can be applied to them. Readers should be aware that not all software packages recognize this limitation and so apply operations only appropriate to 'harder' data. Other aspects of this issue will be addressed in the section on analysis and interpretation later in the chapter.

One is often asked the question 'How many constructs should be elicited within a repertory grid?' There is no magic answer to this question, although there are some limits and issues to consider:

(a) The prime prerequisite is that the constructs elicited cover the range of constructs which the individual feels are important to the area under consideration. Construct elicitation should continue until the individual indicates that his/her repertoire of constructs for that particular range of elements is exhausted.

(b) The elicitation of constructs can be tiring for both the person completing the grid and the other person engaged in the grid conversation, the investigator. One should recognize this and not extend the grid interview beyond the limits of tiredness for both parties.

(c) In many circumstances there may be time limit constraints on behalf of either the participant or the investigator which may well impose a limitation on the number of constructs which are elicited at any one session.

(d) For those who wish to make use of the various computer program facilities available for analysis of grids it is important to be aware of the limitations with respect to numbers of constructs which any individual program might impose.

(e) Some investigators may feel it is desirable to consider every possible permutation of triads when eliciting constructs by triadic elicitation, and may be concerned about the large numbers of constructs that might evolve if such a procedure were adopted. It is, of course, desirable that the elements are considered in various groupings but, in practice, the participant will often tend to repeat constructs and will have exhausted his/her sub system of constructs for the particular universe of discourse long before all possible permutations have been considered.

(f) It is important to remember that the aim is not to encapsulate the whole of an individual's construct system but only that part of it which is relevant to the defined purpose.

The number of constructs which are included in the final grid will, therefore, be a result of some or all of the limits which have been mentioned above.

Figure 4.3 provides a flow diagram which may help the reader to capture the essence of the ebb and flow that may occur during the grid elicitation. It is provided as a guide only and should not be seen as a rigid formula.

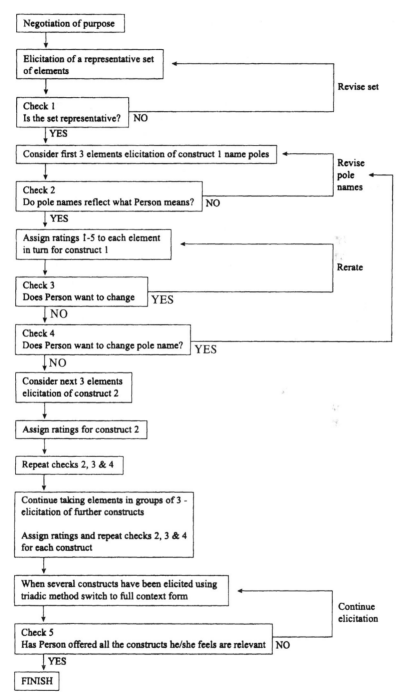

Figure 4.3. Flow diagram for grid elicitation.

Beyond the matrix

So far we have considered element and construct selection and issues that may occur when asking the person to describe the elements along the construct dimension. Constructivist investigators adopt an hermeneutic approach and the art of the repertory grid elicitation should encourage such exploration. One way in which individual constructions are refined is through iterative interactions with the constructs listed. One example is through the use of laddering. Laddering can either be used as a grid is being elicited, when it is completed, or after is has been analysed. During completion, laddering is used when the investigator or participant feels it would be helpful to push the level of construing to a different plane. For example, in considering effectiveness in teaching, the participant may offer a construct *punctual* v *does not turn up to class on time*. It may be informative to ask the participant which is more important, being punctual or not turning up on time, and *'why'*. The participant may then offer 'It is important to be punctual because the teacher demonstrates commitment to the students versus uncommitted to students.' Continuing to ask to ladder up with the question 'why?' may result in superordinate constructs which identify critical dimensions of the person's value system regarding effective teaching.

The opposite process of laddering down (sometimes called pyramiding in other texts) can also be useful. Consider the overarching construct *effective versus ineffective*. When asked to say *what* it is about the effective teacher that is important, the individual may ladder down through such constructs as *commitment to students*, and *aspects of punctuality*. This gives information about how effectiveness can be recognized.

In reviewing a completed grid, the participant or investigator may wish to ladder one or more of the resultant constructs. When the grids are analysed for similarities between elements and similarities between constructs, it may be possible to ascertain further superordinate constructs by asking the person to comment on the connections that seem to be indicated. This going beyond the grid to encourage the participant to act as a co-participant in the enquiry process is an essential part of constructivist procedures. As Lincoln (1992: 381) notes, 'the aim of constructivism ... is deep understanding that is directed towards reconstructions of previously held constructions'. The participants' commentary on their grids provides a fruitful vehicle for such deep understanding. The joint exploration and discussion of grid data is, in our opinion extremely important. The investigator should not rely on his/her interpretations alone. We will return to this issue later on.

Two further suggestions are relevant at this stage. The assigning of elements to one or other of the construct poles in no way, of itself, indicates which pole of the construct the individual prefers. The investigator may wish to collect such information by having the participant mark the grid form in such a way that this is indicated, by a rank order of preference for example. Likewise, one cannot automatically infer which of the constructs the person finds the most important for the purpose under consideration. One can ask the person to rank order the constructs in terms of importance by, for example, picking out the five most important constructs from the grid and rank ordering them. These are but two examples of where it is important to extend the discussion around the grid in order to maximize its potential.

So far, we have discussed issues that may arise when eliciting a grid on a one to one basis. However, a number of studies using repertory grids have used group grid elicitation. This often arises when the investigator wishes to or has to collect a large number of grids from a group of participants on one occasion. We have already identified the fact that it is important to elicit elements that can be personally construed. If the aims of the intervention are such that it is necessary to have the same element set in order to facilitate comparison between grids, then it is important to allow sufficient time for the negotiation of the element set among the group of participants. For example, if one was interested in teachers' thinking regarding appropriate methods for teaching, it would be important to recognize that not all teachers in the group may share the same wide range of teaching techniques that they can construe. There may need to be some negotiation of the final set that goes in the grid or the investigator would have to have a dual approach where there is the negotiated set plus a personal set. Denicolo in Kalekin-Fishman and Walker (1996) provided some useful examples of these techniques in practice.

Of equal importance is the recognition that, on a one-to-one basis, one gains the opportunity to have a full conversation with the individual regarding the meanings of the constructs and can tape record this discussion. This material provides valuable contextual information that can be lost in group work. Another difficulty with group elicitation is that it is difficult to help each individual grid-maker to split constructs or to cope with a situation where 'not applicable' may be most relevant. The investigator may need to discuss these while circulating among the group while the grids are being completed. Of course, these conversations with individuals may be overheard and therefore there is a potential danger of people writing down constructs that they overhear rather than focusing on their own. If such circulation among the group does not take place, one can often find oneself in the position of collecting incomplete grid data, say with empty cells, and therefore it is extremely difficult to utilize these within an intervention. [Practical hint: one method of handling the empty cells would be to give these a rating of '3' if one was using a five-point scale. However, this does not truly reflect what the person was actually thinking at the time of construction.]

It is possible to collect data from grids through a postal survey technique. However, very explicit instructions regarding filling in the grid should be given and, once again, one loses much of the richness of the grid conversation if one uses such an approach. Such grids may give some indication of the views of individuals but a conversational approach will provide a much richer data base and a firmer ground for interpretation, so again the intended use of the grid information should be taken into consideration when making methodological choices.

The grid technique provides a flexible methodology and used with sensitivity can provide illuminating material regarding professional thinking. As indicated above, there could be a variety of data collection methods and it is part of the investigator's craft to decide which is appropriate for the problem under review.

The next section will consider analysis and interpretation of grid material.

Analysis and interpretation

Once elements and constructs have been elicited, and perhaps assigned ratings, the result is a matrix which is open to several different types of analyses. One possibility is a content analysis of the types of constructs offered which is based upon assumptions about the similarities of meaning of the constructs, as indicated by the verbal labels used. A visual inspection of the similarities of pattern between rows and between columns of ratings will give some indication of possible relationships between constructs and between elements in the grid.

The type of analysis chosen will depend on the purpose of the study and the practical feasibility of implementing particular analyses. At this stage we would like to offer some initial comments.

Although there is much to be gained by considering the raw data of a grid and visually or manually extracting relationships from it, the advent of computer program packages for the analysis of grids allows for the ready extraction of the simple formal structural relationships between elements, or between constructs, which may be obscured by the detailed raw data matrix.

Traditional methods of grid analysis have been factor analysis and principal component analysis (Slater, 1977). These analyses are based on two matrices of similarity measures – an element matrix which includes the measure of similarity of every element with every other element, and the construct matrix which shows the measures of similarity between all pairs of constructs. These measures of similarity are viewed as distances in space or dimensions. As these matrices get larger one may have difficulty conceptualizing the geometry of a n-I dimensional space which might maximally require n-I dimensions. Factor analysis extracts the major dimensions or factors and then proceeds to describe each item by defining its position along each dimension, thus yielding factor loadings. Most matrices can thus be expressed as a series of factor loadings which are significantly less in number than the similarity measures in the original matrix. The usual procedure is to consider this 'simplified' expression of the raw data and place a label on the major factors.

Although this method is widely used it has some drawbacks. First, the different forms of mathematical 'pushing and shoving' can isolate different dimensions or factors. Secondly, we feel it is presumptuous for the investigator to name the factors; we consider it best to allow the participant to be involved in this process. Thirdly, it would seem that some people find it difficult to conceptualize or experience their construct system as a series of co-ordinate reference points along a limited set of axes. They find it difficult to conceptualize what has been done to their original data in order to arrive at this reductionist mapping of their system.

Cluster analysis also works with the two similarity matrices but instead of extracting the major factors, groups or clusters of similar items are extracted and the patterning of the original data can be exhibited. FOCUS, see Shaw (1993), is based on a type of non-inclusive two-way cluster analysis. This program produces a linear reordering of the elements to highlight similarities in the way in which they are construed and also reorders the constructs in a similar fashion. Analysis of grids, whether one uses manual or computer methods, will give a structure to the original responses which can be the basis for valuable further discussion with the individuals concerned.

The reader can obtain more detail on FOCUS and principal components in Pope and Keen (1981), on a variety of computer programs in Shaw (1980), on principal components and INGRID in Slater (1977) and in Fransella and Bannister (1977). Stewart and Stewart (1981: 65) gave a useful table which indicates seven of the differences between cluster analysis and principal component analysis. Three of these are worth summarizing here:

1. *Cluster analysis* – Throws away no detail of the relationships between elements/constructs in its visual presentation of the data. *Principal*

component analysis – Throws away some details of the relationships between elements/constructs in its visual presentation of the data.

2. *Cluster analysis* – Uses non-parametric statistics on the data, that is, treats 4 as more than 2 and less than 5, but makes no assumptions about the absolute size of the differences. *Principal component analysis* – Uses parametric statistics on the data, that is, assumes that the distance between 5 and 4, and 4 and 3 are equal, and that a score of 4 on a construct indicates twice a score of 2. This is seldom likely to be the case.

3. *Cluster analysis* – Relatively easy to demonstrate what the computer has done to get from the Grid to the map. *Principal component analysis* – Rather more difficult to demonstrate what the computer has done to get from the Grid to the map.

We prefer the use of cluster analysis particularly because of the three points given above. Here we will show a variety of analyses using data from our research on teachers' views of teaching effectiveness.

The level of the analysis which one conducts with the grid data depends on the purpose of the intervention. In our research on teachers' views of teaching effectiveness, at one level we were able to identify, through content analysis, a range of recurrent themes among the teachers we studied. Themes emerged such as time management, listening skills, integrity, ability to cooperate within a team, administrative skills, pastoral care skills, instructional skills, and a variety of 'personality' characteristics, e.g. *adaptable* versus *rigid*, and *approachable* versus *stand-offish*.

Although, in our research we have often collected full grids, including ratings, at other times we have conducted studies using the triadic method without ratings in order to elicit constructs and then used content analysis to identify the themes that teachers within particular groups have deemed to be important for the issue under consideration.

However, if one does use full rating, the grid throws up a wealth of data and there can be a danger of being overwhelmed by it. The computer helps to structure the information, but the investigator still is left with the task of interpreting the outcome. We have already indicated above that we prefer to use cluster analysis to analyse the data from our rated grids. In one of our studies our purpose was to encourage student teachers to articulate their views regarding effectiveness in teaching and then to explore the extent to which they see themselves as similar to or different from their current constructions of 'an expert teacher'. For staff development purposes, while one can utilize the whole of the grid, it was particularly instructive for each of the students to consider a part of the grid where they could compare themselves with both the expert teacher and the worst teacher they knew.

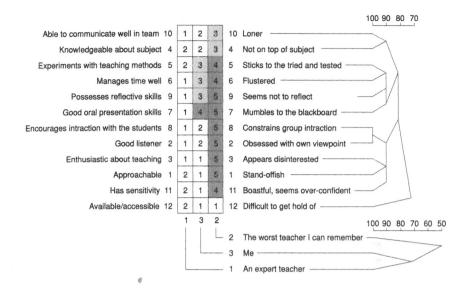

Figure 4.4. A portion of student teacher L–'s grid.

Figure 4.4 shows a portion of L–'s grid, in which one can see that she sees herself as more like the expert teacher than the worst teacher she could remember. However, there are some areas where she sees herself as different from the expert teacher; particularly in terms of her oral presentation skills, she sees herself more towards *mumbles to the blackboard*, and also she is still not possessing sufficient *reflective skills* or *time management skills* and still needs *more experimentation with a variety of teaching methods*. One can also note that, for example, she sees herself as more *available/accessible* as a student teacher than the expert teacher. She indicated in conversation around the grid that she recognized that there may be a limit to accessibility and availability and that teachers need to accept this, and this would link with their ability to manage time more effectively.

Most grid studies, however, utilize the full grid. Figure 4.5 shows the complete grid for the student teacher L– and one is able to see the fact that, at the moment, she is somewhat isolated from the rest of the elements in the grid – see element number 10 in the dendogram attached to the grid at the top. She does, however, veer towards the 'good or expert' teacher group. The poorer teachers are in a separate cluster. One can clearly see from inspecting the actual pattern within the grid where these poor versus expert teachers fall in her construing. The constructs also give a good indication of her current values regarding effectiveness in teaching. You will note some of the themes we alluded to earlier. One can

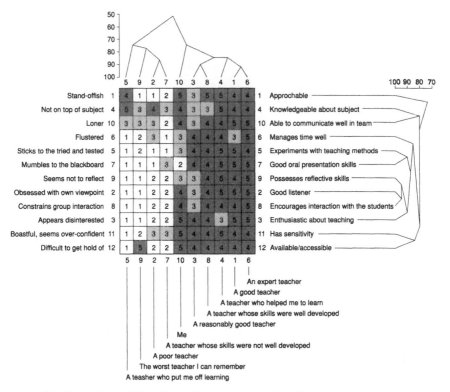

Figure 4.5. Complete grid for the student teacher L–'s grid.

see certain connections within her constructs, e.g. teachers she rates as being good listeners are also rated as encouraging interaction with the students. The construct *stand-offish* versus approachable is an isolated 'personality characteristic' not particularly linked with any skills aspect of teaching. The cluster 'possesses reflective skills, good listener, encourages interaction with students, and enthusiastic about teaching' was seen by L– as being those aspects which she felt were particularly connected with effectiveness in teaching.

One of the reasons why we prefer the FOCUS program, is that it allows the initial data to be retained and the patterns explored.

In our own research we have been particularly interested in Action Research with student teachers intending to work in a variety of professional contexts and, as part of our work, we have often encouraged such students to compare theirs with others grids and see the significance of the similarities and differences between their grids. Having the full FOCUS grids available for discussions in pairs and within groups leads to further rich data that can be utilized for research purposes.

The SOCIOGRID analysis allows the researcher to compare grids and identify some of the structural similarities between grids of various participants within the group. The similarity is based on how the participants have rated the elements on each of their constructs (Shaw, 1980). Figure 4.6 demonstrates this with a socionet that indicates that two students, CC and SPe, were isolates. The content of their grid and the way they saw effectiveness was atypical of the rest of the group. The arrows between individuals show the degree of overlap and sharing between grids. HL particularly links with GP, JS and MC. These four form a sub-cluster. MC also links with SF and JM, and, although not complete isolates, RB and DW only link with JM's grid.

Construct links (at least 50% over 80.0)

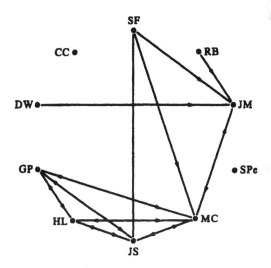

Figure 4.6. Socionet.

Analysis of the individual grids is particularly illuminative while the SOCIOGRID analysis produces useful socionets which give an initial basis for comparing and contrasting and sharing within a group.

We hope that we have, through the use of a worked example, given some insight into how one might begin to interpret grid data. We do find the grid a useful tool. It is a flexible methodology which allows personal meaning to be explored in detail with a public record that is easily compiled. What is more, it is an excellent catalyst towards further conversation. The focused grid can be discussed and participants can be encouraged to interpret their own grids. Figure 4.7 is a schematic outline of a focused grid.

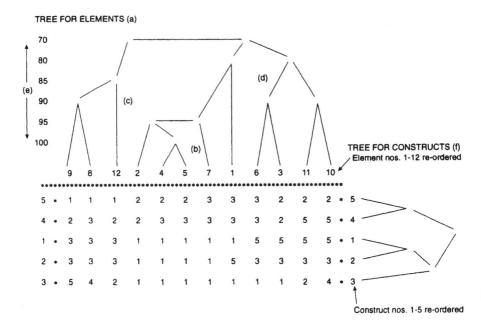

Figure 4.7. A focus grid.

Figure 4.7 is a diagrammatic representation of a printout of a grid with 12 elements and 5 constructs. The elements have been reordered so that the element 'tree' (a) shows the clustering or grouping of elements. In the figure elements 4 and 5 are matched at the 100% level (b). This means that these elements have identical ratings on all constructs. There is a group (c) made up of elements 9,8 and 12 that are separated from the other 9 elements. Element number 1 is least like all the other elements (d). As one 'ascends' the tree the degree of relationship between the elements decreases. The construct 'tree' (f) can be explored in a similar manner and the ensuing conversation often produces further very relevant information about the person's thoughts and feelings. During feedback one should encourage the individual to:

- note high relationships between pairs or groups;
- consider personal reasons why pairs or groups of elements or constructs within the total set may be alike or dissimilar;
- consider the clusters formed in order to ascertain possible superordinate constructs.

However, one should be aware that, for some people, grid methodology may not be the best method of approach for certain purposes. For example, some report that they find assigning ticks or crosses, or numbers, is too formal and structured an approach and thus this constraint interferes with the 'raising of awareness' which can be a major purpose when considering the use of grid techniques. For such individuals a freer discussion may be a more useful method. We elaborate on a range of possibilities in the next chapter, though at this point we note that a grid-like conversation without the formal compilation of a matrix may be one substitute.

If any form of repertory grid technique is used, and especially if feedback sessions are aimed at getting the individuals to think more deeply about their constructs, it is important to be aware of the need for some system of ongoing support for the individual. There are times when appraising one's construing of people or events can be very disturbing and thus some ongoing empathetic support is needed throughout this period. This is an important ethical consideration and we will return to it in Chapter 6.

Before concluding this chapter it is necessary to point out some other subtle dangers. For many, numerical analysis seems to be equated with absolute truth. The existence of numbers in repertory grids, and the ensuing development of computer programs for analysis, must be treated with caution, and considered in the context of the epistemological framework of the investigator.

The repertory grid, with its heavy reliance on numerical analysis, has been used by some investigators as a definitive measure of the persons concerned. This is totally unjustified on both statistical and philosophical grounds. The grid is perhaps best seen as a catalyst within a conversation between investigator and the individual. It can allow insight into some of the ways in which the individual construes the particular aspects of his or her world which is being investigated. It is certainly not a psychological test which accurately pigeon-holes the individual into a neat category system. It provides only a partial record because much process is still in mind of the individual. We are reminded, at this point, of a comment made by Don Bannister in his Foreword to Beail (1985: xii):

> At least two fair statements can be made about the development, to date, of grid method. First the grid has powerfully drawn the attention of psychologists to the central importance of persons' interpretation of their worlds and thereby forced them to take heed of the central tenets of Personal Construct theory. Secondly, grid method is a Frankenstein's monster which has rushed away on a statistical and experimental rampage of its own, leaving construct theory neglected, stranded high and dry, far behind.

We would urge readers to avoid such a rampage. In Chapters 2 and 3 we drew attention to the central tenets of Personal Construct Psychology. We firmly believe that the grid must be underpinned by a sensitivity to these tenets.

It is important to recognize that the grid only provides information and a basis for structural/content analysis – it does *not* provide *solutions* to *problems*. Furthermore, the grid throws up a wealth of data and there can be a danger of feeling overwhelmed. This is where the computer can help. However, being familiar with the technique and having suitable analysis software should not be seen as a panacea for all constructivist research agendas nor for every staff development problem.

The process of grid elicitation is very time-consuming, for instance each grid may take between one and three hours to complete, and this often places an unacceptable burden on the 'investigator' as well as on the 'participant'. Additionally a high level of skill is required to 'sense' the progress of the elicitation and to give 'prompts' and assistance when required, while not becoming over-directive in the approach. This kind of skill comes from practice and really cannot be learnt from books! The reader who is about to embark on such a data-collecting exercise will, therefore, find it essential to have some 'dry runs' eliciting grids to develop this sensitivity to what is actually happening during an elicitation session. It cannot be stressed too strongly that the grid is a powerful instrument and should not be used indiscriminately by folk who are not adequately prepared to use it.

Friends and colleagues can be encouraged to participate in practice sessions and will often give useful feedback about when they are confused about requirements or feel constrained or forced along a particular track by your comments. Listening to tape recordings of such practice grid interviews can be a salutary experience!

In our view the most efficient way of learning to elicit a repertory grid is first to sit in on an elicitation session with an experienced investigator and secondly to elicit some grid data oneself in the presence of a guide and mentor. We run seminars and training sessions for interested potential users. We would welcome any reader who has no 'struggling other' who can help to contact us at the Centre for Personal Construct Psychology in Education, University of Reading. We would be delighted to be of service.

However, in the majority of our work, we feel it is important to exploit the use of a variety of methods, but still within the framework of constructivist research.

The next chapter elaborates these constructive alternatives.

CHAPTER 5

Beyond the grid

We pass the word around; we ponder how the case is put by different people;
we read the poetry; we meditate over the literature; we play the music; we
change our minds; we reach an understanding. (Thomas, 1995)

Introduction: in true spirit

to the constructive alternativist the next step is to see if he can improve his
hypothesis, perhaps by formulating his questions in new ways or by pursuing
the implications of some fresh assumption that occurred to him when he was
writing up the conclusions of the last experiment. (Kelly, 1969b: 126)

For us this quotation embodies the spirit of Kelly's writing and the
challenge that is presented to all users of a Personal Construct approach to
education and research. Kelly put forward his theory, his methodological
argument and descriptions of tools or instruments as tentative
hypotheses. Central to his epistemology was the 'invitational mood' – the
presentation of ideas *as if* they might be a useful way of looking at things.
He encouraged us to look at his theory in this light and to modify and
discard aspects of it which do not prove useful to us in our endeavours.
Thus we are specifically invited to engage in theoretical extension, elaboration and, indeed, reformation to inform our practice by extending our
horizons.

In Chapter 4 we explored the use of grid methodology as one means of
extending our horizons having first identified which ones we were bound
by. We also raised some caveats about uninformed or uncritical use of this
family of methods, recognizing that different tools may be required in
different contexts, for different tasks, and certainly to suit the needs and
skills of different people. In this chapter we respond to Kelly's invitation
to extend method as well as theory. We will discuss alternative methods
which we have discovered, invented, borrowed and amended, learnt from
colleagues and students, or selected and adapted from other theoretical

91

frameworks. As have other Personal Construct psychologists, we have recognized common themata and consonant practice in, for example, ethnomethodological approaches (Garfinkel, 1967; Patton, 1990); symbolic interactionism (Mead, 1934; Blumer, 1978) heuristic inquiry (Douglas and Moustakas, 1984) and Rogerian humanistic psychology (Rogers, 1965). All of these provide a variety of lenses with which to view the perspective of the personal so that a Kellian framework can be seen to fit within the tradition of a *verstehen* approach, one which seeks to come to an understanding of the view of the world held by the actors in any particular situation.

Novak (1983) suggested that other approaches, those which use a 'personless' framework for studying and working with humans, negating their perceptual worlds, missed the essence of personhood and lacked respect for the integrity of people. He recognized in PCT the potential for justice to be done to the uniqueness and complexity of the perceived world of the person. We do, of course, recognize that *potential* deserves to be realized in *action* but such action may not be easy to undertake; coming to understand our own worlds is challenge enough while attempting to enter the world of others is an awe-inspiring task. Not everyone has the ability, inclination or time and technology to embark on grid elicitation for themselves or with their colleagues/ students/ clients while each of these latter may present challenges to the endeavour in being, for instance, limited in language skills (see Chapter 6) or alienated by approaches which require formally structured interventions. Equally significant in the choice of technique to explore personal worlds is the purpose of the exploration. Earlier we emphasized the need to be clear about purpose with participants when using a grid, but there will be times when the purpose itself precludes the use of a grid and demands exploration by other techniques.

Nevertheless, whether we are engaged in exploring our own or the worlds of others through research or evaluation, or whether we are helping others to understand and expand their own worlds through education, guidance or therapy, we should heed the words of Kelly (1969b), referred to in Chapter 3, when he urged his students that they: 'should not overlook what their subjects have to contribute'. What we need are processes and tools which encompass 'helping a person to build for himself a viable system of ideas, on the basis of which he can find meaning in his own life, discover new aspects of reality for himself and help to enrich the ever-growing heritage of human experience' (Salmon and Bannister, 1974: 26). The problem is to find suitable ways to help people to access and represent their ideas or constructs of reality.

For Eisner (1993: 6) representation is the 'process of transforming the contents of consciousness into a public form so that they can be stabilised, inspected, edited and shared with others'. While we recognize that any form of representation is only partial, that the nature of each form will inevitably filter, organize and transform the contents of consciousness, we suggest that each technique described in this chapter has the potential to contribute a small tile to the mosaic which displays personal meaning. The realization of that potential depends on the skill of the individual in selecting an appropriate form of representation, implementing it and interpreting the outcomes. The following sections provide some ideas, a little guidance and a few caveats. Let us preface these with a general warning: we can only present a summary here of the techniques and how they might be used. Each one deserves a manual in its own right and certainly each will require further exploration and practice. We have provided references to the work of others which we have found useful as a stimulus to resource building for others. (At the end of the previous chapter we referred to our Centre for PCP in Education. As part of this we have a Resource Base which includes the literature referred to here and to which we allow access to interested others.)

The techniques described and illustrated in the following sections allow us to explore further our own worlds and are conduits through which other individuals can illuminate for us their construing of themselves and the worlds they inhabit. As a prelude we present the words of Connelly and Clandinin (1990: 5):

> Data can be in the form of fieldnotes of the shared experience, journal records, interview transcripts, other's observations, story telling, letter writing, autobiographical writing, documents such as class plans and newsletters, and writing such as rules, principles, metaphors and personal philosophies ... The sense of the whole is built from a rich data source with a focus on the concrete particularities of life that create powerful narrative tellings.

Narrative techniques for exploring constructs

It is not our intention here to provide a detailed examination of the nature and role of narrative techniques in education, research and professional practice, nor to debate the semantics of 'story', 'discourse' etc. Others have done that ably before us and readers are referred to the compendium compiled by McEwan and Egan (1995) which addresses the theories which underpin the use of narrative in those contexts and abounds with examples of both its use and the work of others who have made it a special study. A useful text to read in contrast to the latter is Goodson's (1996) chapter in which he urges caution, while nevertheless valuing the antidote that narrative-based methods provide to the misrepresentation or over-simplistic representation of reductionists methods. We should not, he contended, reify narrative techniques such that they become a new orthodoxy. In particular, he warned that stories should not just be narrated but also located:

> Stories and narratives are not an unquestioned good: it all depends. And above all it depends on how they relate to history, and to social context . (p. 215)

He went on to remind us that consciousness is constructed rather than produced completely autonomously by the individual so that, if narrative is divorced from the social context, we are in danger of perpetuating ideological pressures which influence thought and behaviour. Kompf (1999) also recognized as a major issue the limitations of selected disclosure in narrative methods of research. He made a particular point that what is experienced, and thereafter revealed, by the participant has its own character and tensions. He provided a summary (see Figure 5.1) of contrasts between the researcher and participant about what engages them at different stages of the research process. These provide subtle but nutritive food for thought for anyone choosing a 'storytelling' approach.

We will return to these authors' concerns in the last section of this chapter, having served our purpose here, which is to describe and illustrate a range of techniques which we and others have found to be productive alternatives to grid methods for elucidating personal constructs. However, to set the context and to provide our rationale for grouping certain techniques within this sub-heading, let us loosely define 'narrative' techniques as those: giving a connected order to a series of events in a verbal form; an organized text.

We contrast this with the techniques portrayed in the next section which owe much of their power to pictures or diagrams. In those the verbal accompaniment is usually spoken rather than written, as it is in those described in this first section. All of these, though, could be termed 'stories', and are derived from human experience. Perhaps we can be forgiven for repeating just a few of McEwan and Egan's (1995: viii) words here:

> A narrative, and that particular form of narrative we call a story, deals not just in facts or ideas or theories, or even dreams, fears, and hopes but in facts, theories, and dreams from the perspective of someone's life and in the context of someone's emotions. It is helpful to remember that all the knowledge we have has been gained in the context of someone's life, as a product of someone's hopes, fears, and dreams.

	Participant	**Researcher**
Pre-activity (Anticipation)		
Pre-contact	N/A	issue and focus development of methods
Initial contact	thinking about being chosen	thinking about choice
	thinking about what to say and how to be	impression formation
Inter-activity (Reflection-in-Action)		
Interview	anxiety to provide desired information	focus on issues and questions
	demarcation of areas of disclosure	methods and accuracy
Journal: Private	stream of consciousness	N/A
Public (e.g. coursework, therapy)	self report	assigned activity
	marked domain of comfort with occasional stretching of boundaries	pre-analysis of text, context and subtext
	development of self-as-learning partner	formation of classifications
	enhanced ability to represent self	increased richness of data
	ability to discriminate more finely between and among experiences	
Post-activity (Reflection-on-Action)		
Deconstruction	how did I represent myself?	analysis of text
Incorporation	what do my words mean to me? what does it mean to the researcher?	determining classification
Interpretation	what did we learn? what did I learn?	co-constructing meaning
Transformation	how am I different?	distillation of content
Reconstruction	how do discovered differences in self affect my life?	analysis of findings
Anticipation	where do I go from here?	who's next?
Disengagement		
Residual from process	effects of 'being studied' main point in reflective life psychological motion	additional data

Figure 5.1. Participant and researcher reflections on the narrative process (after Kompf 1999).

If this is not constructivist enough, then we can do no better than to turn to Mair (1989: 2), who argues that all our psychological reporting is story telling, although often of *very limited, stilted, impoverished kinds*. He contends that PCP is particularly *story-valuing* and invites us to consider rewording the Fundamental Postulate and the Corollaries in playful recognition of this, thus:

- Persons' processes are psychologically channelized by the *stories that they live* and the *stories that they tell.*
- Individuals differ in the stories they live and the stories they tell.
- A story is convenient for the anticipation of a finite range of events only.
- A person's story varies as he successively construes the replication of events.
- A person may successively employ a variety of stories that are inferentially incompatible with each other.
- To the extent that one person construes the stories of another, he may play a role in a social process involving the other person. (Mair, 1989: 5; original emphasis)

With this in mind, let us now review some of the alternative ways in which other lives might be storied.

Seeking constructs in text and non-text documents

There are many textbooks devoted to research methods which provide detailed descriptions of the diverse forms of content, discourse or narrative analysis so it would not be appropriate to reiterate them here. (Our students have found Mason (1996) a useful basic introduction, Patton (1990) a comprehensive and comprehensible guide and Denzin and Lincoln (1984) a detailed encyclopaedic resource.) Instead we want to alert readers to the wealth of constructs to be found in written documents of all kinds: recourse to specific and special methods for eliciting constructs is not always necessary. Constructs, like the colour green, can be seen all around us once we have been alerted to them. The more obvious ones can be seen in descriptive words, adjectives and adverbs, which of course tell us about how the authors of documents, or the people whose words are portrayed in the document, see their worlds. We can find in interview transcripts and official documents, such as government papers, organizational procedures etc., similar evidence of world views.

We may only find the emergent pole of a particular construct within any one document – but this is still a clue! Sometimes the contrast pole can be found elsewhere but caution has to be exercised in linking the two without checking with the person whose construct it is.

Less obvious, but still worth looking at, is the way in which words are used. We will note in Chapter 6 that great care must be observed in interpreting language use, because words do not always mean to the user what they mean to us so that an exploration of *how* they are used in documents is as important as noting which actual words are used. Patton (1990: 394) provided an illustration of this when discussing the examination and analysis of interview data. He had found that a group of teachers all categorized the students who skipped class as either 'chronics' or 'borderlines' but individual teachers used different criteria to distinguish them. It was not so much that one teacher's *chronic* was another's *borderline*, for each teacher would categorize the same students under each heading, but that each had their own defining characteristic for the terms. Earlier Patton had noticed that no matter what the variation in ingredients or method of preparation, most people recognize a hamburger.

Further, there is usually a consensus on what fits the hamburger category and what are cheeseburgers. He suggested that what people say about them enables the analyst to discern how they experience them. We would suggest in addition that constructs can also be observed in action – so that a record of a screwed up face or a contented smile in observation notes can add to our evidence about the apparent constructs of others – or even ourselves (have you ever suddenly become aware of a silly grin or a frown on your face which made you realize what an incident meant to you – a construct creeping up behind your mask?!)

They say a picture paints a thousand words. Although in the second part of this chapter we will probe the deliberate use of pictures as aids to elicit constructs, while we are investigating the constructs inherent in public record documents it is relevant to note that these texts often contain diagrams, pictures and other non-text material. These have been chosen by the authors or compilers of the document to illustrate points and they, too, contain evidence of what is considered important by them and of what they think their audience might find useful, or might not understand readily without this form of support. To build on the hamburger example above, consider what the public relations officials of a chain of fast food outlets are attempting to convey by their illustrations on menus, posters etc. What significant features of the food are emphasized, and what does this say about the view of public requirements held by the purveyors? Another example comes from the work of one of our students who was investigating recruitment and retention in the profession of nursing. She surveyed the recruitment literature over a period of years and was surprised to find that although the rhetoric conveyed a developing professional image, and was couched in non-sexist language, the photographs of nurses used in illustration were predominantly of women, in poses by the bedside which reflected a more historic public view of the role. This led her to consider further how nursing is generally conveyed by the media, resulting in an overview of television programmes over the last thirty years which portray the profession in different ways. She argued that these both reflect and influence its public image (Pope and Denicolo, 1997).

When describing roles, events (past or prospective), activities or experiences, people frequently compare or contrast them to other things with which they are familiar, or those they think others might relate to. You might think of how you would explain your job to a young, inexperienced person, or how you would describe a foreign holiday venue to someone who has never been there. To provide an image of the job or venue, you select aspects which are significant to you and try to capture the essence of them. What you choose and the way in which you present that essence is informed by your own constructs of both the job/venue and of what the other's comparable experience might be. Of course, there will be some influence too from what impression you wish to convey by your description – think of choosing postcards on holiday to send to different people. Why do you choose different cards for different people and select different views to convey how you see the context while rejecting others? How would you describe your job to a new recruit, to your child who wishes to follow your footsteps, to someone who wants you to change your job, to your boss who wants to add to it? All of these provide different kinds of evidence about your own constructs and need to be considered in relation to the context in which, and purpose *for* which, you are forming the description.

At different periods in our previous research, we have been interested in the metaphors which people use, either deliberately or inadvertently, in discussing aspects of their world. (Here we are using 'metaphor' to stand for any figurative language form – similes, analogies etc.) For an in-depth and fascinating treatment of this topic, see Lakoff and Johnson (1980). In their book, *Metaphors We Live By*, they contend that metaphors, far from being just the province of poets and those who like to use rhetorical flourish in their speech and writing, are pervasive in everyday life, governing as well as describing our experience and actions. They invite us for example to consider the metaphorical concept of *time is money*. They present examples of the kinds of phrases used commonly in Western contexts:

> You're wasting my time ...
> This gadget will save you hours ...
> How do you spend your time these days? ...
> I've invested a lot of time in her ...
> You need to budget your time ...
> Is it worth your while?...
> He's living on borrowed time.

Later in that discussion they suggest that this concept of time 'as a valuable resource' is culturally specific, but where it exists and pervades language use it also structures how we act and conceive of time. Others too have found it instructive to become aware of the metaphors which permeate descriptions, and to consider how they represent and influence world views. (See Martin Cortazzi's (1993) excellent book *Narrative Analysis*.) In teacher training and professional development courses we have devised activities based on the work of Dennis Fox (1983). In summary, he asked teachers to describe their role and the process of teaching/learning, and what methods they use for different aspects of their role, for instance in lessons, in assessment etc. From the data, he identified four prevalent theories:

- the *transfer* theory, in which words like convey, impart, transmit information were used in conjunction with lecture-type methods and assessment of received knowledge;
- the *shaping* theory, in which words like mould, model, demonstrate, prepare were used in conjunction with exemplar and case study activities with assessment of practice;
- the *travelling* theory, in which words like lead, point the way, guide, help were used in conjunction with exploratory activities and descriptive/ discursive essay assignments;
- and the *growing* theory, in which words like cultivate, nurture, foster, enable were used in conjunction with student centred, experiential activities and assessment.

Although he found that the more novice teachers tended to subscribe to either or both of the first two theories, he noted that experienced teachers were able to apply all the theories flexibly, at different times, and appropriately, according to the needs of the students and the subject content – much as we urge you to apply judiciously the techniques discussed in this chapter. His work does demonstrate that constructs are discernible in the way in which people describe aspects of their worlds. The activities we have devised based on it follow this through. For instance, we have encouraged students early in a course to write such descriptions, to store these away and then to compare them with similar descriptions they write having completed the course or a particular experiential aspect of it and their chosen occupation. They can then discern for themselves whether or not they have changed their orientation towards their activity, what they understand by it and how they implement procedures. In addition, by noting the kinds of words used, categorizing them in terms of coherent themes and discerning the metaphors that underpin their use, we can gain some access to the shape and texture of their worlds (or the taste and smell of them, if you prefer that metaphor!).

Of course, a specially designed activity can provide a focus for exploring particular issues in which you and your fellow participants are interested. On the other hand, you may now be alert that data collected previously, perhaps in the form of interview transcripts or observation/ behaviour records, can contain information on constructs through the words used and images conveyed. Do remember, though, that the questions you chose to use in the interview, the language in which you couched them, and the observations recorded say much about your own constructs of the situation and may have influenced those who were the intended focus of attention. Psychology text books dealing with the limitations of eye witness evidence provide examples of this. One that sticks in our mind is the variation in speeds attributed to cars when the question changes from 'How fast was the car travelling when it hit the other car?' to 'How fast was the car travelling when it smashed into the other car?' The wording of your interview questions or the categories of behaviour you note may have a similar biasing effect which you need to be conscious of. This effect may be reduced when participants have a more general remit to respond to, as in the sources of data described below.

Accounts, logs and process descriptions

In education and training, the purpose is to help others examine their own ideas and practice in order to identify those which are useful and those which could bear some critical review or, indeed, those which are detrimental and need to be discarded. In research, the purpose may be to review such things either with or on behalf of others.

Whatever the purpose, the exercise should not be undertaken lightly because, to be effective, some considerable reflection on and in practice is required of participants and this process is seldom easy or free from potential hostility or resistance to change, as we have noted earlier. Tools are required to aid this reflection, especially reflection on deeply held core assumptions, and these tools need to be managed with sensitivity. Consciousness can seldom be raised without having implications for support and guidance, something to be expected perhaps in an education/training context but also something to be aware of in a research setting. Although as constructivist researchers we do not expect to take the traditional 'fly on the wall' stance, and do expect that our presence will affect the system we explore, we should nevertheless not leave our participants in a worse state than that we found them.

Thus, we introduce first the least 'invasive' of techniques for helping people to reflect on their ideas and practice.

Encouraging or requesting people to provide an account of their practice, or to compile a log of activities or to describe the process they engage in may at first appear to be a relatively easy task for them to undertake and may not seem particularly indicative of their construing. Possibly only trying this for yourself can convey the complexity of the task, and the load it either imposes on memory or on simultaneous recording and acting. Perhaps you might like to try now to provide an account of what you did on your most recent day at work, or imagine how you might cope with logging each of your various activities as they occur, or with describing the process of your work – teaching, managing, etc. You, like us and those we work with, might find it helpful to concentrate on a particular occasion or to focus on a particular subset of the activity ... to make it more concrete, as we advised in relation to element selection for grids, and to limit the 'universe of discourse' to a manageable entity. On the other hand, you might be interested in the very complexity of a life activity, and its manageability. Again, purpose should determine choice although the time allocated to the task will have a considerable bearing on results! Respondents will, though, report what they deem to be significant to the declared purpose within the bounds of what they perceive as salient. One of us had a notice pinned to the office wall which said – 'I used to complain about all the interruptions to my work, until I realized that the interruptions were my work!' Such consciousness raising has its place in many spheres of activity, be it classified as ongoing work, research or teaching/learning.

We have long had a policy of encouraging research students to keep a fieldwork log or research diary. This has not been a prescriptive activity and the forms that these have taken have been as various as the students concerned. One common factor, though, has been that each has perceived the activity as valuable in some way: for documenting how their ideas and skills have developed; for illustrating the opportunities and constraints they have encountered; for providing information about the tone and tenor of situations they have been in. Perhaps most relevant to the discussion here is that they have provided them with salutary reminders of their own constructs, the spectacles through which they have perceived their fieldwork and all the participants in it, how these have changed over time and how these might limit their interpretations.

Learning logs involve the tracking of personal development through the writing up of what are considered to be influential learning experiences drawn from everyday incidents. This both provides a structured way of reflecting on practice for some people who are rather more inclined towards activity and alerts others to the learning potential inherent in what were previously viewed as mundane activities.

Participants often ask if certain activities 'count' – for instance, passing conversations in the corridor or cogitations during the journey to a venue. A constructivist response would be that it counts if it is considered important or salient by the person conversing or cogitating. Thus, the categories of what might be logged might be better elicited from the person whose log it is, rather than imposed by those seeking the information. This is just as we advised for constructs in a grid, bearing in mind that some negotiation might preserve the focus of interest. That negotiation itself, though, forms part of the data. Similarly, negotiation might be relevant in relation to the level and detail in a process description. It might be more productive to ask for a general description of a process and then to elaborate the detail by further probing of how and why particular aspects were undertaken, in the form of laddering described in relation to grids.

Although they can be very informative in their own right, accounts, logs and process descriptions can usefully be used as a basis for deeper exploration in interview with individuals. In contrast, they can provide a means of exploring situations with a large group of people who compile them individually in their own time and then share the results. This sharing can be direct, perhaps by pairs exchanging products and then by 'snowballing', perhaps at that point only noting main similarities and differences. An alternative is that one person, the researcher, investigator or teacher perhaps, analyses the main points for group discussion. Our colleague Jon Roberts (personal communication) has used logs in his teaching of Masters students:

> I offered an MA group a foreign language learning plus logging course. They reviewed their logs and selected insights which they wrote on cards for the 'reflection on action' activity they presented, explained and discussed these, and then arranged all their cards into thematic sets on table tops. It worked really well, producing categories of insight/issue and contrasts.

We reported one version of the latter process in a text about developing active learning in Higher Education (Denicolo *et al.*, 1992). In a workshop, we asked lecturers to think of some specific situations in which they had been learners, both ones in which they had felt actively engaged and ones in which they had felt inhibited from learning actively. We then asked each of them to describe those situations, paying particular attention to factors which seemed to enhance the active learning process and those which detracted from it. From these individual descriptions we produced lists of 'positive' and 'negative' factors and shared these with the group. The lecturers were interested to find some factors in each list that they shared in common, some that individuals saw as significant whereas others perceived them as trivial, some that individuals had experienced frequently and others seldom or never, and some that they disagreed about in terms of which list it should be in! 'Getting negative feedback on efforts' and 'feeling on the edge of security' appeared in both aggregated columns, for instance. The group involved went on to discuss avidly and in great depth the individuality of learning and how to create learning environments which provide a variety of stimuli to suit a range of needs. Over the course of many such workshops, we were able to collect numerous such lists and review them for recurring themes. For interest, these are listed below. Note that they are not in any order of priority for it will be different for each person, depending on experience, context and personal constructs about learning.

Groups of factors influencing degree of active learning

- perceived salience of subject matter;
- the communication skills of the teacher;
- the degree of expected participation of the students;
- the structure of the learning experience;
- the social perception skills of the teacher;
- the subject expertise of the teacher;
- temporal and environmental factors;
- degree of security felt by the student;
- the amount of content of the session;
- the amount of excitement/interest generated;
- the personal style of the teacher.

You might like to consider the order of priority which you would allocate to these in a traditional course setting, and then think whether the priority might change if you were having a practical flying lesson. In the latter case, personal safety might perhaps become a higher priority.

Diaries and journals

Personal safety, or at least firm assurance of confidentiality, becomes a significant factor when asking people to share with you their diaries or journals whether it be for their own personal development or to inform research. Few people would be willing to share personal diaries compiled for their own purposes, though they may be prepared to share 'edited highlights'. Many professional registration courses, especially in the health and caring services, currently encourage students to keep a reflective journal so to encourage reflection on practice and to provide assessable evidence of their ability to engage in such a process. Obviously it is important and good practice that students are alerted in advance about which parts, or how much of such a journal, will be required to be shared with the tutor and others and about how such information will be confidentially treated. We would urge such good practice whenever asking others to share such personal reflections.(See section on Ethics in Chapter 6.)

As with other techniques and tools described in this chapter, diaries and journals provide examples of what is considered significant in a person's life, even if only through what is included as being of note, and what opinions are brought to bear on recorded events. However, it would be less than sensible to expect that everyone is equally adept at recording events, or has the same amount of time or commitment to such an activity. Since different people have different previous experience of keeping diaries or journals and differing purposes for doing so, then clarity about what is being requested in such an activity is paramount. Some people use diaries to record appointments only, others may include a list of most activities to be undertaken. Others see diaries as reflections on what is past rather than to aid future planning. Each form is informative about a person's lifestyle and experiences but each serves a different aim and set of expectations.

Anecdotes, life histories and autobiographies

We have combined these three, anecdote, life history and autobiography, under one heading to emphasize some important aspects that they have in common. Whether written by the person at their centre or transcribed verbatim from oral accounts, they provide a rich text from which to discern constructs. They include what is considered to be of importance from a complex stream of events. As Dilthey noted (see also 'Snakes, rivers and connecting threads', below, p. 111), much of what we do or experience is lost in the complicated and intricate, if not perplexing, rush of survival in the present. Only specific examples from our past are selected out for special attention. Others may be stored in memory but it takes special stimuli to bring them to consciousness. Even when they are retrieved, they may be re-interpreted unconsciously by the individual concerned to make better sense in the current context or to suit the purposes of recollection and the audience with whom they are shared. They may be elaborated or played down in their telling, but nevertheless that telling has a subtext which allows the discerning listener/reader to identify constructs, perhaps for further exploration.

To elaborate on some of those points, it might seem that an autobiography provides a supreme example of the way a person views her/his life and of the constructs which orientate it. However, given the size of the task, it is clear that some selection must take place and that selection is likely to be determined by a particular perspective. Each of us could write a range of autobiographies, depending on whether we intend to write a best-selling book or an historical account (though one may not exclude the other necessarily), whether we intend to inform or entertain, with the same caveat, and depending on which life role perspective is in focus at the time. Different emphases, examples and, yes, anecdotes would seem salient to us if we were writing our autobiographies as academics, as women academics, or simply, but not merely, as women. Just as a CV might have some things in common whatever the purpose (for different jobs or for a job as opposed to for an adoption agency), so too an autobiography, life history or anecdote is tailored to fit purpose, context and audience. It is important when interpreting such information to find out what these distinguishing factors are.

Ely *et al.* (1997) provide illuminating and sometimes touching examples of these 'multiple selves' that determine autobiographical work. They also describe the 'nuggets of meaning' embodied in and represented by anecdotes. The choice of outstanding event which is used to make a point or illustrate a perspective, what is emphasized and what is ignored in its telling and the language used, all contribute to the formation and sharing of meaning.

Some researchers are less attracted to autobiography being concerned that, in the confines of a research project, limited time to build rapport, seek out reflections and reminiscences etc. necessarily also limits the insight it can offer to any of the parties involved. Some researchers, and we would include ourselves when supervising higher degree students, consider that a brief autobiography which demonstrates the developing interest in a project of a researcher, the concerns and prejudices which are brought to bear, is helpful in providing readers with a frame of reference and some clues about the lenses through which the problem is viewed. It is also worth considering, even in relatively formal written presentations, whether brief anecdotes might encapsulate for the reader the tone or ambience of a research context.

Self-characterization sketches

Kelly (1955: Vol. 1, 239–67) wrote a whole chapter on this technique which we cannot better here, so we will only present the main points as an appetizer. We have already alluded to the notion that some requests for information about self produce rather self-conscious, sanitized responses. Kelly's well-honed version of the self-characterization sketch, originally for clinical interventions, has much to commend it for research and staff development activities, especially in cases in which a role relationship is sought in which the other person's personal outlook is valued as part of the interaction. He suggested asking the person to write a character sketch of him/herself from the perspective of a friend who knows him/her very *intimately*, perhaps better than anyone really could, and is *sympathetic*. It should be written in the third person, beginning something like – 'name of person' (e.g. Jo/Joanne) is ...'.

The phrasing of this request:

- permits people some latitude to use their own constructions of self;
- emphasizes that it is structure rather than detail that is important;
- allows them to make themselves plausible from an outsider perspective;
- indicates that something more than a superficial description of appearance is required;
- frees them from feeling threatened into providing either an incriminating description or a litany of what they 'ought' to be like.

We will provide in the chapters which follow some examples from practice of this technique. These will illustrate how replete with constructs, the emergent poles at least, such sketches can be, not only about how people view themselves but how they perceive the worlds that they inhabit. While these can then be explored further in a subsequent discussion, perhaps using laddering techniques, analysis of the sequence and linking of ideas, the organization of them, shifts in emphasis, the emergence of themes and the repetition of them, all provide evidence of personal viewpoints.

When we wrote earlier of autobiography we recognized that each of us is capable of providing several versions of our own, depending among other things on the role perspective from which we re-create it. This is also true of self-characterization sketches. This is addressed by Millar Mair (1977) who posited that each of us sees ourselves as a community of several people – our family roles interacting with our professional and social roles – so that a self-characterization sketch might be drawn up for each of these, for the combination (very difficult to do though) or only one of them, depending on the purpose of the exercise.

Some of our fellow researchers have sometimes been concerned with one particular aspect of human frailty, asking 'but what if people lie, or exaggerate or miss out really obvious things about themselves?' Kelly did consider this, but invites us to consider a credulous stance. For the contexts in which we recommend the use of this technique, we are not in the business of scoring the sketches for accuracy – that is, our version of accuracy – we are concerned rather with how the individual seeks to project him/herself. We might wonder why anyone would go to the trouble of 'lying' or whether their 'truth' might be different to ours. We might also consider if another technique might be more helpful in stimulating a particular person to express his/her experience of the world.

Reflection on practice activities using pictorial artefacts

So far in this chapter we have concentrated on analysing documents which already exist or on textual representations such as transcripts of interviews or solicited written material such as autobiographies or self-characterization sketches. These fall into what might be deemed the traditional tools of research. These latter can be useful when the sequence of events is as important as a description of what happened.

Stimulated recall

In situations in which such experiences may be difficult for individuals to recall or when the interest is in how things were done, why did something happen and why at that time, then it is frequently helpful to use a family of techniques described as 'stimulated recall' (Bloom, 1953; Woods, 1985; Pope, 1981; Dolk *et al.*, 1999). Some forms of this require some advance preparation. An activity, practice session etc. may be audio- or video-recorded, or still photographs may be taken at intervals during the activity. These are then used, as the name suggests, to stimulate recall by the examination of exemplar sections or scenes accompanied by questions perhaps about what was happening, why it was, what had led up to it, what followed and why, how could it have been different and so on. Just like Marcel Proust's (1922) madeleines, a taste, smell or recreated experience can bring back memories thought long vanished and these are not just scenes and events but physical sensations and moods as well. Sometimes a small snippet from a tape or a photograph is sufficient to trigger a flood of recollections about what one was thinking and feeling at the time. These artefacts can also be used by an interviewee who took part in the activity to exemplify or illustrate what they meant by answers to interview questions of this nature. Using the control button on the video player need not be the prerogative of the interviewer!

Nor need the stimulus materials be actual records of an experience. Sometimes evocative material can be obtained from sources such as advertising material, archived photographs or general pictures of a professional activity. Similarly they can be manufactured, perhaps by collecting photographs of similar situations or by drawing or making diagrams to represent a scene. One research student (Sexton and Denicolo, 1997) used photographs which illustrated a broad spectrum of the situations a practitioner in a particular profession might meet in everyday life. Each was capable of being interpreted in a variety of ways and participants were invited to examine the photographs and relate any recent events in their professional experience which were brought to mind by the photographic image. This is an example of retrospective examination of a real incident through a representation of it. The selection and review of critical incidents within work or education settings is valued as both a staff development and a research activity since it illuminates aspects of actual practice, allowing details about meaning and effectiveness etc. to be unpicked. Cormack (1996), addressing the setting of research into nursing, particularly notes the versatility of such techniques. The next sections deal with other examples of the genre.

Illuminative incident analysis

This technique was developed by Cortazzi and Roote (1975) as a means of investigating the thoughts and feelings of members of teams working together in the health and social services. It is based upon the notion that team development can be encouraged by frank interchange of ideas and feelings about incidents which have happened while the team have been working together. Cortazzi and Roote use as their starting point the illustrations of incidents drawn by team members. They point out that, since there is often a great deal of emotion connected with certain incidents which often blocks verbal discourse, the drawings help clarify the position of each team member. They suggest that words can hide reality whereas feelings, as every art therapist knows, are more accurately portrayed in drawings. The drawings encourage each team member to confront her/his own feelings about the incident and allow, by comparisons between drawings, each one to come to an understanding of the others' perspectives. Thus the drawings are a conduit from the non-verbal to the verbal. Revans (1975), in his foreword to Cortazzi and Roote's book, agrees that such a method allows individuals to convey to others what we sincerely feel and what we honestly fear. He also emphasizes its value in helping each of us to understand why we say and do the things we do, helping us to interpret what we mean by them. We include here an example (Figure 5.2) of an Illuminative incident drawing produced within an educational context. The drawing was produced by a postgraduate student and could be entitled 'The Postgraduate's Dilemma'.

The postgraduate, dressed in the Sex Pistols T-shirt, was attempting to portray a problem which he encountered when joining an educational research institute. Having been outside a formal educational system for many years he felt that his vocabulary was not adequate to communicate fully with other members. The 'sophisticated' members of the institute (the wine-drinking French man and woman) spoke in a language which, to him, was 'foreign'. Words like 'epistemology', 'phenomenology', 'heuristic', 'paradigm' and 'ethnomethodology', to name but a few, to him posed a problem of translation. This drawing was originally produced as

Figure 5.2. An illuminative incident example.

an overhead transparency with which he introduced a student seminar. During the course of the seminar with its consequent discussion, the student was relieved to find that he was not the only student with this particular problem. This was the seed from which grew our own introductions to research methods courses, in which we combine glossaries of terms with opportunities for students to express and listen to each other's concerns. It also acts as a reminder to us as tutors that we must not leap to conclusions about the meanings that others attribute to experience. Analysis of such drawings requires the combined efforts of the listener and the producer of the drawing to interpret the nuances encapsulated in the lines and to tease out their full significance. In other words, the drawing in its production provides the first step in expressing ideas and feelings and then acts as a catalyst to the verbal commentary.

The use of drawings is particularly useful in this respect with children. Ravenette (1997) provided many examples of the power of this method for shedding light on the worlds of children, especially children who had had difficulty in articulating their fears and worries. Both Ravenette and Dalton and Dunnett (1992) advocate drawings as a relief from intensive verbal explorations, which can push children back into their protective silence, and also as a method for opening up levels of personal knowledge that were not previously available at higher levels of awareness. One form that all these authors have used is to encourage the drawing of scenes which record happy (positive) times and those which capture sad (contrast) occasions. By exploring what it is that makes the difference between these in the drawings, a route is provided to the identification of what 'makes the difference' in real life.

For adults who are more self-conscious about demonstrating their artistic prowess than most children, it is worth emphasizing that it is the simple, unrefined nature of the line drawing which allows it to capture the essence of meaning. It is this very simplicity which underpins the valuable contribution that the following technique also affords to understanding how others interpret the world.

Interview about instances

Osborne and Gilbert (1980) used this technique to explore students' views of the world in relation to scientific concepts. They generated a series of cards on which there are drawings representing situations in which some aspects of areas of science are depicted. Normally the cards included situations which contain an instance of the concept under investigation (say, force or energy) and others show situations that do not contain an instance of the concept. The cards were used as an initial stimulus to generate a conversation about the concept and these conversations were audio-recorded, then transcripts were prepared. From analysis of these the alternative, but coherent, understandings that both children and adult students have about the concepts were demonstrated, and these frequently diverged from scientists' views. Awareness of such alternative frameworks by a teacher is an important step in helping the students move from the understandings they bring to the classroom towards understandings held by experts in the field. An example of an Interview about Instances card is provided here (Figure 5.3) with an extract from the transcript of a conversation between our colleague Mike Watts and a young teenage boy about the concept of force.

Figure 5.3. An interview about instances example.

Boy: He's forcing it on the ground... forcing the golfball for when he
                hits the ... golf club onto the ball ... um ... there's force *on* the ball
                and that sends the ball away.

Interviewer: Mmmm mm and so if you were just talking about forces on the
                ball at the moment?

Boy: Yes.

Interviewer: What would you say was there?

Boy: Well it's still got force of the golf club and it's still going along ...
                hmm and you've also got force of gravity pulling back down to
                the ground again.

The scientist's view would be that there is no 'driving' force on the golfball
in mid air. There is gravity and the friction of the air which combine to act
against the ball. The 'driving' force of the club on the ball ends as soon as
they lose contact, though the boy still thinks that the ball has 'got the force
of the golf club' because it is still moving on. Clearly the boy's and the
scientist's views are at odds and this would be a good point for the teacher
to begin negotiation between the two viewpoints.

Such uncomplicated stick figure drawings encourage a focus on the
action in which they are engaged and this method can be readily adapted
for use in a variety of situations in which understandings about what is
going on and why could be explored. As the drawing here demonstrates,
what is going on now has its roots in the past and the next technique uses
a simple drawing technique to explore the influence of the past on the
present.

Snakes, rivers and connecting threads

Contradictory as it may seem, the anticipatory power of constructs lies in
the past. In order to come to an understanding of the present we need to
compare and contrast it with experiences we have had previously and use
these to predict the future. Merleau-Ponty (1962: 297) expresses it thus:

> Experiencing a perceived truth, I assume that the concordance so far experi-
> enced would hold for a more detailed observation; I place my confidence in the
> world. Perceiving is pinning one's faith, at a stroke, in a whole future of experi-
> ences, and doing so in a present that never strictly guarantees the future; it is
> placing one's belief in the world.

The success of our predictions will depend on our selecting appropriate
and relevant constructs and being willing to contemplate adapting them
to fit current circumstance or amending a network of constructs to meet
new situations.

It is clear that biography has an important influence on the constructs we bring to bear on any situation we find ourselves in at present. The ones that predominate while engaged in a particular activity are likely to be ones that have served us well in what appear to have been similar circumstances in the past. Since much of life is hectic, encouraging us to act rather than reflect, we are often unaware of the constructs which are guiding that action and from whence, in our pasts, these are derived.

Unfortunately, though they served us well in the past, some constructs may now be redundant or even counter-productive but, unless they are explicitly noticed and challenged, they remain influential in orientating our being.

To illustrate this notion, one of us for most of her life perceived herself as 'no good at Maths'; relative to a brother who won prizes and gained a degree in the discipline, her struggle to gain a mere 'A' level in the subject stood out as indicating poor ability. For many years, although she successfully solved complex equations with and without the aid of a calculator, each confrontation with batches of numbers was accompanied by a sense of dread at expected imminent failure. Our career development work with mature health service professionals, who were successfully completing postgraduate degrees without having gained a first degree, alerted us once more to how long past school experience influenced the self-concept of adults. Many described themselves as 'non-academic', 'not likely to make much of themselves', 'a bit of a dumbo'. It sometimes took considerable unpicking with sensitive interviewing to discover why they saw themselves that way and to encourage them to challenge their current self-concept.

This experience, coinciding with reading others' reflections on similar phenomena, led us to what we then termed 'career snakes'. The essence of the rationale for these drew on our recognition that constructs evolve over time and are particularly influenced, consciously or unconsciously, by formative experiences. Only by understanding these constructs by reflecting on their origins can the opportunity be provided for contemplating alternatives and breaking free from biography.

In a search for a means to facilitate this process we were impressed by an observation by the philosopher Dilthey, writing at the turn of the century and quoted by Rickman (1976: 215):

> The person who seeks the connecting threads in the history of his life has already, from different points of view, created connections which he is now putting into words ... The units are formed by the conceptions of experience in which present and past events are held together by a common meaning. Among these experiences those which have a special dignity, both in themselves and for the passage of his life, have been preserved in memory and lifted out of the endless stream of forgotten events.

The metaphors of 'connecting threads' and 'streams of life' reminded us of a method used in social skills training called the 'snake' technique by Priestley *et al.* (1978). It also resonated with a description of an image or construct described by Connelly and Clandinin (1984: 47) as reaching 'into the past gathering up experiential threads meaningfully connected to the present. And it reaches intentionally into the future.' Our first efforts at designing a simple process for our students to engage in was described in Denicolo and Pope (1990). It involved participants in drawing up in private a representation of their lives in the form of a winding snake, each turn of its body depicting a personal experience which influenced the direction that their career took. These turns were annotated briefly and formed the bases for later discussion and elaboration, with us, about their significance as formative experiences both for career decisions and for their personal style as practitioners. One example is provided in Figure 5.4.

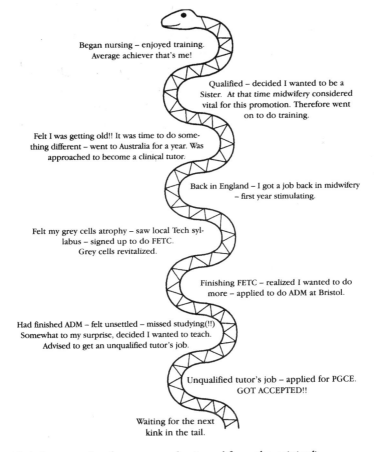

Began nursing – enjoyed training. Average achiever that's me!

Qualified – decided I wanted to be a Sister. At that time midwifery considered vital for this promotion. Therefore went on to do training.

Felt I was getting old!! It was time to do something different – went to Australia for a year. Was approached to become a clinical tutor.

Back in England – I got a job back in midwifery – first year stimulating.

Felt my grey cells atrophy – saw local Tech syllabus – signed up to do FETC. Grey cells revitalized.

Finishing FETC – realized I wanted to do more – applied to do ADM at Bristol.

Had finished ADM – felt unsettled – missed studying(!!) Somewhat to my surprise, decided I wanted to teach. Advised to get an unqualified tutor's job.

Unqualified tutor's job – applied for PGCE. GOT ACCEPTED!!

Waiting for the next kink in the tail.

Figure 5.4. An example of a career snake (typed from the original).

We were impressed by the process for it seemed to require little input from us other than interest as the participants went through a personal interrogation of themselves about the reasons for isolating a particular incident and why it was still influencing their practice and professional identity. They reported feeling empowered by the recognition of potential which had previously been untapped or constrained not because of circumstance as it now is but because of how it had come to be perceived or construed. Our intervention with the technique had provided what might be a form of disorientating dilemma which results in perspective transformation as described by Mezirow (1990: 13–14). He suggests that our meaning schemes may be transformed by reflection on anomalies, providing as an example the housewife attending an evening class and finding to her amazement that other women do not have to rush home to feed their husbands as she does. He concedes that such dilemmas may also be invoked by eye-opening discussions which challenge presuppositions and act as catalysts to critical reflection.

In the last decade or so, we and our students (see Chapter 7 and 8) have used the technique in a variety of contexts and for a range of purposes, both to enhance professional development and to research practice. We have acceded to those who are sphiophobic (hate snakes) and used a river of life analogy, a useful one to explore for converging tributaries and undercurrents. At other times needlework metaphors have emerged with threads being composed of many strands which can link things together in an intricate patchwork – but still become knotted. Whichever form we use, we encourage the use of artful image making as substantiated by Diamond and Mullen (1999: 30):

> a vital experience stands out meaningfully in our minds because of contributions to an ending. The culmination and the path chosen to reach the ending make the experience meaningful. The quality that pervades the experience often emerges only after being represented in artful form.

As our lives flowed, wriggled on and became more tangled, we received feedback from former participants who had fruitfully continued to use the technique to illuminate their own and the lives of colleagues and students. The most affirming incident was one which occurred some twelve years after our first trials of the technique. One of the original participants who had been on one of our teacher training courses, having successfully developed her career, returned to undertake a doctoral degree. At that time we were interested in the impact that such study had on the lives of our students and several of them engaged in a range of techniques, including 'snakes', to share their experiences with us (Denicolo 1996a). The focus of the snake exercise was to identify critical incidents in their lives which led them eventually to embark on PhD studies. It was salutary that, though she could recall drawing and talking about her snake in relation to her deciding to become a teacher, she could not remember which incidents she had chosen. After she had completed the new version, a rake through old files in the attic unearthed the original. The incidents chosen to represent her life up to teacher training were almost identical in both versions. It is clear that the selection of incidents is more than serendipitous; as Dilthey suggested, they stood out in the endless stream of forgotten events.

Another technique which we used with our research students was the development of concept maps, which we describe further in the next section.

Concept maps

In 1984 Novak and Gowin introduced a technique, which they termed concept mapping, to help learners identify the links they made between concepts and what the nature of these links was. In a more recent paper, Novak (1995: 1) made more explicit link between his ideas and those of constructivism:

> Concepts are perceived regularities in events or objects ... designated by a label ... humans have the innate capacity to perceive regularities in objects and events ... and to use language labels to designate these regularities. Each person has a unique sequence of experiences and, hence, to some degree, each person's concept meaning will be idiosyncratic even though they use common labels to represent meanings ... Moreover, concept meanings derive primarily from the relationships that are perceived between concepts ... Because human beings are unique in their capacity for using symbols or language labels to represent concept and propositional meanings, I have called the process of knowledge acquisition *human constructivism*.

We need only substitute our technical labels 'elements' for concepts and 'constructs' for relationships or propositions to identify common ground here, which is further exemplified as he goes on to say (p. 3):

> As learners mature in a discipline, their relevant knowledge becomes more and more complex, and therefore, meaningful learning involves seeking integration with a larger and larger framework of concepts and propositions. In turn, the meaning of prior concepts and propositions are altered somewhat by the incorporation of the new concepts and propositions.

Thus our use of concept maps has involved the identification by participants of relevant elements in a realm of discourse. These are then ordered on a page (or screen for those who are computer literate) in such a ways as to demonstrate their relationships with each other. The linking lines between elements are annotated with labels which identify relationships.

We present here (Figure 5.5) Novak's own concept map about concept maps to demonstrate their major characteristics.

These can be produced in a simplified form using thickness of lines and proximity to demonstrate relationships or can be very elaborate, using extended labels for lines/constructs. We have found them particularly valuable to help identify novice ideas on a topic at the beginning of a

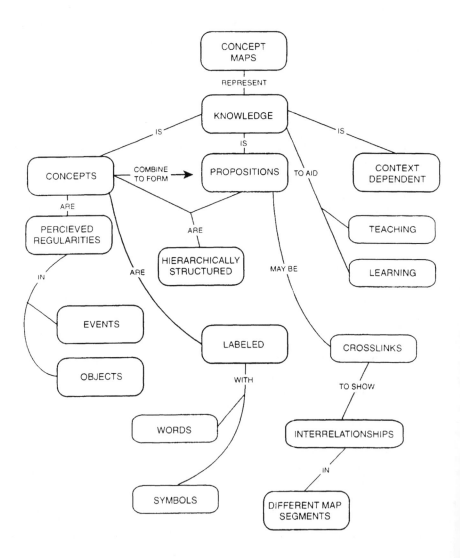

Figure 5.5. Novak's 1995 concept map about concept maps.

course, as a prelude to building on these. Another benefit can be drawn from encouraging learners at the end of a course to repeat the exercise so that they can make comparisons between previous and current understandings. This also serves as an evaluation for us of the success of our teaching activities.

The flexibility of concept mapping as a tool is demonstrated in the research with doctoral students mentioned in the previous section. The elements were significant roles in their lives, with the central one for this exercise being the research student role. Through this exercise we were able to share together how this latter role impinges on other roles or is influenced by them. This was by no means a trivial experience as regrets became apparent about how the significance of some roles had faded, how others appeared to require reviewing if their research role was to be successful, how yet others had crept up in importance to them as their lives changed. Nevertheless, though we gained in information about our research area, the participants reported that they too had profited in having an opportunity and means for re-assessing their priorities. An example of one of these concept maps (Figure 5.6) illustrates these points.

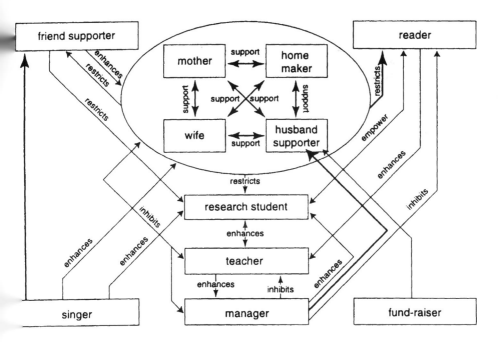

Figure 5.6. An example of a research student's concept map about life roles.

Lawless *et al.* (1998) provide a thorough review of concept mapping and related techniques (e.g. semantic networking – Stewart, 1980) in a paper which describes their application in business contexts as well as in education. They conclude with an observation that this family of techniques has potential for development and elaboration in many fields of endeavour where understanding the meaning systems of others is critical. We would endorse this evaluation for this and all the techniques described in this chapter but add that each provides a glimpse of only one facet of that meaning system. It may be useful to use more than one technique to gain a fuller understanding.

In the concluding section of this chapter we raise other caveats relevant to such explorations.

Interpreting others' perspectives – health warnings

Sometimes we are confronted with the cry – 'I tried that but it didn't work.' The problem often lies with the inappropriate choice or implementation of the technique or both! That is one of the reasons why we have been so assiduous in emphasizing the importance of purpose in our descriptions. It is important that a tool which is 'fit for the purpose' is chosen; one which seeks the answers to specific questions, for human beings are so wonderfully complex that we might learn much about them using one particular instrument, but not what we want to know. Just as important as the enquirer knowing the purpose and nature of their enquiry, is the requirement that the respondent is let into the secret too! This is not just an ethical consideration, as we discuss in Chapter 6, but is also a practical one. Kelly suggested that if we want to know something about a person then we should ask him/her but he did not suggest that if we want to know about some aspect then we should ask about another. Apart from common sense and ethical objections to such subterfuge, he recognizes the power of the respondents as 'personal scientists' who will form hypotheses about what is required, what questions are leading up to, what will fit the bill in a particular encounter, and will respond accordingly. (It is salutary to remind ourselves again at this point that participants and enquirers are following different agenda as was noted by Kompf in Figure 5.1.)

Similarly, we have emphasized that each tool provides an insight into a particular aspect of the person's complex construct system, so that if we wish to expand our outlook then we might want to combine information derived from an array of techniques – triangulating methods to add dimensions or to gain different perspectives to enrich what we learn. It is important to remember, too, that what we learn is very dependent on what the other wishes to teach us. This underlines the need to build rapport and a justified sense of safety and begs us to consider that our interpretations of another's constructs are dependent on our own. If we truly want to understand their interpretation of the world then it might be better if we checked our interpretations with them and would be best if we allowed them to work with us in the process of interpretation.

Nor should we neglect to account for the affects of context (see Goodson referred to earlier) of both the enquiry environment and the one in which constructs are formed. Mud, which is construed practically and even joyfully when having a dig and delve in the garden, is viewed differently when attired in best bib and tucker on the way to a professional meeting. Equally, we have not all had the opportunity to acquire and elaborate our constructs freely; they may not be so much of our own choosing as they are the result of our not realizing that alternatives might exist. It is well worth considering the opportunities and constraints on elaboration that confine or limit others' constructs or how they express them. A simple example might suffice here. We cannot assume that people do not have emotions or complex ideas about something just because they do not have the vocabulary to express them. We will elaborate on this in the next chapter.

Interpreting others' perspectives might seem a time-consuming business; something we cannot nor would not deny. All of the techniques we have described do take time to implement. They also demand skill for successful use so practice is a significant factor in planning the process, and the most appropriate guinea pig to use at first is yourself. Like repertory grids, these are sharp instruments which can do much damage if not employed carefully so practice should not be conducted on the innocent or unwary. The examples we have given, or will provide in later chapters, demonstrate their power. Nevertheless, many might seem fun or illuminating for those who take part and they can be that too, but are more likely to be so when they are used with discretion and dexterity. It is wise not to assume that because participants are willing to work with you, and are likely to gain greater access to their own meaning systems as they do so, that they will find this a pain free process. Nor will you, if you try the tools on yourself. We recommend that in both instances you ensure that support systems are available and offered, either from your own resources or with the help of others.

In this chapter, although we have used short examples to explain methods, we have attempted to introduce the techniques in a relatively context free way so that the main tenets stand out. In Chapters 7 and 8 we will provide and elaborate on some applications of Personal Construct

Psychology techniques within education practice, but first it is important to consider some of the practical points and ethical issues raised in this and the preceding chapter.

CHAPTER 6

Developing an appropriate climate

Silence is the one great art of conversation.

William Hazlitt (1778–1830)

In the preceding two chapters we have introduced techniques which encourage others to explore their constructs and share them with you. The focus so far has been on asking the right questions in such a way that constructs are revealed but contaminated as little as possible by the form or style of the question. In this chapter we will address some further important issues. The first concerns reception rather than transmission problems, the latter being dealt with later in the chapter.

Listening – a fundamental skill which underpins all interactive techniques

In the normal course of a face-to-face interactive process the researcher, teacher or staff developer receives copious information, much of it through the auditory channel.

This is more than simply a process of hearing it. Hearing is concerned with the reception of auditory stimuli whereas listening involves the additional intellectual and emotional aspects which support meaning and understanding. Listening is, therefore, a more complex act that involves not only hearing but also selecting, attending to, and processing or interpreting what is heard.

> We hear with our ears, but we listen with our eyes and mind and heart and skin and guts as well. (Ekman, 1969: 295)

There are a range of things which act as blocks to listening, not the least the strong motivation to talk. This can result in a preoccupation with one's own thoughts and the diversion of attention from what is being said to what might be contributed to the communication. One of the more difficult tasks within a construct elicitation process is that of keeping quiet. The dilemma is that participatory activities demand input from both parties to be maintained. The listener must encourage the flow of communication while not significantly contributing his/her views to it. Continual verbal interjection on the part of the listener serves to disrupt the flow of the process even though it may help to clarify particular parts of what is being said.

It is useful to practise non-verbal signals which convey encouragement, such as nods and smiles, while listening in non-critical situations and to have ready a series of neutral responses to interject if the flow ceases, such as 'tell me more about that', 'what does that mean to you?', 'can you give examples?'. It is important to allow for pauses for thought. A little silence often prefaces a further flow of ideas so it is worthwhile being patient to allow for thoughtful responses.

Skilled counsellors will be adept at these techniques but those with less experience need to get used to this form of elicitation before they use it for a special occasion such as data collection or a staff development workshop.

It is also a salutary experience to tape record an informal or trial interview for careful listening at a later time to check on:

- how much talking is done proportionally by the interviewer/interviewee;
- how frequently an interesting theme is curtailed by interruptions;
- whose ideas are being pursued in the interaction etc.

There is a tendency for all of us to hear what we want to hear or to focus on what is familiar to us, hence the 'cocktail party' effect when we suddenly pick up a mention of our own name among a hubbub of chatter around our own particular conversation. Care must be taken about not solely picking up and pursuing particular constructs that we are interested in or expect to be there to the detriment of unpredicted ones.

When there is a great deal of information available, listening can become a very selective process. Sometimes the taking of notes can aid listening, directing attention to what is being said, and aiding the possibility of going back to pick up points that were dropped as others came into focus. However, it is not easy to listen, interpret the message and write legibly at the same time, while the non-verbal signals of the interviewee may be missed while concentration is on the writing paper. The grid process can be helpful with this because the structure can allow and encourage agreed main points to be written down. Even during a grid elicitation and certainly during the less structured elicitations described in Chapter 5, it is very helpful to audio-record the session, if the interviewee gives permission, so that elaborations and asides that provide further clues to meaning can be extracted later.

A variety of things can interfere with a listener's ability to concentrate on what is being communicated. Such distractions, or 'noise', can have internal or external sources and may affect the sender as well as the receiver of communication. Concerns about the time, whether the session can be overheard, and anxiety about whether you are being taken seriously are examples of internal 'noise' whereas too warm a room or a distracting view as well as a busy environment can constitute external 'noise'. This means that the physical environment and the timing of the interaction need careful planning and consideration. However, even the best laid plans can go awry so that it is wise to have contingency plans. If this is not possible or these fail, then later interpretations need to take account of these limits on the data.

Honest and meaningful communication can only be achieved in an environment of respect, trust and openness. This demands an ethical framework, an issue which will be considered after the next section which explores how misinterpretations can arise even when we have carefully listened to what is being said.

Common words, uncommon meanings – the problem of language

Robert Burns, the poet, assured us that by any other name a rose would smell as sweet while George Bernard Shaw reminded us that Britain and the USA are nations divided by a common language. Both writers recognized that language of any kind is merely a system of symbols, arbitrarily chosen and signifying different things to individual users. A mundane example follows.

A handbag to us is a life-support system, to our husbands it is a place to deposit keys and odds and ends when a jacket pocket is unavailable, to others it might be merely a decorative fashion accessory while to Oscar Wilde's Lady Bracknell it was a source of disdain. Thus the cry 'I have lost my handbag' has different import to different people.

Thus we must be careful when interpreting the meanings of things communicated in words. Descriptions of entities such as 'stressful' or 'fabulous' depend very much on an individual's experience of stress or astounding things as well as on popularity of usage. Twenty years ago few occupations would have been described as 'stressful', perhaps brain surgeons and air traffic controllers, whereas many people describe their work roles as stressful as the century turns. Without further exploration it would be precipitate to assume that the work itself has changed rather than the popularity of the term. In our very young years 'fabulous' was a term used to describe, say, Fabergé eggs. In our teens it became common parlance, was shortened to 'fab' and applied to pop groups, clothes and innumerable other artefacts.

The discriminating power of these words was lost, one might say, and other words for other generations are used to describe extremes. It is not sufficient and can be considered patronizing, though, to adjust interpretation of word use according to the perceived age and social context of the participant because individual idiosyncrasies derived from abundant experience also have a part to play.

Some people have a rich and varied vocabulary with which to discriminate between things while others tend to use a restricted range of words. Some people have a tendency to use extremes of descriptions while others are more conservative and so on. If a person, object or event is seldom part of their experience, or is of little interest to them, then people are likely to have fewer constructs about it than one with which they are familiar or very interested in. One of us has few constructs for cars and a multitude for shoes, another has a wide range of vocabulary to describe ballet and a restricted range to describe a game of football. Such information tells us something about our construct systems, but more so if the focus is wider than just one universe of discourse. It might be important to explore in some circumstances whether a restricted range of constructs derives from a lack of interest, a lack of experience or a lack of vocabulary, or any combination of these.

Many of the techniques used in personal construct elicitations are specifically designed to help with this problem. We have emphasized earlier the importance of trying to elicit a description of the submerged pole of a construct. Finding that 'stressful' contrasts with 'restful' for one person and 'boring' for another gives us clues about how the term 'stressful' is defined. Exploring the links with other constructs helps us further – activities which are seen as stressful might also be seen as 'imposed' or 'stimulating', for instances. Laddering techniques also help us not to jump to conclusions about which is the preferred pole and why and so on.

Of course, it might be that individuals are 'lost for words' to describe something but it should not be assumed that they do not experience it deeply. It could be that their vocabulary is inadequate to the situation or it might be that they choose not to share it. The latter might be through natural reticence, because of distrust, or because they are unused to sharing such ideas or are unfamiliar with the techniques employed. Robert Browning, in Rabbi ben Ezra xxv, clearly recognized the former problem:

Thoughts hardly to be packed into a narrow act, Fancies that broke through language and escaped.

The next section deals with issues related to the ethical procedures which may serve to allay distrust while methods for helping people to become familiar with the process and techniques are described in the last sections of this chapter.

Building an ethical framework

How we interpret our world, and how those interpretations are structured and organized is a personal and generally private thing. We may choose to give our opinions on some aspects of our world readily while others we only share with significant and 'safe' companions. Why we hold such opinions or construe the world as we do might not even by shared with close companions, indeed we may not always recognize in our daily lives from whence such constructs derive, or even that they exist at all to influence our being.

Thus, asking people to engage in processes which are intended to reveal, for us and for themselves, such intimate details of their thinking, whether it be for research or for developmental purposes, demands that a special duty of care is espoused and an ethical framework adopted.

The first aspect of this framework is the need to respect a participant's right not to participate at all or to restrict participation. An individual can only effectively make such a decision if they have had both the process of elicitation and how the data will be stored and used clearly explained to them. In medical contexts the equivalent notion would be that of 'informed consent'. This issue of voluntariness is an ethical stance on our part but is also related to the practical value of what can be obtained using personal construct procedures.

People will only share with others their version of the 'truth' if they feel that their views are respected and if they experience trust in the situation. This is why we advocate the negotiation and establishment of a contract with participants. Such a contract should involve:

- an honest declaration of the aims and intent of the research or developmental activity;
- an overview of procedures with a recognition that the instruments are powerful and incisive;
- a commitment to complete anonymity unless specific agreement has been reached about in what contexts identification of source is permitted (in group work, for instance);

- the confidential storage of data, so that identification codes are stored separately from the data;
- the planned and accessible provision of support should the process or what is revealed prove to be distressing in any way;
- an acknowledgement that any instrument/interaction can only be a partial record of a person's perspective.

The last point is emphasized by Kompf (1999: 6) in his paper 'There is more to me than my story':

> In spite of all cautions we can only see that which we can seek and perceive. What the participants see remains, for the most part, invisible to the researcher. We are allowed glimpses through self-report and disclosures made but only as edited prior to utterance by the informant.

It is clear that how partial that record is will be dependant on the level of trust developed between individuals as well as on the power of the instruments used. While we recommend the use of a variety of techniques, used in triangulation, to explore a particular aspect of the world and achieve rich data, it is also our experience that the use of such instruments spread over a period of time is also beneficial. This allows for an atmosphere of trust to be developed so that ideas and constructs are elaborated on in subsequent sessions.

A further caveat is worth raising in this respect. Unlike some means of enquiry, it is not assumed within this approach that participants will be left 'unchanged' by the intervention or that data collected on one occasion will necessarily be reliably replicated on another. Indeed, it is recognized that the act of exploring constructs encourages re-assessment and perhaps revision of them. The recommendation about support provision being part of the contract is in recognition that such re-assessment and revision may not be a pain-free process. It is important that a concern for doing no harm is substituted within this paradigm of work for that of instigating no change within other paradigms.

Indeed, it may be that the investigation aims to monitor change by exploring constructs before and after a certain intervention. The techniques themselves cannot but be part of such an intervention, perhaps raising issues for conscious deliberation which were previously submerged or went unnoticed, and such an acknowledgement should be part of any interpretation made.

Similarly, any interpretation made by another of an individual's construct is, in the last analysis, informed by that other's constructs. We alluded earlier to the alternative interpretations that we impose, for instance, on specific words. Especially in the case of an in-depth study which aims to have a significant influence on practice, we would recommend that interpretations are taken back for checking to the original participants. Only they can confirm that a correct rendering of their meaning has been achieved though it is wise to be prepared that they might have developed or changed some ideas in the intervening period. The emphasis may need to be on an agreement that the meaning 'as it was meant at the time' has been accurately conveyed.

Not everyone is comfortable with the notion that their ideas or constructs might change, even if only at the peripheral level. Some people prefer to see themselves as stable and consistent in their views and would prefer not to be confronted with any paradox in their thinking. They may need a particularly supportive atmosphere and environment in which to engage in reflection. We will explore how that might be established in the next section while the following one extends that idea by discussing mechanisms for helping participants to focus on experience, especially suited for those, as mentioned in the previous section, who are unused to sharing verbally their experience with others.

Stimulating reflection

As we indicated when discussing the grid procedure, there is no magic formula, or swift means, for accessing the rich and significant meaning which people attribute to their experience. All the techniques which we explored for doing so in the previous chapter require for effective use a degree of trust between participants, a process which itself eats time, and a suspension of engagement with the hustle and bustle of work and other survival activities. The context in which they are implemented should be conducive to reflection – some physical comfort helps but relative safety and confidentiality are critical. It is a rare, and perhaps foolish, person who will voluntarily and frankly divulge their inner feelings, attitudes, beliefs and anticipations to a stranger in a busy venue with no guarantee of, or respect for, privacy. Nor yet will those meanings reach the surface of consciousness while discomfort or threat take the centre stage, or when other urgent tasks demand attention.

When we attempt to stimulate others to reflect, or to foster self-reflection, it is important to note the 'iceberg-like' properties of the process – far more is contained in the hidden portion than will be revealed on the surface. Mezirow (1990: 13) contended that:

> By far the most significant learning experiences in adulthood involve self-reflection – reassessing the way we have posed problems and reassessing our own orientation to perceiving, knowing, believing, feeling, acting.

This cannot, therefore, be an objective (in the sense of unemotional or unpartisan) activity nor one that is undertaken without commitment. As we have argued earlier, this does not make it unscientific, but it does mean that a particular epistemological position is espoused. Both Kelly and Koestler (1976) in his article 'The vision that links the poet, the painter and the scientist' demonstrate the similarities between the scientist and the artist in their desire to construct meaning from experience and subject these constructions to reconstruction. Further, Magee (1973: 68) in discussing Popper's philosophy of science, noted that Popper suggested that there are not two distinct cultures:

> One scientific and the other aesthetic, or one rational and the other irrational – but one. The scientist and the artist, far from being engaged in opposed or incompatible activity, are both trying to extend our knowledge and experience by the use of creative imagination subjected to critical control.

Magee further emphasized that such an enterprise 'puts the greatest premium of all on boldness of the imagination'. We suggest that there are at least three enterprises in which people who adopt constructivist approaches must apply their imagination:

1. in allowing that their own world could be interpreted in a different way than the one they are used to;
2. in recognizing that others may see that world very differently;
3. in devising ways to access the alternative frameworks, or world views, of others.

In order to introduce this notion to our students and collaborators in exploring constructivist approaches, we have found it helpful to engage them in a thought experiment. This activity not only demonstrates the pervasiveness and commonness of alternative constructions of reality but also provides reassurance that holding different perspectives is derived from different prior experience and priorities and so is internally rational and can be useful. It stimulates for many people interest in what other possibilities for construing the world exist, and why. It also indicates to those whose constructs we hope to share that we are open to learning from them rather than seeking to judge their apparently 'strange' views. Readers might like to try the thought experiment for themselves and perhaps adapt it for use with others.

Activity

Imagine yourself standing on a hilltop looking out over the countryside. Further, imagine that you are a farmer contemplating your land. What catches

your attention? What is important for you in what you see? How do you interpret some of the specific things you see?

Now, blink hard and look at the scene again, but this time as an artist planning a
picture. Ask yourself those same questions again.

And for good measure, blink hard once again and examine the landscape from
the point of view of a property developer, again thinking through the
questions.

When we and others have tried this we found the 'farmer' in us focusing
on such things as the kinds of crops that were growing or the animals that
were feeding off the land. We thought about the fertility and drainage of
the soil and how we might improve it. We wondered if it was time to plant
or harvest.

The 'artist', on the other hand, concentrated on appreciating light and
shade, colour and texture, wondering how to capture form and structure,
intensity and subtlety. Our 'property developer' had different interests and
concerns. The accessibility of the land, how it could be subdivided into
plots or reshaped to make room for more units predominated these
thoughts.

From this simple, preliminary exercise we can recognize readily that
different roles, motives and experience, among other things, lead us to
deem some things more important than others even though the object of
our attention remains the same. Indeed, some things may be ignored or
not noticed at all, depending on where we are 'coming from'. Other things
will be interpreted differently. Friable soil may be the farmer's joy and the
property developer's problem. The action that such interpretations lead
us to is, of course, equally diverse. We may seem to inhabit the same
world, but each of us construes it differently.

All experience is the product of both the features of the world and the
biography of the individual ... influenced by our past as it interacts with our
present. (Eisner, 1985: 26)

Focusing on experience

We have noted on several occasions that many constructs are not readily
available for inspection. They may seem so obvious to the people who
hold them that they refrain from articulating them – they convey how the
world is, surely? Equally, they may seem irrelevant or trivial to them. They
may, on the other hand, be difficult to articulate, for all sorts of reasons.
For some people formal interviews or very structured techniques are not
appropriate. For instance, young children, people with learning disabili-

ties or the many adults who are not used to expressing their ideas or even
having other people interested in what they say, might find the traditional
grid techniques constraining. This is one reason why we have been interested in exploring the alternative techniques described in the previous
chapter.

Many of us are unused to airing personal opinions and ideals which
have a strong emotive content and some cultures have a tradition of not
talking about oneself or revealing the thoughts that guide action. Burr and
Butt (1992: 80) refer to the technique called 'McFalls Mystical Monitor'
which Don Bannister used to help people elaborate for themselves their
reasons for doing things. This involves having a continuous conversation
with oneself into a tape recorder for a fixed period of one hour and 15
minutes, any periods of 'drying up' being explained on the record. The
recording is then reviewed and the tape erased. The exercise is repeated
for a further thirty minutes, with the tape again being reviewed and
erased. The revealing thing about this exercise, which the authors emphasize, is that, despite the only audience for the conversation being oneself,
it is still difficult to say certain things. It may be that only with practice
using such freewheeling methods are some, perhaps preverbal, constructs
accessible even to ourselves.

In the latter part of the last chapter we focused on methods which help
people to express their ideas, values, perceptions of their worlds by using
stimulus materials other than words. Since our objective in this book is to
review PCP methods for use in education, training and professional
practice, rather than in therapeutic settings, we concentrated first on
those which enable the sharing of personal meaning with peers. Whatever
the intended technique(s) within a peer learning environment, some
preliminary steps might facilitate the process.

Initial exercises

In situations where people meet for a short period, say a day or two, for
the purposes of sharing in an educational or professional development
activity it is useful to have activities in which they get to know each other.
In some contexts these are known as 'ice-breaking techniques'. When the
session is underpinned by a PCP philosophy then it is important that the
activity should involve some sharing of personal constructs in a relatively
safe form, allowing participant control of what they choose to reveal.

However, we recognize that an invitation to 'say something about
yourself' to an audience of strangers can be a paralysing experience; or at
least one which makes one deaf to others contributions while one collects
one's own thoughts. We have found it helpful to ask people in advance to

bring with them a small object which demonstrates some aspects of themselves which they feel comfortable in sharing. This allows for advance preparation, is generally regarded as quite fun and is less threatening since the object of attention is, on the surface at least, the chosen artefact. People have brought a plant to describe their interest in gardening, their ability to change with the seasons, their sensitivity to environmental conditions such as blossoming in a conducive context, etc.; others may choose a picture frame, a particular book or a ring that has a significance to them and says something about their taste and preferences.

In our higher degree research training classes, we have asked newcomers to introduce themselves by means of a simple drawing which conveys how they currently view their research activity. They are assured that artistic ability is not important and they are invited to describe what the choice of scene means in terms of their research. This metaphorical exercise has produced, for example, a ship setting out on a voyage of adventure, a map of an island with only a few known landmarks, a view of some foothills with mountains shrouded in mist beyond, a dense wood with creatures lurking behind trees and some sunny clearings.

We introduced this activity because we remember clearly our own experience of joining such a group, convinced that everyone else knew just what they were doing and where they were going. We have had reports from students who successfully completed their research projects long ago that this was a turning point for them in becoming members of a mutually supportive research group. Each year it is pleasant to see the serious, and sometimes tense, faces which enter the room, leaving it bearing smiles or at least more confident expressions. We contend that we would have less positive results if we had asked each person to summarize their research interests for the group before engaging in this exercise, though they are sometimes eager to do so afterwards having contacted the humanity in each other. Bridges have been built through the process.

In the chapters which follow we describe examples of the application of PCP approaches and techniques in different educational contexts and for different purposes. We hope that, now you are familiar with the basic tenets, these will act as planks in a bridge between your current experience and practice and what might be possible using a constructivist framework.

CHAPTER 7

The learner as personal scientist

A little learning is a dangerous thing;
Drink deep, or taste not the Pierian spring:
There shallow draughts intoxicate the brain,
And drinking largely sobers us again.
Alexander Pope, *Essay on Criticism* (1715), ll. 215–18.

Introduction

So far in this book we have concentrated in Chapters 1–3 on the theory and philosophy of alternative perspectives on education and research and in Chapters 4–6 on the basic practicalities of espousing and putting into action a personal construct approach to education. Brief examples from practice have been used to illustrate particular points in those chapters, but we now endeavour to provide a greater insight for the reader into lived experience of those who have sought to transform education practice and research using constructivist approaches.

In our work with colleagues and research students we have been afforded privileged access, literally or 'virtually', to the complex world of teaching and learning in schools, colleges, higher education and professional education in the public and private sector. We will draw on that experience to demonstrate how constructivist approaches can inform perspectives in education and assist in professional change and development. We hope that the examples provided will speak to the reader, providing inspiration for future practice. The intention is not to provide a full and detailed account of the results of others initiatives, rather it is to note the diversity of issues that have been addressed in specific contexts using some of the tools and techniques described earlier in the book.

References are provided so that readers can explore further details of results and procedures for themselves from the original authors' texts, where these exist. However we are also concerned to describe work which

132

is current at the time of writing so when detailed reports are not yet available for reference, readers are urged to contact the investigators in person through the Centre for Personal Construct Psychology in Education, The University of Reading.

In making this selection from the potentially enormous range of research and development activities using PCP in education, we have focused on those interventions with which we have had personal involvement of some kind – as supervisors, co-researchers etc. – though we will occasionally refer to some publications by colleagues known to us through our work for the European Personal Construct Association, the International PCP network and the International Study Association on Teachers and Teaching. We are particularly indebted to all of those who provided us with summaries of their work for this purpose. In gathering the pieces together for this and the following chapter, we were at first struck by their diversity although, gradually, overarching themes emerged as we sifted through the wealth of ideas submitted. While we have presented work that reflects constructivist approaches to education within the UK we have also included many other examples of work in a wide range of other countries. We have presented work that is ongoing and we have also included work that has been conducted in the past but which has had a seminal influence on later work applying constructivist approaches to teaching and learning. This chapter is concerned with work aimed at understanding the learner's perspective and the following chapter reveals work aimed at understanding the teacher's perspective. In both chapters we have chosen as headings the general focus of the work under which specific topics are explored using a range of techniques. The first of our foci concerns studies which are concerned with learners' personal meanings in science education.

Constructivist science education

We have already alluded to our interest in science education in our prologue and in Chapter 2 the important work of Bell and Gilbert (1996) was discussed in terms of the implications of constructivist approaches in relation to pupils' conceptual development in science. In Chapter 5 we introduced you to a particular technique, the Interview-about-Instances (IAI) approach, and gave an example from the work of our colleague Mike Watts. We will give further examples in this chapter. Pope and Gilbert (1985) gave a detailed account of the influence of Kelly's epistemology and theory of personal constructs within science education, drawing on the work of the Personal Construction of Knowledge Group (PCKG) then based at the University of Surrey. As members of that group, we were able to note that much of the cohesion of the research was related to the use of the epistemological base and constructivist research methodologies implied by Personal Construct Psychology. One unifying theme in the group was the recognition that philosophers of science, practising scientists, curriculum planners, teachers of science, students in colleges and children in schools may have differing views with respect to the nature of science and concepts within science. We argued that, potentially, many of these views will need to be negotiated within the design of the science curriculum.

Knowledge in science can be seen as progressing from the personal construction of the individual scientists, seeking to make sense of their experiences and anticipating events, towards some consensus of construing a topic by a community of scientists. Kelly's commonality corollary allows for overlap between personal views and therefore a full or partial consensus. Along the way the journey taken by scientist is fraught with conflicts, personal and interpersonal, and in a sense the journey is one that will not end because they must be prepared for and open to transformation of the consensus developed.

The initial work of the group was focused largely on the importance of recognizing pupils' *alternative frameworks*, or naive constructs, prior to formal instruction and which need to be considered within the teaching process. Many studies based on constructivist perspectives have been documented and their implication for science education discussed (Driver *et al.*, 1985; Watts and Pope, 1989: Bentley and Watts, 1992: Frensham *et al.*, 1994; Pfundt and Duit, 1994). Henessey (1993: 8) considered that 'constructivist theories of learning, which hold that forms and content of knowledge are constructed through active interaction with the environment, have long been established in the research literature and are now part of the conventional wisdom'. However, she went on to suggest that classroom situations are not being devised to help pupils perceive what they are doing as a construction of knowledge. She regretted that the views of many science teachers conflict with a constructivist stance. Aguirre *et al.* (1990) investigated student teachers' conceptions concerning the nature of science, teaching and learning and found that almost half of those questioned still believed in a transmission model, i.e. the passive accumulation of a body of knowledge which has independent reality. In the next chapter we too discuss student teachers' epistemologies and those of teachers of science. Smith and Neale (1989) drew attention to the 'alternative frameworks' in relation to key concepts in science held by primary school teachers and noted that these mirror the alternative conceptualizations of pupils from within their classes. We will explore the pupils' conceptions further in this chapter.

The example in Chapter 5 based on Watts's work provided alternative frameworks of the concept of 'force'. In addition to force, Watts (1983) explored pupils' alternative frameworks related to energy, heat and light. In the same year, Zylbersztajn researched alternative concepts of light, colour, force and movement. Pope and Watts (1988) provided a number of examples of alternative frameworks which arose during conversations using the Interview-About-Instances approach. We give one example below.

Kathy was a 14 year old talking about heat. She had developed a model of the earth's atmosphere where the temperature gradient is such that temperature increases with distance from the earth's surface. At the beginning of the interview, Kathy made a commonplace comment that 'heat rises'. When asked what she thought happened as distance from the ground increases she responded 'it gets hotter and hotter'. When this was explored further by asking 'what happens at altitude in the upper reaches of atmosphere?', Kathy commented 'It gets very, very hot. That's why things burn up when they come into the atmosphere. That's why that space shuttle needs those heat-resistant tiles on it.' Kathy retained her model in face of further questioning. For example, Kathy was asked how she would explain, in terms of her heat model, why there is snow on very high mountains. After a puzzled moment she said, 'No, I'm not sure. But I do know it's hot up there ... my friend went skiing at Christmas and she got sunburnt.'

Colinvaux (1992) developed an interesting variant on the IAI approach. Instead of using stick-like diagrams of people or other drawings representing a concept area, Colinvaux used actual pictures. Her study explored the issue of 'change'. She examined the philosophers' and scientists' theories of change as identified in the literature. Her fieldwork compared these perspectives with the personal meaning held by students. Colinvaux presented 20 photographs and asked each individual whether the various photographs represented an instance of change. These photographs included such items as a river, plants, a butterfly, the moon, lightning and baking a cake. She then explored their concepts regarding non-change and also what meaning they ascribed to change and the process of change. Her fieldwork was carried out in Rio de Janeiro, Brazil and involved children from the age of seven, university students and partially schooled adults. While the pictures provided an initial stimulus for conversations regarding change, Colinvaux always provided an opportunity for the individual to add their own examples. We reproduce a few of these below:

A thick hair that can be straightened and thinned by using special types of creams.

A person who is good but becomes bad under the influence of another.

A slim person who wants to become fat and eats a lot to change to achieve this aim.

When one's hurt oneself, it opens [the wound]and then it heals... then it changes.

A rich person who goes bankrupt. (Colinvaux, 1992:15)

These demonstrated individuals' everyday conceptions of change.

The Interview-About-Instances technique has proved fruitful in eliciting pupils' implicit theories. However, this technique involves pupils discussing situations that have been presented to them. Gilbert and Pope (1982) extended the approach asking the children to respond with pictures. Figure 7.1 (Ghost) is an example given by one child to exemplify his idea of energy. It is the pupils' instances that were being elicited. Conversations about these personal pictures proved a fruitful source of the alternative frameworks which the young people used to construe 'energy'. This development led Swift (1987) to evolve an approach akin to the Illuminative Incident Analysis we mentioned in Chapter 5. Swift was investigating secondary school science students' epistemological stances.

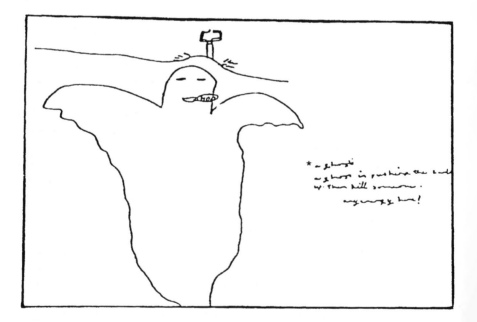

* A ghost is pushing the earth up. Then kill someone. Any energy here?

Figure 7.1. Ghost.

He felt it was important that science teachers have some understanding of their students' epistemological stances because these views would pervade their appreciation of their science lessons. He asked the students to do a sketch of what has happened outside school in which they did something scientific. Some examples included a drawing of a girl with her hands on her head and she inscribed: 'I am dyeing my hair. Because in hair dye there are chemicals.' Another included a stick person drawing, under which it said: 'here I am smoking but lighting the fag with a lighter. The lighter is scientific because inside it is complicated and scientific.' Swift's work is a good example of a multi-method approach from a constructivist stance, influenced by the work of George Kelly. He critically examined the curricula response to contemporary notions of truth, objectivity and knowledge. In addition to the Responding With Pictures method, Swift used IAI, interviews, lesson observations and repertory grids in order to explore students' and teachers' personal meanings of science and scientific method.

Although Swift used an extensive array of techniques in his study, he did not use concept mapping. As we indicated in Chapter 5, this technique can be a powerful one for gaining insight into the way a person conceptualizes a topic and the interconnections between various ideas in their repertoire of understanding. Within science education, concept mapping has been used to understand pupils' constructs about a number of topic areas (Novak, 1998). Novak and Gowin (1984: 15) claimed that concept maps are intended to represent meaningful relationships between concepts in the form of propositions. They characterized the concept map as 'a schematic device for representing a set of concept meanings embedded in a framework of propositions'. They suggested that it is a 'kind of visual road map showing some of the pathways we may take to connect meanings of concepts'.

One interesting area of study is pupils' understanding of the meaning of 'food'. What follows is an account of an ongoing study of one of our research students, Parla-Petrou, who is investigating this concept:

> Recent research (Driver et al., 1992) concerning the children's prior conceptions about science issues related to food has revealed that the meaning of "food" is not consistent in children's thinking and they have different concepts of food in different contexts. Additionally, Turner (1992), who dealt with the development of nutrition education as part of the school curriculum and the teaching and learning about food as part of science and health education, indicates, that children's ideas about nutrients differ from scientific views.
>
> The following section describes the concept mapping technique used in my research.

Concept maps help children to capture their thoughts on paper. It is a way by which a teacher gets to know what any individual child's presuppositions are, about some given topic.

There are many ways that exist for constructing concept maps. All the methods involve the learner putting concept labels on a page and linking them with lines and words to show the relationship between the concepts. Their construction requires considerable creativity in organizing their structure, selecting important, relevant concepts to add, and searching out salient cross-links, indicating relationships in different sections (Novak, 1998: 192).

My study involved a sample of nine and ten year old children participating in the Royal Society of Arts (RSA)/Waitrose Endowed Research Project. This project is part of an RSA initiative called "Focus on Food", which aims to influence policy makers so that cooking becomes part of the entitlement of all children in school. It aims to identify the extent to which Sustained Planned Practical Food Education is taking place and includes the experience of practical and social engagement with food, children taking responsibility for their own learning based upon their own understandings of food and cooking, the variety of teaching approaches being used and the policy planning and implementation.

The children were introduced to the process of producing a concept map by being involved in several activities, which helped them to understand what are concepts and what are linking words, what is a concept map and how it is produced, as well as its importance for the project. They were then asked to produce their own concept map about food, by being given the general concept word *food*, which they wrote in the middle of a blank sheet of paper. The children understood that they had to choose a second word, which they could relate meaningfully to the first and write it nearby. Both words were placed in boxes and joined by a line. They wrote along this line what the relationship between the two concepts was. Then further words were added to the map until all meaningful links had been shown.

The concept mapping activity has been done in two different ways, because I had to work with two different age groups of children (9–10 year olds and 5–6 year olds). The first concept mapping activity, outlined above, was done with the older children, the 9–10 year olds.

The second way the concept mapping technique was used was with the young children participating in the research project, the 5–6 year olds. It was introduced differently because children of this age are unable to read and write fluently. Children were told that they were going to play a game with pictures and words, all related to food. They were asked individually to think of concepts related to food and link them with the word "food" and between one another. These concepts were represented by pictures (clip art images) which the children arranged on a big surface, around the word *food*, building up in this way their concept map themselves. I helped the child to write on a piece of paper both the concepts as arranged and the linking words the child used to link the concepts together. The use of pictures was motivating and stimulating for these young children.

Examples of the concept maps produced by both five- and nine-year-old children (see Figures 7.2 and 7.3), show that children do not come to learn a

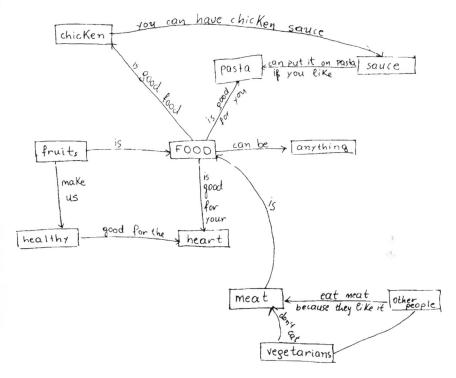

Figure 7.2. Concept map by Year 1 pupil.

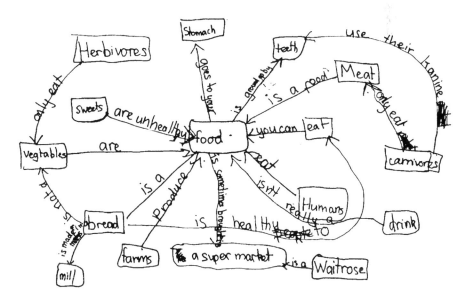

Figure 7.3. Concept map with focus on food, created by Year 5 pupil.

topic with "blank slates" for minds but approach experiences presented in classes with previously acquired notions. In this case it has been shown that children hold alternative concepts about food compared to the "received" scientific view. Some of children's views are common and some distinct for each child. My research shows that the concepts children hold are enriched and progress with time. The concept maps are both idiosyncratic and rich and therefore vary substantially in their extent and complexity. They demand a qualitative scoring technique for their analysis, so that no data is neglected.

The concept maps offer a preliminary insight into children's existing ideas about food, an important first step for this research project, which was set up to explore the effects that the RSA's sustained and planned practical food education intervention programme has on children's learning and their attitudes to food. This data collected at the first part of the project will be compared with the data that will be collected after the intervention programme takes place, in order to explore and describe its implementation and effectiveness in promoting conceptual change and development.

The final example in the 'constructivist science' section explores an often neglected area – the teaching and learning of design and technology. Our colleague, Trevor Davies, provided us with the following account of his research in this field.

As a case study for the research a single-sex girls' school was chosen. The school was selected on the basis that there was reasonable evidence of "sufficient relevant experience" of the central phenomena of "creativity in design and technology education". To set the context for the research, school documentation was examined and an interview conducted with the Deputy Headteacher in charge of the curriculum to establish the geographical, social and overall institutional factors influencing the climate and culture associated with the teaching and learning of design and technology at the school. Subsequently, three design and technology teachers with specialisms in resistant materials (male), textiles and food (both female), were interviewed followed by eight girls of ages between 12 and 15. Following individual interviews, group discussions with the staff were held during the process of data analysis to test findings and judgements.

There is little commonality about the way in which key terms, such as design, technology and creativity, are used and understood in their relevance to teaching and learning activities. A phenomenological approach was adopted which included bracketing out my experience and pre-conceptions of the central phenomena of creativity as the researcher. There was a serious attempt in this research to recognize and value the individuality of each participant's construct system while attempting to elicit deeply held constructs relating to their personal (and in the case of teachers, professional) experiences of the central phenomena. Repertory grids were therefore chosen as a means for eliciting those constructs, derived as part of a semi-structured interview conducted with each participant.

Most definitions of design and technology include the requirement to manufacture a product (real or abstract). Products were chosen as the vehicle to examine creativity in this study for the following reasons:

- they contain physical evidence of creativity;
- they represent a culmination of the application of knowledge, skill and understanding;
- they reflect choices and decisions made by teachers and learners within a framework of constraints, such as those associated with working in a school, constraints of prior achievement and experience and psychological constraints;
- they offer a useful concrete focus for conducting a meaningful repertory grid interview that allows rapid access to the higher order constructs of interview participants.

Initially, teachers were asked to select six to eight student products which they found "interesting" to bring to their interview. They were subsequently used as elements in the construction of a repertory grid. Around 12 bipolar constructs were generated during the course of each interview using the triadic method. Three to four products were then jointly selected during each interview on the basis of their giving evidence of most creativity. The student "owners" of these products were then interviewed. A simplified elicitation procedure was conducted based on "the Salmon line" (Salmon, 1984) where students identified emergent and contrast poles for each construct, then graded each element on a scale of 1 to 5.

The following stages of analysis were then used to process the data:

1. Analysis of repertory grid through a) focusing the data and b) principal components analysis to identify strong relationships between constructs and/or elements for each interview using RepGrid software to aid the analysis;
2. Formal transcription of interviews developing codified data using NUDIST*4 software to aid the extraction of common constructs and categories of meaning for each interview;
3. Summary accounts (narrative) for each interview produced from combining 1 and 2;
4. A set of common themes extracted from the teachers' interviews and a separate set from the students' interviews;
5. All of the themes identified in 4 used to generate two tables summarizing factors perceived as relevant by the participants to each of the following:

"the nature of creative *teaching* in support of creative learning" included:

- teacher/learner relationship construction,
- teachers' personal attributes,
- teachers' approaches to knowledge in design and technology,
- teachers' delivery style,

"the nature of creative *learning*" included:

- learners' personality factors;
- learners' cognitive factors;
- opportunities for learners;
- learners' approaches to learning in design and technology.

The study benefited from the use of Personal Construct Psychology in a number of ways. Adapting the instruments of PCP to the needs of this study allowed an "in depth" examination of teachers' and learners' constructs and the interpretations they placed on their experiences. These were accessed rapidly once good relationships were built with the participants who were able to maintain control and gain empowerment through the data gathering. They were able to use the interviews and meetings as opportunities for clarifying their own thoughts and perspectives given the complex, multi-variant nature of the research focus. Hence the research was perceived as a good source of professional development by the school.

The benefits I gained as a researcher included:

- rapid access to participants' deeper levels of understanding;
- working with individuals at their own level;
- enabling individuals to change their value positions as they became more sophisticated during the research process;
- having efficient ways of recording and processing data;
- being able to incorporate methods of PCP analysis comfortably within a phenomenological framework for the research;
- the opportunity to identify shared understandings and disparate meanings.

A range of patterns and relationships existed in the data that has raised serious questions about the nature of creative teaching and its relationship with creative learning, in the context of design and technology education.

Davies's work concludes our selection of examples from science education. In the next section we will explore some examples from different areas of the curriculum in order to demonstrate the diversity of PCP approaches used to investigate personal meanings.

Different and challenging worlds

The title of this section is developed from one that Burnard (1999) used in her exploration of children's experience of musical improvisation and composition. It is, however, apposite in that it embraces the wide range of privileged access we have been afforded to other educational experiences, including learning English as a foreign language, adolescents' views on smoking and health education, the perspectives of adolescents about drugs and the challenges inherent in the education of able children.

First we will return to Burnard's (1999) work. Her study explored children's experience of improvising and composing music and sought to discover how children participate and reflect on creating music. She used a constructivist-interpretative perspective, employing a multi-method approach including individual interviews, focus group interviews and video-graphic stimulated recall. She also observed a number of music sessions over a period of six months. These sessions took place with a group of self-selected children from a middle school, aged 12. Burnard's interviews were semi-structured and included what she referred to as 'Musical Rivers of Experience' and an image-based technique, both of which were based on Personal Construct Psychology. Burnard was able to use these techniques to compare the pupils' recollections of their personal experiences before their work in the music sessions with their reflections after these sessions were finished. The initial interviews allowed Burnard to understand the pupils' previous experience and relationship with music, revealing vital information about their musical orientation and self-conceptions as musicians. The music sessions included experience with improvisation and composition. At the end of the study Burnard was able to explore which aspects of the pupils experience of improvisation and composition were recalled and was able to identify the pupils' final conceptions of the nature and the relationship between improvisation and composition. She has provided us with the following account:

> It was considered important to provide the children with the opportunity to give voice to the attitudes and orientation implicit to their musical worlds. My experience as a teacher taught me that children tend to explore more "real-life" dimensions when they are talking about things they consider important. Thus, the tool of critical incident charting was used to encourage a reflective conversational style of engagement whereby the children would be asked to reflect on their prior musical experiences and recall a specific incident, situation, person or event which they considered to be of special musical significance. The ensuing accounts of their musical experiences were charted in the form of a winding river where each bend represented an influential incident. Each bend in the musical river was a manifestation of aspects of the child's formative experiences in music. A preliminary one-hour interview provided baseline data concerning the children's musical background, formal instrumental tuition as well as information about their general musical interests both at home and school. This gave me an insight into each child's individual and social worlds based on their own words and self-perceptions. As part of the initial interview the children were asked to recall events of special musical significance. I located key issues of their narration on each bend of the river. Then I asked them to reflect upon their statements.

Burnard provides us with two contrasting pen portraits below:

Introducing Tim. Tim has completed five years of formal instrument tuition on piano and has reached Grade 5 piano, Grade 4 in Theory and Grade 3 in violin.

He has also completed two terms of group lessons at school in percussion. He is a member of the school choir, string orchestra and attended a Saturday morning School of Young Musicians. According to Tim, he has "really got into the rhythm of doing grades" and intends to "go all the way to Grade 8". His mother is a professional piano teacher and father plays the guitar, piano, saxophone and banjo. His younger brother also plays the piano and cello. At home, they have a variety of digital and acoustic pianos.

What strikes me most about Tim's recollections is that they are primarily defined in terms of progress, achievement and competition. As a result, his river begins and ends with expressions relating to "proper pieces like the Allegro by Bach" and the ambition of "getting it right". He also speaks of the pressures of preparing for exams and the "frustrations" of "having to practise".

What is interesting is how he emphasizes the salient issues of experiences that are set by expectations, standards of achievement and success as characterized by subjective values, particular to a set of goals. Tim is an ambitious player who reveals his thoughts and feeling in terms of musical training rather then musical experience. For Tim, musical meaning seems to be based on the highly structured and sequential learning techniques which form the basis of his musical instruction. He is a very confident musician with advanced skills on piano and violin. He is a member of several performance groups and enjoys high levels of motivation and commitment to music.

Introducing Sidin. Sidin is a 12-year-old Asian girl who receives no formal training on a musical instrument. She is the youngest member of the family. There are no instruments to play at home and Sidin is the least musically experienced member of the group. She considers that people fall into one of three categories in terms of musical ability. First, there are those that are "really talented and play good music". Secondly, there are those that are "good but need improvement" and thirdly, there are those who "like music but are not good or looked up to". Sidin conceptualizes her own reality when she says: "When I play, I think I'm the third type of person but I want to be like others and play the way they do. I want to play it but I think I shouldn't play it."

Despite her self-consciousness and shyness, Sidin indicates a strong desire to play music as evident in reflections relating to her musical experiences. This is shown in her Musical River.

The qualities that characterize Sidin are her self-consciousness and low self-esteem. Her great admiration of those with performance skills is a reflection of her interest in music. Her reflections relate to private and "imagined" performance at her house within the security of a home environment. Clearly, she feels intimidated by performing in a school context whereas her private musical world was a safe, non-threatening place where she can find expression in a way such that "it doesn't matter if it sounds silly". Part of her fear of public performance is a result of the difficulties she has with reading notation, which required her to "look at it and think and play it".

Burnard's (1999) research showed that the 'music-rivers' revealed diverse experiences although at times they conveyed sameness identified as an interest in playing instruments and a desire to be involved in music. This was a common characteristic of all the participants recollections. The music-rivers also illustrated some key issues relating to the experiential knowledge of music. These representations highlighted the influence of prior experience on artistic activity as in 'ways of knowing' that involve reflection, production and musical perception.

Many commentators have drawn parallels between learning music and learning a foreign language. Both, for instance, involve imbibing a different culture. It is to foreign language teaching and learning that we now turn.

While the learning of English is considered as extremely important in Turkey, there has been continued dissatisfaction among teachers, students and parents regarding foreign language teaching. Research into the teaching of English as a Foreign Language has suffered from the lack of coherent framework within which to integrate educational aims, theories and concepts in education and strategies of data collection and analysis (Sendan, 1995; Saka, 1995). Pope and Saka (1997) argued that Personal Construct Psychology could prove a useful theoretical framework for research on the teaching and learning of English as a Foreign Language and gave an account of a study that used repertory grids and individual interviews with pupils studying English as a Foreign Language in Turkish schools. Two repertory grids were completed by all students. The elements of the first grid were different school subjects including English. The second consisted of video clips of actual classroom activities that had taken place during English lessons. The use of video clips is a novel application within repertory grid technology. Saka had engaged in a large amount of videoing of classroom activities in order to eventually derive a series of nine classroom episodes which were representative of the type of experience the students would be able to construe. These elements were:

> Teacher explains grammar, choral repetition, students work in pairs, student does oral corrections, teacher reads aloud, teacher explains vocabulary, students work in groups, students write a composition and teacher asks questions.

The repertory grids were analysed using the RepGrid program (Shaw, 1993) which both provided a cluster analysis which focuses individual grids and produced a mode grid which allowed the extraction of some common terms with which the students construe the elements. Students had been identified as strong or weak by their teachers. Pope and Saka (1997) found it interesting to note the different terms used within the mode grid of the strong students and those designated as weak when describing English as school subject. We list below some of the mode constructs used by the strong students followed by those given by the weak students:

Strong students

- useful for lots of jobs;
- more enjoyable;
- essential for my higher education;
- more logical;
- I am good at;
- you can make new friends;
- it is a social benefit.

Weak students

- I tried to memorize what the teacher teaches us;
- I am a failure;
- essential for a career;
- I cannot get good marks in exams;
- necessary for my higher education;
- I feel nervous.

Of particular note in the weak students' grids was their frequent reference to 'trying to memorize what the teacher tells us'. There were differences between the strong and weak students in terms of how they clustered the various classroom activities. The strong students clearly valued classroom activities in which they were actively involved as opposed to just listening. They showed a clear preference for *students working in groups, students working in pairs, students writing compositions* although they clearly recognized the latter as very demanding relative to other activities. The strong students did not value activities such as *teacher explains grammar, teacher reads aloud, choral repetition* and *teacher does oral corrections*. The following verbatim quotation from one strong student supports this analysis:

> I generally like all the activities in the classroom with the exception of some grammar exercises and choral repetition. I sometimes find grammar a bit boring. There are lots of rules to remember. It is important for our learning but not very encouraging. For example it often happens that when I want to say something in English I cannot put things together at once. I would prefer to be taught how to speak in English. I like to speak in group work and pair work. These activities give you the opportunity to use what you know already. It is encouraging. I mean when I talk in class I feel also can speak outside class. (Pope and Saka, 1997: 323)

The weak students in Pope and Saka's study showed a marked contrast with this perspective. The weak students preferred *choral repetition, teacher explains vocabulary, teacher explains grammar* and *teacher reads aloud.*

The case study presented of one of the weak students in their study showed that the student found *students working in groups* and *pairs* embarrassing and she felt nervous and tense in such situations. During the interview the student gave a very clear indication that she had a very low esteem in relation to herself as a language learner. She was only comfortable in situations where she was not actively involved. She perceived the presence of her friends in class not so much as an opportunity for exchanging knowledge or practising her language skills but more as a threat causing embarrassment in the class. This was clearly evident in the extract from her interview which we give below:

> I get angry with the teacher when she puts us into groups. I like it when she teaches us new words. But in group work, there is nothing to write or to memorise. Good students talk English amongst themselves, and the poor ones like me, we just sit and wait for the school bell to ring. Most of the time we talk in Turkish or look up the words in the dictionary ... I am frustrated. I want to leave the class. Successful students do not talk to us in English. On the rare occasions when they attempt to talk to us we cannot reply at once ... I think the teacher is fed up with us failures. She only wants to make her favourite students happy. Depressed. I feel useless. I have given up the idea of being good at English in the future. I only want to pass the exam. (Pope and Saka, 1997: 326)

These two examples of comments made by students demonstrate the power of the repertory grid as a catalyst for generating conversations which tap into very personal concerns of the learner. Pope and Saka felt that it was important to stress that the aim of the study was not to stereotype weak or strong students but to gain an understanding of the perspective of each student. It is salient for teachers to recognize the important influence such perspectives will have on learning. The students' comments regarding the various activities is useful information for the teachers who need to take into account the differing views of students within their classrooms and try to balance activities. Saka (1995) interviewed the teachers but they seemed unaware of the differing perceptions of their students. They appeared to see the class as a whole group while their duty involved the successful management of the whole group. One of the outcomes of her study was a Staff Development Programme for teachers of English as a Foreign Language in Turkey. The classroom episode video developed by Saka is now used as an awareness raising device. Teachers are able to use it with their own students. Personal construct psychology has generated methods of providing an alternative framework for use within Turkish schools. It is hoped, that through adopting this alternative, the disillusionment felt by many teachers and students will be overcome so that eventually there will be conceptual change in foreign language education. In the next chapter we present the work of Sendan (1995) who, having completed his work with student teachers, is helping to effect this conceptual change.

We now return to this country and provide two different examples within the area of Personal and Social Health Education. These studies exploit the rich variety of techniques which fall under the umbrella of Personal Construct Psychology.

Lynch's (1996) study was concerned with adolescent smoking and health education practice. A variety of techniques was used with a group of 16–17-year-old smokers and non-smokers, including repertory grids which used pictures (drawings and photographs) of smoking situations as elements and 'critical incident pathways' or snakes. A PCP approach was chosen because it takes a holistic view of the person. It does not isolate smoking from other personal experiences but attempts to explain smoking from an individual perspective and in relation to other aspects of life. By using sociogrids which include smokers and non-smokers, the study demonstrated many facets of the young smokers that contradicted conventional wisdom – they, for instance, tended to have idiosyncratic thoughts about smoking unlike non-smokers who tended to concur in their views. Young people who smoked also knew as much, and sometimes more, about the health hazards of smoking than their non-smoking peers. Smoking was strongly associated with exerting a sense of self-identity, perhaps an important part of their maturation process and, though they tended to associate together, this had as much to do with being with 'like-minded others' as it did with copying the behaviour of others. There was no evidence to suggest that smokers and non-smokers were different personality types – socializing or fun-loving, for instance – since they had these and many other constructs in common with each other.

The implications of this research for Personal, Social and Health Education (PSHE) are that much more emphasis needs to be placed on the psychological maturation process of adolescents and far less on simple information provision. The goal of PSHE should be to increase self-awareness and the development of a positive self-identity. Lynch contended that too much school-based health education time is spent in telling pupils what they already know, or what does not really matter, and insufficient time is spent in helping them to explore and understand what personal meaning this information has for them. He advocated the use of PCP techniques for eliciting and confronting that meaning.

The second study related to Personal and Social Health Education explores the perspectives and meaning systems of teenagers and their parents about drugs and the communication they experience with each other on the topic, so to improve that communication. Mallick's research, which is now drawing to a conclusion, consisted of a review, and further development, of the drug education programme 'drugsbridge: enabling understanding between parents and youth'. Her work is an excellent example of action research using a case study design and two small groups, one each of teenagers and parents of teenagers. The main PCP technique used was the self-characterization sketch. For this each participant wrote about themselves in the third person as the main character in a film, in which the context was drugs. They were encouraged to write it both intimately and sympathetically as if from a best friend who knew them better than anyone.

The sketches provided, firstly, a baseline measure of the perspective and understanding of the participant and secondly it provided characters for role-plays, using composite types to ensure anonymity. These role-plays involved 'family groups' of a parent with two children, the young people playing character roles which contrasted with their presented selves while the parent character was a composite, used to produce a rather extreme character compared to the 'typical' parent involved in the programme. The role-plays were based on a Rogerian listening exercise. Further opportunities to listen and interact were provided later by asking the participants to write a self-characterization sketch of the other person, parent or teenager, and again engaging in a 'listening' role-play based on the composite products.

These techniques were valuable in allowing each to have access to the other's perspective and to see themselves from a position 'outside' themselves. The role-plays allowed for the temporary subsuming of another perspective and increased sociality, in an atmosphere which was safe and maintained confidentiality. Mallick, in recognizing that recent research had demonstrated that much drug education is ineffective because it frequently fails to be meaningful and personally relevant for young people, found that this method enabled her to work with the participants' personal and individual perspectives in a spirit of open communication, so overcoming some of the difficulties which teachers, parents and teenagers face in discussing an emotionally laden and socially sensitive topic.

Adolescents who smoke or take drugs are often labelled anti-social and their behaviour can be disruptive within the classroom. We recognize that contemporary teachers lead busy and pressurized professional lives. However, we feel that it is important that teachers engage with their pupils on a personal level. The repertory grids, snakes and self-characterization sketches used by Lynch and Mallick are tools to help this process.

The final example in this section addresses a problem that is often overlooked or disguised. Able children can become disruptive or be socially isolated if insufficient attention is given to their needs. Often able children are not seen as needing an education particularly suited to their needs. It has been assumed by many that their ability means that they would succeed regardless of other factors. Lee-Corbin (1996) and Lee-Corbin and Denicolo (1998) argued that this view is unfounded. All too often the needs of the able child are overlooked while the focus of attention is given to children who are presenting challenging behaviour or who are deemed to be under-achieving. However, as Lee-Corbin has identified, the able child may often be under-achieving because their potential abilities remain unrecognized. She presents in her thesis 'portraits of the able child'. Many of these were under-achieving in their primary classrooms. She recognized that an important aspect of her work was the attitude the teacher had towards his/her pupils and also the way in which the pupils reciprocally perceived the teacher. In order to discover whether the attainment of children was affected by teacher attitude Lee-Corbin found it necessary to find a means of illuminating these personal perceptions. She found Kelly's personal construct theory, repertory grids with teachers and pupils, and children's narrative to be powerful in helping her to interpret situations and elicit personal constructs. One important aspect of Lee-Corbin's work was that, in order to form a complete picture as possible, she also interviewed the parents of able children. In this way she was able to produce vignettes or pen portraits of each child. For the repertory grids with teachers Lee-Corbin asked them to select six able children from their class and these formed the elements for their repertory grids. We will provide a short commentary on Alistair one of the 'under-achieving' able children presented in Lee-Corbin and Denicolo (1998: 97–9).

Alistair had not had a particularly easy school life. He had social difficulties which were exacerbated by his mother's constant monitoring of his progress at school. He was at times argumentative and sometimes violent. Alistair's mother was critical of the school for not trying to improve Alistair's concentration and self-esteem. However, Lee-Corbin's observations of classrooms would indicate that his teacher had worked hard to improve these aspects and, indeed, these had improved to some extent. In Alistair's grid about his teachers he provided the following constructs: *kind/strict, helpful/not so helpful, group teaching/all class, amusing/ grumpy* and *personal interest/not so interested.* Alistair liked a teacher to be amusing, to teach in groups as opposed to the whole class, to be kind, helpful and to take a personal interest in him. In rating his current class teacher he did not find her to be particularly interested in him although she was seen as reasonably kind, helpful, amusing and taught groups for most of the time. In the class teacher's repertory grid she identified the following constructs; *tidy presentation/'dogs dinner', staying on task/off task-loss of concentration, cooperation/aggressive 'anti-adult' behaviour, relating well to group/refusing to listen to others, completing tasks/failure to complete task* and *understanding of work/further instruction needed.* In order to achieve, the class teacher felt that it was important that a child had good presentation, was able to stay on task, was cooperative and related well to peers in the group situation. It was important that work was completed and that there was a good understanding of work. On only one of these attributes did Alistair score highly, i.e. the understanding of his work. He found it difficult to stay on task, he was uncooperative and often aggressive. He did not relate well to a group of children and found it difficult to accept the views of others. This was exhibited in terms of dominating situations or withdrawing from them. For the most part he failed to complete items of work. It was clear that Alistair saw all adults as trying to exert pressure on him as his mother did. Alistair's social problems were possibly exacerbated by over-anxious parents. All three of the case studies of 'under-achieving' able children in Lee-Corbin and Denicolo's book had difficulties with concentration and with completing tasks. The two boys described in the book found hand writing laborious and this added to their reluctance to engage with work. Lee-Corbin and Denicolo suggested that achievement and under-achievement are the result of a combination of factors. In their book they propose a number of techniques and suggestions founded in personal construct theory for improving the collaboration between parents and teachers and for each to gain an enhanced awareness of the pupils' perspective.

The examples we have shared with you in this section have acted as reflective mirrors to give you some insight into a variety of worlds experienced by pupils in school. In the next section we will give you a glimpse of the perspectives of students in Further and Higher Education.

Beyond the school gate

There has been relatively little research on students' perspectives in Higher Education other than the student teachers' perspective which we will address in the next chapter.

In Chapter 5 we gave an example of a concept map from a postgraduate research student of ours. This work (Denicolo and Pope, 1994) demonstrated the importance of considering the personal challenges faced by doctoral students while the study as a whole exemplified the value of a multi-method approach. In addition to the concept map which was built around roles which were particularly relevant to each individual, including the research role, we also used repertory grids that contained two family members, two social members, two professional colleagues, two other individuals, two community roles and the research student role as elements. The students also completed a 'winding river' chart on which each bend denoted critical incidents in their lives which had culminated in their taking up the research student role. They also wrote self-characterization sketches describing themselves and their reactions as research students. The outcome of this research has shown that students are able to reflect upon, and articulate their views on the postgraduate role in which they are submerged. Some participants have taken advantage of the optional personal feedback offered; many want to meet as a group to discuss the results and decide on the next stage. We feel that supervisors should encourage greater engagement in such group activity among postgraduate students to promote increased understanding of the process. It has been our view that such active participation in research can be emancipatory for those involved. The various tools used within the enquiry can be taken further to form useful conversations about the process of supervision itself.

The following quotations indicate that the students who participated in the research had found the process illuminating:

> This has been a fascinating activity – many things become clearer for me now.
> I can't believe how much I have told you here, things I haven't even shared with my nearest and dearest.
> This hasn't been an easy exercise. If we had done this earlier I would have made different choices.
> Revelatory!! The more I got into an activity, the more I wanted to stop doing it, for it was scary, but the less able I was to. (Denicolo and Pope, 1994: 127)

This demonstrates that research can indeed be an emancipatory experience. The concluding three examples we give in this chapter are the work of doctoral students, and now colleagues, who have also found working with Personal Construct Psychology, using a variety of techniques, to be a positive experience. First we will give Paul Ashwin's account of his work in a Further Education college:

> I used Personal Construct Psychology in my doctoral research into Peer Learning in Further Education. Peer learning involves students facilitating other students in their learning or in studying within a particular institution. I defined peer learning as: occurring in any formalized interaction where students are facilitated by other students who are studying, or who have recently studied, the same learning material or at the same institution, and where the support

offered reflects the manner in which the students are peers and is mutually beneficial to the students who act as facilitators and the students who are facilitated.

I examined the implementation, operation and significance of peer learning in a Further Education college. In looking at how the implementation of peer learning developed, I examined a case study of peer learning operated on one particular course in the college, and I examined whether peer learning had any significance for how students understood the roles of teachers and learners.

In examining this implementation and operation of peer learning it was George Kelly's view of persons as personal scientists that I found particularly useful. This view of persons helped me to examine my activity as a researcher and implementer of peer learning in a way that was consistent with the way that I viewed the other participants in the research process.

However, it was in the examination of the significance of peer learning for students' constructs of the roles of teachers and learners that I found PCP most helpful. I used repertory grids to examine whether involvement in peer learning influenced the understanding of the roles of teachers and learners of the seven peer facilitators involved in the case study mentioned earlier. I elicited two grids with each of the peer facilitators, one before they started to run peer learning sessions and one after their last peer learning session. In their grids the participants compared and contrasted an number of teachers and learners that they had known. They then ranked the resulting constructs in terms of their importance in teaching and their importance in learning. I examined how these rankings changed over time. I found that, through their involvement in peer learning, the peer facilitators developed their understanding of their roles as learners. Before their involvement in peer learning the peer facilitators saw learning as an individual and solitary process. After their involvement in peer learning, the peer facilitators began to see that the social elements of teaching and learning situations were important to good learning. In this way they had developed a view of learning that was closer to their views of teaching. However, the peer facilitators' views of teaching did not change and these seemed to be defined by what teaching they had experienced in their educational careers.

The use of PCP methods allowed me to examine the way in which the peer facilitators understood the roles of teachers and learners in their own terms. Rather than using pre-defined notions of the roles of teachers and learners, my analysis was based on the constructs that the peer facilitators used to compare and contrast different teachers and learners. The resulting division in their constructs, of teaching as a social process focused on others and learning as a solitary process focused on the self, was not one that I had anticipated.

It was the opportunity that a PCP approach offered in terms of the way participants involved in the research were viewed, as well as the insights offered by examining the participants' constructs of teaching and learning in their own words, that I particularly valued. I felt that my research benefited from this approach and that this approach deepened my understanding of how different people approach teaching and learning situations.

In Chapter 4 we discussed the practicalities of using repertory grids in educational research. The following example demonstrates the flexibility of the repertory grid technique. Quinn is using the technique to facilitate reflective learning by what she terms 'reluctant learners'. She explains it as follows:

> Reflective learning requires active, motivated learners, and stimulating reflective learning when the student is uninterested in the subject is problematic. In the case of social work students an example of such disinterest is their negative attitude towards work with older people. (Many studies have shown a hierarchy of students' client group preferences with children and families at the top and older and disabled people at the bottom.) In Britain, older people are the major group of users of social services. There is a mismatch between users' (and agencies') needs and social work students' client group preferences. Students' negative attitudes about work with older people also conflicts with the social work professions' ethical base.
>
> I introduced a repertory grid technique to enable students to articulate and reflect on their views about work with older people. I used:
>
> 1. triadic elicitation in small groups, with a list of different social work posts (covering work with older people and work with children, in a range of settings);
> 2. feedback of constructs to the full group, and development of a list of constructs;
> 3. individual grids completed by students, and submitted anonymously; the elements of the grid were the posts used in 1, plus 'my ideal social work post'; the constructs were ten that students selected from the list developed in 2;
> 4. feedback to the whole group of the results from the individual grids, in terms of
>   • constructs selected, and frequency;
>   • a list of those posts seen as most like the ideal social work post;
>   • a list of those posts seen as least like the ideal social work post.

The use of the repertory grid technique gave a structure which supported students' reflection on their attitudes to work with different client groups and in different settings, with the focus on attitudes towards work with older people. The initial elicitation of constructs helped students compare attitudes to different social work posts within the members of their small groups, and encouraged reflection about the basis for these attitudes. There was the benefit of personal reflection alongside an anonymous sharing of group responses. In these ways, a dialogue about work with older people was started. Enabling students to critically reflect on their own attitudes towards work with older people is a necessary first step in eliminating barriers to their learning in this area.

Quinn also provided a reflection on the value of using PCP in this circumstance that readers might like to consider if they encounter similar situations in which there exist blocks to, or problems with, learning:

> I think PCP techniques are of considerable use in facilitating reflective learning.
> Even in the absence of specific barriers to learning, not everyone starts with the
> necessary skills for reflection. The technique of triadic elicitation, exploring
> similarities and differences, provides a structure within which reflection can be
> developed in dialogue with others, and completion of a grid can enable
> individual and private reflection.
>
> When there are barriers, and students are reluctant to engage with the topic
> at all, PCP techniques can encourage them to explore aspects of that viewpoint,
> and have the advantage of starting where the students are – that is, disinterested
> in work with older people. By discovering similarities as well as differences
> between social work posts with younger and older people, negative judge-
> ments can begin to be questioned; the basis for judgements is also scrutinized.
> The approach is non-threatening – it engages students in examining their
> attitudes, but without labelling such attitudes unacceptable. Students can
> discover that some views are inappropriate and discriminatory for themselves.

The students in Iantaffi's (1999) study often feel the brunt of discrimina-
tion. Her study is a sensitive account of her work researching the academic
experiences of disabled women students. The practical tool that she
selected for her work was the 'river of experience' which she found
extremely useful and powerful in her ongoing dialogues with disabled
women. Iantaffi did not select any particular disability but encouraged
volunteers who had identified themselves as disabled to take part in the
study. She felt that by selecting one or several disabilities over others
would have implied a reinforcement of the medical model of illness and
impairment. She was sensitive to the fact that many disability studies have
adopted such models and have been carried out by non-disabled
researchers acting as experts. She was aware that as a non-disabled
researcher herself there was a critical need to ensure that she provided a
climate of trust within her research. Reflecting on the conversations
around the 'river of experience' Iantaffi found that she was able to develop
a dialogue of discovery which uncovered what she referred to as the 'lost
tales' of some disabled women students in higher education in England.
In highlighting not just the 'struggle' involved but also the 'survival'
achieved, Iantaffi's aim was to use research tools which would encourage
active involvement from the participants in an emancipatory and democ-
ratic manner. This led her to the choice of personal construct theory and
methods. These 'lost tales' are indeed poignant. Readers are encouraged
to read these for themselves. However we will finish this section with a

quotation from Iantaffi produced while she was in the process of her dialogue with her participants. We think that this demonstrates the importance of a reflective stance in research:

> Researching disability is a winding river of experiences in itself, and at each bend, I feel thrown 'off-balance' a little, discovering new, interesting affluence to explore. It is always new and challenging, and at the same time, it is slowly becoming familiar as patterns start to emerge, linking those individual, different tales I am collecting like pearls on a thread. The different shapes and colours harmonise, at least in my eyes, and I continue to look for new and old words to describe them, together with my participants, trying to reconstrue ourselves and the world in a freer, more democratic, embracing way. The solos and chorus flowing from the rivers can, in this way, create a *powerful ensemble*. (Iantaffi, 1997: 7)

In this chapter we have focused on the learner as personal scientist in a range of contexts. Exploring the students' personal meanings is critically important within the teaching and learning process. In the next chapter we put the spotlight on the teacher. The studies we present in that chapter and the range of techniques we address are aimed at encouraging teachers to be reflective and recognize the importance of adopting a teacher-as-learner perspective throughout their careers. Part of that learning is developing an understanding of the students' perspective, so that the studies in both these chapters inform the education process.

CHAPTER 8

Teachers' perspectives

And gladly wold he lerne, and gladly teche.

Chaucer, *The Canterbury Tales.*

In the previous chapter we have focused on the learner as the main actor in the process. This was not to deny the central role of the teacher in the process of teaching and learning. Indeed we have argued on many occasions that the titles 'teacher' and 'learner' are often a matter of administrative convenience. When one looks at the activities involved in teaching and learning the processes are often symbiotic. We agree with Goodson and Hargreaves (1996:22) who suggested that 'at the end of the day teacher professionalism is what the teachers and others experience it as being, not what policy makers and others assert it should become'.

The curriculum that teachers present to their learners represents their interpretation of it. In this chapter we acknowledge the importance of these interpretations. We have chosen examples of the implementation of various techniques that we have discussed in Chapters 4 and 5 which give voice to the teacher's perspective. In choosing our selection we have deliberately started at the beginning – with the novice teacher. We have then continued the journey by revealing the implicit theories held by experienced teachers in a wide variety of educational settings. We have been privileged to work with a number of research students who have conducted their research overseas and also been able to draw on the experience of colleagues who form part of the International Study Association on Teachers and Teaching in order to bring to you a flavour of teachers perspectives throughout the world.

Beginning teaching: the start of the journey

We believe that the development of a personal model of teaching is an integral part of teacher education. The formal concepts presented university or college courses need to be transformed and assimilated into the particular frame of reference held by the student teacher. Student teachers, as learners, need to become aware of their frame of reference from the outset and continue to explore their developing assumptions which will underlie their teaching behaviour. They benefit from reflecting on the way they construe teaching. With this in mind an early application by Pope (1978), which has been cited by many researchers wishing to adopt a PCP approach to teacher education, carried out a study aimed at monitoring the viewpoints of student teachers during a period prior to, during, and shortly after a major teaching practice. The aims of her work included the evaluation of the repertory grid as a means of monitoring changes in the students' perspectives and as a vehicle for feedback to the student teachers. This would thus provide them with an opportunity for reflection on changes in relation to experiences during teaching practice. Volunteer participants within two teacher training establishments were randomly assigned to one of three groups:

• Group 1: participants interviewed before and after teaching practice;
• Group 2: participants interviewed before and after teaching practice plus the completion of three grids, one before teaching practice, one during teaching practice and the third on return to college;
• Group 3: participants completed the same schedule as Group 2 with the addition of feedback sessions during which the analysis of their previous grid was discussed.

Each person in Group 2 and 3 provided their own elements and constructs. This was important given that the major purpose of the study was to determine what the individual student thought was relevant to his or her teaching. The elements chosen were those aspects which the person thought of when he or she had 'teaching' in mind. Tape recordings of the interviews and the feedback discussions were made. The grids were analysed using a precursor to the FOCUS program (Shaw, 1993). The grids provided a useful basis for developing an insight into the students' frameworks. At one level of analysis, Pope was able to categorize types of constructs generated by the group of students. We would suggest that this approach may well throw light on issues such as school ethos or organizational climate. However, it is important to remember our 'health warning' given in Chapter 6. Construing someone else's construing has its limitations. Nevertheless, Pope was able to identify some common constructs. The most common type of constructs elicited reflected concerns for or an awareness of, external constraints in teaching, for example *governmentally controlled/no government control*. Another common construct indicated a concern for pupils, e.g. *to do with the broadening of children/less to do with*.

Discussion with students about their constructs and the elements raised issues about their personal philosophy of education and their aims. The two sets of elements given below indicate a divergence in ideas about teaching held by two of the students in Pope's study.

During conversations with participant No. 19 she emphasized the need to have an atmosphere of fun within the classroom and to establish good relationships with each pupil. However, participant No. 8 made no specific reference to classroom atmosphere or relationships with the pupils. Her emphasis was on achievement and concern for 'the state of their homework' and 'whether they give it in on time'. In Chapter 4 we indicated that there are only guidelines for elicitation of elements and constructs when one uses repertory grid techniques. You will see from these two examples of element sets that they vary in 'concreteness' and degree of homogeneity. Nevertheless, for Pope's study it was important that each student teacher defined his or her own 'universe of discourse' as the element set itself became the main vehicle for extended conversations with the student teachers.

Student No. 8	*Student No. 19*
Children	To broaden a child's knowledge
Books	Widen child's interests
Chalk	Build a bridge between home and school
Headmaster	Work in an atmosphere of fun
Classroom	Try to get on with the rest of the staff
School	Relationship with the head
Ability	Plenty of space
Board	Trying to adapt method to suit child
Pens	Be where the child is at
Exams	Happy relationship with children
Worry	Understanding each child
Sense of achievement	Making allowances for individual problems
Film	
Attitudes	

Figure 8.1. Two student's divergent ideas about teaching.

Figure 8.2 shows the hierarchical element 'tree' or cluster diagram from a participant from Group 3. At the outset Pope was immediately struck by the fact that despite many conversations with student teachers before this study she would not have provided 'needing adult company' as an element. This, however, proved to be a very important element as far as this student teacher was concerned. It was one of the reasons behind her decision to enter teacher training. 'Family commitments' were also important, as these could affect her performance as a teacher. This particular participant was divorced, with a young child.

The 'tree' diagram (Figure 8.2) was shown to the participant during the feedback session and she was asked to comment on it. Individual groupings, for example 'marking at home', 'extracurricular activities', 'probationary year' and 'area in which I teach', were discussed. The emphasis was on the participant providing the label or rationale for the cluster rather than the researcher naming the factor, which is often the case in other studies. As Pope was interested in monitoring possible changes due to experience and reconstruction during teaching practice, the participant was given her

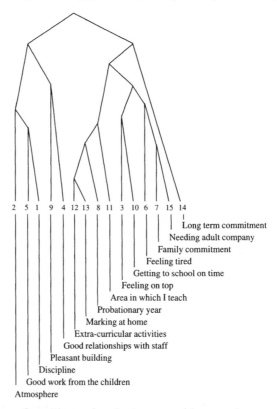

Figure 8.2. Element tree for grid completed prior to teaching practice.

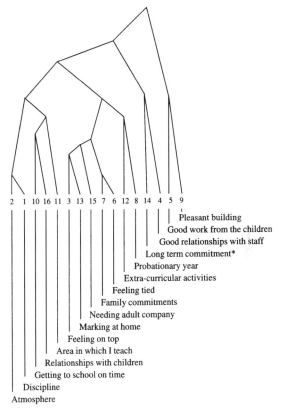

2 1 10 16 11 3 13 15 7 6 12 8 14 4 5 9

Pleasant building
Good work from the children
Good relationships with staff
Long term commitment*
Probationary year
Extra-curricular activities
Feeling tied
Family commitments
Needing adult company
Marking at home
Feeling on top
Area in which I teach
Relationships with children
Getting to school on time
Discipline
Atmosphere

Figure 8.3. Element tree for grid completed during teaching practice.

original list of elements and constructs, was allowed to add any elements or constructs and was then asked to rate the elements on the constructs again. Thus a base comparison was available between original elements and constructs on each occasion alongside a monitoring of any additions.

Figure 8.3 is the same participant's second grid, completed in the middle of her teaching practice. She decided to add 'relationships with the children' to her element list, because she now realized this was an important factor in teaching. A tight cluster is evident, consisting of 'feeling tired', 'family commitments', 'needing adult company', 'marking at home' and 'feeling on top'. In describing this, the participant explained that she was very pressurized during teaching practice and found it difficult to cope with both family and school work. She now realized how important the 'atmosphere' in the classroom was for the general 'discipline' of the children. She commented on the fact that 'good work from children' and 'pleasant building' seemed to be linked – she was not surprised by this and felt it represented her feelings and experience during teaching practice, as the following extract from her tape recording indicates:

> It was a Victorian school with very high ceilings, and very little display space and it was very difficult to organise the classroom so that it looked attractive. The vast ceilings, and you had to stick things on the wall with sellotape and it looked messy. There weren't any nice display boards. You felt you wanted to – it would be more incentive to get the classroom looking nice and get the children producing stuff if you could in fact have displayed it nicely, but it was very difficult.

Her comments on the new link between 'good relationships with staff' and 'long term commitment' were also revealing:

> When I was at the school that I was on teaching practice at I found that staff ... well I just was not compatible with them at all and I just couldn't imagine teaching for a long time in that situation with that kind of company. I would really find it very off-putting unless there was staff there that I felt I fitted in well with. I don't think you can isolate yourself in the classroom all day, I think you need to have some kind of feedback from the staff which I just didn't have at that school ... I really do think I need to be, feel inspired. You know I just found the staff exceptionally dull, exceptionally unimaginative and I just felt completely an outcast. You know they weren't antagonistic towards me, I just had absolutely nothing in common with them at all which is quite horrifying. I couldn't consider doing a job if I felt like that about people.

Boei *et al.* (1989) were concerned with what they referred as to the 'subjective theories of student teachers'. The aim of their project was to investigate student teachers' perspectives about good teaching. They assumed that these subjective theories would influence teaching behaviour. Boei *et al.*, whose research was conducted in the Netherlands, suggested that knowledge of these subjective theories would be useful for pre-service and in-service teacher training. They argued that traditionally the task of teacher training was seen as one of teaching students objective theories which could be put into practice. However, they proposed that 'to be able to apply the taught objective theories, student teachers must convert them to their idiographic practice' (Boei *et al.*, 1989: 175).

They used the repertory grid to investigate the students teachers' theories. However, unlike Pope (1978) they decided to use a selected number of provided elements. Since their interest was in student teachers' views on good teaching, they first conducted open interviews with 27 student teachers during which their ideas were discussed. These interviews were analysed and ideas expressed about good teaching were extracted and categorized. Boei *et al.* initially extracted 57 consensus statements which were further categorized into five main clusters as follows:

- conditions for good teaching;
- objectives/goals to be reached;
- qualities of teacher;
- interactions/classroom climate;
- didactic process teaching – learning process (Boei *et al.*, 1989: 177).

When deciding on the provided elements, Boei *et al.* (1989: 179) were anxious to remain 'as true as possible to the formulations that were made by the student teachers'. The statements were reformulated in terms of teacher behaviour, for example 'the teacher pays attention to individual children'. The triadic elicitation method was used with a fixed number of randomly selected triads. In addition to 'teacher behaviour elements'. The researchers provided two further elements: 'I as a teacher' and 'I as an ideal teacher'. These were not included in the triadic elicitation procedure but were used by the researchers in order to ascertain the student teachers' views of self as they saw themselves at present and the ideal teacher to which they aspired. Boei *et al.* provide a detailed discussion on the methodological decisions they used prior to the repertory grid elicitation. For example, they were concerned to provide a standardized set of instructions for each student and, given the size of their main sample (64 first-year student teachers from 12 teacher training colleges), the researchers had to train a number of interviewers. In addition to being interested in the differences individual students had with respect to how they saw their 'current self' and 'ideal self', the researchers were interested in what similarities could be found in the constructs of the first-year student teachers. The common constructs they identified were:

- teaching and learning (of knowledge) versus social/emotional relationships and development;
- teacher centred versus pupil centred;
- goals versus means;
- teaching and learning (of knowledge) versus persons/personal;
- individual pupil versus group;
- professional activities inside class/school versus (professional activities) outside class/school.

One interesting result was that the differences between 'I as a teacher' and 'I as an ideal teacher' were most marked in terms of the final category in the above list. Boei *et al.* (1989: 189) suggested that in their opinion:

> this points to a rather narrow perception of the professional teaching role; it
> should be incorporated into teacher training to avoid what Zeichner (1981)

calls 'utilitarian teaching perspectives' in which teaching is separated from its
ethical, political and social dimensions.

The research of Pope and Scott (1984) was concerned with the teaching of
psychology in relation to student teachers' epistemology. They argued that
student teachers should be encouraged to adopt a reflexive stance with
respect to their learning and to consider the inter-relationships between
their own views and those inherent in formal statements regarding the
nature of knowledge offered in psychology lectures and educational texts.
It was clear from Pope and Scott's research that student teachers do have
personal epistemologies. Some of these are reminiscent of those we
identified in Chapter 1. Unlike Pope's study and that of Boei *et al.*
discussed earlier, which both used repertory grids as a vehicle for the elicitation of student teachers' constructs, Pope and Scott's work was based on
a more conversational approach. Students were asked to talk about their
beliefs about knowledge and learning and the role of the teacher. These
conversations were tape recorded and transcribed verbatim. Many of the
students saw the teacher as 'expert transmitter of knowledge'. The two
quotations we give below could be seen to fall within the cultural transmission mode:

> As a direct imparter of information because I think something's can only be
> learnt and taken in by being told or educated by another, by a person who is
> experienced as that other thing.

> I think knowledge should be built upon itself, so that it sort of builds up like
> building blocks and it has to have a very firm foundation to build on. So a child
> has to be taught the basics ... so knowledge is built up step by step.

This latter quotation could be seen as fitting an accumulative fragmentalist
view of knowledge. The quotation below represents a contrasting view:

> [Knowledge] It's experience. I don't think knowledge is a body of facts. I don't
> think that it's true. I think knowledge is when you have experienced different
> things, different things in life ... attitude, values, beliefs and you accept or ...
> understand those beliefs even though you don't accept them ...

Many of the student teachers commented that they had found the process
of talking about their epistemology and ideas about teaching and learning
during the interviews to be helpful in focusing and clarifying their
thoughts.

> It's [the interview] been of great value to me actually. I've not really had to sit
> down and think about things like this as much. I do wrangle about it with other

people but not just sit down and me think and no one else come back with a counter-argument. So it's helpful, very helpful. Perhaps we could do with more of it.

Pope and Scott's work indicated that student teachers can, if encouraged, become aware of their initial epistemologies. Constructivist teacher educators would seek to continue this process by encouraging the student teacher to challenge his/her initial epistemology and explore the potential of alternative views.

Thomaz (1986) took up this challenge in her work with student teachers of science. She recognized that the practice of a constructivist approach in science teacher education was a fruitful alternative to the prevalent practice in Portugal. In her work she discussed the aims for physics teaching in general education derived from the psychological perspectives of George Kelly and his constructivist view of knowledge. Her work fell into three phases. First she provided a course in 'physics didactics' to 13 student teachers in two consecutive years at the University of Aviero. In the next phase five student teachers were followed throughout their year of teaching practice and, in phase three, three of these students were followed up in their first year of professional life as teachers. During the first phase Thomaz encouraged her student teachers to read a number of articles which emphasized the importance of understanding pupils' perceptions and the students explored uses of approaches such as the Interview About Instances method we described in Chapters 5 and 7.

Thomaz encouraged the student teachers to consider for themselves the value of seeing the learner as a personal scientist. They were also encouraged to reflect on their own conceptions of concepts in physics, for example, concepts of 'light and its properties'. She developed a diagnostic questionnaire for students to use in order to investigate the pupils meanings for words such as 'mass', 'weight' and 'force' before formal teaching. She also included a series of questions aimed at eliciting the distinctions pupils made between various concepts for example 'mass', 'volumes', 'weights', 'force', 'motion' and 'velocity'. The student teachers were asked to reflect on their own meaning of 'teaching physics' and to consider how their views may have changed before and after the first phase of Thomaz's course. All 13 of the students considered that their view of teaching physics had changed. We offer a few examples below:

> Before the course, 'to teach physics' was, for me, to convey knowledge which we can get in books without seeing the link between that knowledge and the reality around us, memorise knowledge, formulas and definitions. Now I can see that link.

At the beginning I had a very traditional view of teaching. I mean, for me, teaching was only the transmission of content. The task of the teacher was to 'give' the subject matter.
I think that, concerning our expectations 'teaching physics', something has changed after the course. We understood, at last, 'teaching physics' isn't a matter of transmitting or explaining physics knowledge, but it is a matter of stimulating, guiding and helping pupil's evolution in their physics learning. (Thomaz, 1986: 510–11)

It is clear from Thomaz's work that the students shifted their epistemology and views about the nature of teaching. They had also adopted a more constructivist image of science itself. Thomaz found that the three novice teachers in phase three were able to maintain a constructivist perspective in their schools despite different institutional contexts during their teaching practice and their first year of professional life.

Sendan (1995) also adopted constructivist theory as the conceptual framework for his study. He saw learning to teach as a complex process of change in student teachers' personal theories during which they develop, test and reconstruct their own hypotheses about teaching. He used overlapping, cross-sectional and longitudinal samples and repertory grids and interviews were conducted with 54 student teachers attending an 'English as a Foreign Language' programme in Turkey. Sendan (1995: 2) suggested that student teachers need to be encouraged to reflect on their own theories during teacher training if they are to be prepared as 'reflective and autonomous practitioners'. His study was concerned with the nature of and changes in student teachers' personal theories regarding teaching effectiveness throughout their initial teacher training. Like the Boei *et al.* study, which we discussed earlier, Sendan also included the elements 'self' and 'ideal self' as teacher. However, unlike Boei, Sendan elicited both elements and constructs from each participant on a personal basis. Prior to the data collection process, student teachers were provided with detailed information regarding the purpose of the study and commitments expected. This was important given the fact that some students would be interviewed on several occasions. The participants were provided with a set of nine cards each with codes (E1, E2 and E3 for effective teachers; T1, T2 and T3 for typical teachers; I1, I2 and I3 for ineffective teachers).

We commend Sendan's rationale for using codes. The participants were asked to think of actual teachers who fulfilled each of these roles but, given the fact that some of their choices may be derived from persons who were still their tutors and/or may have been known to Sendan, the codes preserved anonymity.

The personal constructs were elicited using the triadic elicitation technique we discussed in Chapter 4. Sendan decided to record the constructs on the grid form himself in order to reduce the heavy demands on the participants and to ensure appropriate recording of constructs offered. He occasionally used the laddering technique to obtain higher order (superordinate) constructs. The elicitation procedure was brought to an end when participants indicated that they were not able to propose further constructs or when they started repeating constructs already offered. The participants were allowed to check the constructs labels written down by Sendan and make any alterations they required and participants were also asked to mark their preferred construct pole on each of the constructs elicited. The data was analysed using the RepGrid 2 computer program (Shaw, 1993). Sendan was able to obtain a FOCUS grid for each participant and produce socionets of construct links for each of the cohorts. He carried out an iterative process of classifying the various constructs elicited, deriving seven categories:

- planning and preparation;
- lesson presentation;
- lesson management;
- instructional methods, techniques and materials;
- teacher/pupil relationship;
- teacher knowledge and characteristics;
- evaluation and feedback.

Sendan discussed a pattern of change which he observed in his cross-sectional data. The change between the first two occasions was mostly in the area of *teacher knowledge* and *characteristics*. There was more focus on *lesson management* between the second and third occasions and on *lesson management* and *teacher/pupil relationship* between the third and fourth occasion. Sendan (1995: 121) saw this as 'indicating a pattern of "deconstruction" of personal theories in the early years of training and "reconstruction" towards the end'. In the case studies Sendan was able to focus on both the change in content and structure of the student teachers' construing. His experience of using the repertory grid technique confirmed his view that student teachers are capable of 'reflecting on their personal theories and training experiences when given the opportunity and a supportive environment'. Sendan (1995: 229) alluded to the negative influence of assessment on experimentation and reflection. He argued that the student teachers' active involvement in the research process helped them to have a greater consciousness of their personal theories about teaching and their views of themselves as a teacher. This participation also helped them to reflect on various experiences during their period of training. We provide below two examples of comments made to Sendan during his follow-up interviews:

> I am not sure how much help I was to you, but I found it extremely useful to articulate my thoughts and feelings about teaching. I now feel more aware of who I am and who I would like to be.
> My participation in your study [has] broadened my views about the teaching profession and helped me become more aware of myself. (Sendan, 1995: 237)

Cabaroglu (1999) also investigated the beliefs of student language teachers. In her study the student teachers were Postgraduate Certificate of Education (PGCE) teachers engaged in a one year course in Modern Foreign Languages. Cabaroglu's particular interest was the sources of their beliefs about teaching on entry to the course and how these beliefs developed through the year. She was particularly interested in what factors promoted change and development. She gives her own account of her study below:

> A constructivist approach to the investigation was adopted. The data collection strategy included open-ended, semi-structured interviews, "snake"s, language learning autobiography and student teacher fact sheet. In this account I will focus on the "snake" technique. The rationale behind the use of this technique was twofold:
>
> 1. To answer the research questions in depth and to elaborate some of the issues that arose from the interviews.
> 2. To triangulate the data gathered from standardized open-ended interviews.
>
> In relation to these two points, the aim was to collect data that would enrich and strengthen the interview data. Additionally, as beliefs and attitudes are difficult to explain and measure, and different people have different ways of showing their attitudes and beliefs, the use of the "snake" technique would hopefully make it easier for the participants to express themselves.
> The "snake" technique was used with three student teachers out of the 20 participants from the main study. The justification for the selection of these case studies was made after the preliminary analysis of the first and the second interviews, and before the third interview was conducted. The preliminary findings from the first and second interviews suggested that there were remarkable differences between what some student teachers said in the first and second interviews. Two of the student teachers construed teaching, teacher and pupil roles in a significantly different way. Their views of teacher and pupils' roles were almost completely different at the time of the second interview when compared to the first interview conducted with them. When asked the reasons behind those remarkable changes in their beliefs, they only referred to their teaching practice experiences.
> Contrary to these two student teachers, another student teacher seemed not to have changed the way she had construed teaching, teacher and pupil

roles. Could these extreme situations be the result of the interviews conducted? What were the reasons behind these extreme cases? In order to investigate the answers to these questions further, the "snake" technique was chosen for use with these three student teachers, and it proved to be very useful in explaining further the reasons behind these three cases.

- The "snake" technique allowed the participant to identify her/his own agenda (i.e. what to talk about, and when in her/his life to start the "snake" chart). In the case of one of the participants in particular, it was revealed that the way she construed teaching before the PGCE course completely different. Although an interview was conducted with her on entry to the course, the interview alone was not very helpful in identifying her beliefs regarding teachers and teacher roles.
- Employing two different data collection strategies was helpful to me in investigating further the reasons for change/developments in beliefs, but it was also helpful for the participants to reflect on their experiences and to express themselves better with the help of a different technique.

On reflection, the value of the PCP approach and the "snake" technique of my studies can be summed up as follows:

- The data provided a deeper and a better understanding of why the beliefs of those three student teachers from the main study group showed a different development pattern. In a way, the data from the "snake" activity filled in the gaps in the complex puzzle I had in front of me.
- The "snake" technique was invaluable from the point of view of the participants. One of them indicated that she was not a "good speaker". During the semi-structured interviews conducted with her, she found it difficult to express herself. However, she indicated that the "snake" activity (i.e. drawing the chart; the visual aspect of it; reflecting on the incidents, people, and so on that brought about changes in her beliefs) made her task easier.
- It was invaluable for me too: I had the summary of the aspects of the participants lives in front of me with annotations. I could see developments and what had contributed to them. I could "dig" further by looking at them.

So far we have presented research on student teachers' thinking which describes such matters as their views on effective teaching and their personal theories of learning. We have recognized that student teachers' experiences during training will have an impact on their thinking when they enter the profession. In the UK, there is evidence of increasing stress in the teaching profession and student counsellors have reported stress among student teachers during their training. Excessive stress may lead to undesirable effects such as frustration, depression, deterioration in work performance and interpersonal relationships.

We finish this section with a study which addresses this important issue. In his review of research on student teachers and teachers' stress research, Yeung (1992) confirmed Blase's (1986) earlier suggestion that such research had primarily relied on quantitative methods using highly structured instruments. Participants' responses were excessively controlled and most of the instruments used to measure stress were developed from stress inventories based on theoretical ideas developed from stress studies outside the area of education. Using a Personal Construct Psychology perspective employing the repertory grid technique and interviews, Pope and Yeung (1996) attempted to avoid some of the problems inherent in previous research in the area. They were concerned to identify how stress is perceived by the student teachers themselves, without the constraints of pre-structured questionnaires and stress inventories.

The study was conducted in three phases. During the first phase of the study student teachers took part in open-ended interviews in which they were invited to describe openly and freely what they had done during their course and to identify specific course activities. Pope and Yeung were concerned to allow the students the opportunity to define course activities that they perceived as meaningful; they encouraged them to make clear their own meaning of stress. At the end of each interview, when the course activities had been identified, the student teachers were asked to rate these according to three levels of perceived stress, i.e. low stress, medium stress and high stress. When all of the interviews had been completed with the 16 students in Phase One, a list of 17 course activities was generated that represented some commonly mentioned activities which were distributed across the three stress levels. These became elements for the repertory grid which was completed by a further volunteer sample of 21 students within the same university. The elements identified were:

- lectures
- teaching practice file
- subject specialism
- visits by tutors
- teaching practice self-evaluation
- curricula areas – related studies
- practical work/performance
- lesson plans
- exams
- teaching practice
- seminars
- project
- National Curriculum
- school visits
- essays/assignments
- education and professional studies (EPS)
- classroom teaching.

These 17 elements were ordered in a sequence that alternated the expected levels of stress based on the students perceptions in Phase One of the study. Students were free to add elements or discard any elements they felt were inappropriate. The triadic elicitation method was used at the beginning of the interview while towards the end of the interview the full context approach was used so that students were free to offer any combination of elements in contrast to others without the constraints of particular triads. Since no student availed themselves of the opportunity of discarding any of the 17 elements it was possible to obtain both a focused grid for each individual using the FOCUS program within RepGrid and socionet diagrams for different groups following the SOCIO program. The student groups varied in terms of their year of study and also whether they were on a four-year course of initial teacher training or on the one-year postgraduate certificate in education (PGCE) route. A supplied construct 'a lot of stress' versus 'a little stress' was used. This meant that for each individual, the relationship between the supplied constructs and other personally elicited constructs could be identified. Pope and Yeung were able to identify which pole of the construct represented the high stress pole and then the ratings of each element on the high stress end of each construct dimension was calculated. The element stress rank order for the four-year students and the one year PGCE students was identified. Here we will refer only to the four elements for each group that were ranked highest for stress level. For the four-year group the *teaching practice file* was ranked highest in terms of stress level followed in turn by *teaching practice*, *visits by tutors* and *classroom teaching*. On the one-year course *teaching practice* was ranked highest followed in turn by *visits by tutors*, *teaching practice file* and *classroom teaching*. Course-related elements such as *seminars*, *projects*, *lectures* and *education* and professional studies and curriculum areas/related studies were seen as less stressful by both groups.

Using the SOCIO program it was possible to identify mode constructs, i.e. those constructs most commonly used by the participants in the study. A content analysis of all constructs as they were applied to the elements was also carried out and a number of categories emerged:

- *evaluation stress* – this category referred to student teachers constructs that reflected feelings of being 'assessed', 'examined' and 'evaluated';
- *workload stress* – this stress included reference to 'workload pressure and the exhaustion involved in completing tasks';
- *expectation/uncertainty stress* – many students indicated that they felt stressful when they were 'uncertain of what was required of them and uncertain of what tutors expected';

- *efficacy stress* – this included constructs referring to 'fear of failure and lack of confidence and competence in coping with work';
- *course meaningfulness* – this type of stress occurred when student teachers felt that they were 'wasting their time, were bored and irritated';
- *importance stress* – this construct dimension referred to feelings of stress which occurred when the course activity was considered to be particularly important, especially if it were seen as 'important for career prospects';
- *class control and student learning* – constructs classified under this dimension referred to stress that some student teachers feel when they need to accept 'responsibility for students learning and control of classroom discipline';
- *tutor stress* – this refers to constructs where the students indicated that they were stressed when their 'tutors were unsupported or unduly critical'.

During Phase Two the students welcomed the opportunity to talk about their course activities and discuss which aspects of the course they found particularly stressful. It was clear that 'teaching practice' was the major source of stress to student teachers and activities relating to teaching practice, including 'preparation of schemes of work, writing lesson plans, classroom teaching, visits by tutors and writing self-evaluations' were seen as demanding, many of the students viewing them also as stressful. The tutors support during teaching practice was seen as important. Students felt upset and demoralized when tutors' feedback was not given in a constructive manner. Several students talked, most forcibly, about the neglect they felt while being evaluated in the schools and felt apprehensive at being examined on their competence as a teacher within the classroom. Students often felt uncertain about what was expected of them and would have welcomed more advice from college teachers and mentors in schools. Recognition of these concerns is vital, and without support from tutors, students may become overwhelmed, demoralized and unable to cope. If support is lacking they may leave the course prematurely. One of the outcomes of the second phase of Pope and Yeung's work was the compiling a list of all of the personal constructs that students had used when describing the feelings of stress when considering their course. These were grouped under the major categories we identified above.

In the third phase of the project this list was sent to all directors of counselling services in the 62 universities in England which offer both the four-year and one-year teacher training courses leading to qualified teacher status. The counsellors were asked to indicate the extent to which each of the students' statements, under the categories identified, reflected their experience when counselling students with stress. Counsellors responded identifying the relevance of each statement based on their experience and also, as requested, added further statements. This list of statements, derived initially from individual students constructs has proved useful for counsellors, professional tutors and the subject mentors in schools. Pope and Yeung's work, and that of others we have outlined in this section, has drawn attention to the value of a Personal Construct Psychology approach to research on the training of the student teacher. These few examples also point to the importance of using such insights within teacher education. However, the teacher's journey has only just begun ...

On the long and dusty road

The previous section has provided examples of the exploration of the person meanings of students at the beginning of their career. We now move on to gain an awareness of the beliefs about teaching and learning held by experienced teachers. While Oberg (1989: 145) was interested in good professional practice, she argued that:

> goodness is not judged only by looking at the results of teacher actions, but more importantly by looking at what the actions are an expression of. Teachers' actions are understood as expressions of teachers' ideas of the educational good and their ideas on how to move towards that good in the present circumstances. These ideas constitute what we have called the grounds of practice.

Oberg asserts that the 'ground' for professional practice is a complex interplay between beliefs, intentions, judgements about what an action will lead to and the teacher's values related to what results are desirable from their professional activities.

Oberg adopted personal construct theory because she found it consistent with her assumptions about the nature of 'ground' and it had well-established methods for identifying personal constructs. Oberg worked with eight experienced teachers and adopted a method of enquiry which was collaborative in order to build the necessary trust and respect required to achieve a shared understanding of the teachers' views regarding their practice. Oberg and her co-researchers began their initial conversations with the teachers by asking each of them 'what did you do today'. She was surprised that the transcripts of these first conversations were rich in description and contained examples of the teacher's own interpretation of their practice. Oberg used observation to provide additional data to corroborate, refine and extend her analysis. For each participant she was able to construct a table which listed constructs and their accompanying principles of practice, together with actual examples from practice provided by the teachers such as that given in Table 8.1.

Table 8.1. Constructs and accompanying principles of practice

Constructs	Principles of practice	Examples from practice
Learner as able to take responsibility for each other's learning	Arrange for top students to monitor slower peers	I use some of my fast readers who finish the work to provide oral reading experience with the slower children ... I use the fast group as monitors for correcting procedures

Source: Oberg, 1989: 156.

Oberg and her co-researchers used this three-column format together with a short paragraph describing the teacher's practice. Where possible they constructed the paragraph around a unifying metaphor. An example is given below.

> The teacher plays his role like a restrained symphony conductor. He is there to direct the performance of his students ... the teacher's goal is to help each student learn as much as possible, and in order to do that, they must become proficient performers in the classroom ... Some students are good enough to be solo performers, while some will always require the security and direction of the group under a conductor. The good students are allowed to work independently, in a group or individually, with occasional monitoring by the teacher. The others require more teacher supervision ... All these various arrangements are orchestrated by the teacher. (Oberg, 1989: 156)

Oberg reported that the teachers in her study were surprised about the amount of information that was gleaned from the conversations with the teachers and, despite the constraints of the charts and paragraphs in terms of capturing the richness of the teachers construing, Oberg was relieved to find that the teachers received the accounts 'with surprise and appreciation' (Oberg, 1989: 157).

She provided this excerpt from a teacher called Gerry:

> The whole document was something I never had to say aloud before and had never seen in print before ... the fact that it is written down instead of just spoken about, that in itself is a very commanding thing. (Oberg, 1989:157)

The teachers found that the charts and paragraphs represented significant aspects of the grounds of practice. Reflection on and developing these grounds of practice becomes an important part of developing professional knowledge and practice.

The theme of developing professional knowledge in practice was also important in Albanese's (1999) study. However, unlike Oberg's work which focused on elementary teachers, Albanese's context was that of tertiary education. She was specifically concerned with the development of writing instruction and explored if, how and why a dual creative and analytical thinking approach to teaching at this level could enhance academic writing development. Albanese used a Personal Construct Psychology approach within her study and we give her account of how she used PCP and her reflections on the approach adopted below:

PCP critical incident snake charts were elicited from teachers as a supplement to semi-structured interview questions. The purpose of the information was to examine if and how tertiary level writing teachers incorporated or encouraged creative thinking in their students of academic writing. To elicit the PCP information, the participants (teachers) were asked to recount the critical events in their own writing history. As they discussed the major events, insights, or turns in their writing history, the researcher (myself) charted the events on a sheet of paper.

By the time the participant had finished relating their history, a one-page rough draft of the snake chart of their history was also done. Showing these to the participants for further comments allowed them to correct or clarify their snake charts, or further reflect upon their histories *in situ*.

Reflections on the value of the PCP approach/method
I was initially sceptical about the utility of the PCP information. I was concerned that it gave me, as the researcher, less control over the direction of the information volunteered by the participants than could be gathered by direct interview questions. I was afraid it would allow valuable interview time to be spent on off-topic issues and would yield uneven types of responses from the various participants that defied comparison. This is why I used it as a supplemental technique in addition to the semi-structured pre-planned interview questions.

I was surprised at the number of ways and reasons that the PCP data proved useful. These include the following:

1. It confirmed, validated, or provided additional support for ideas expressed in the interviews.
2. It clarified ideas expressed in the interviews and added a further dimension as to how and why the participants arrived at their various beliefs.
3. It "quantified" the ideas expressed in the interviews. By this, I mean it often revealed the depth of the participants' belief in the ideas they espoused.
4. It sometimes provided a response more appropriate to the intention of the interview question than the response received from asking the question directly (if, for instance, the participant interpreted a direct interview question in a way it was not intended).
5. As an added benefit, seeing their personal history tangibly charted occasion-

ally clarified or crystallized the participants' views for them in a way that they had not consciously understood before. To watch a participant experience such an epiphany of self-understanding, catalysed by the research, was a valuable experience. In addition, it taught me much about the value of reflection, which directly and positively affected subsequent aspects of the work (including the development of a learning theory based on the importance of reflection).

Based on my experience with PCP, I now believe that any data gathering effort worth the trouble of an in-depth interview approach would benefit by a supplemental and easy to conduct PCP elicitation such as that described above.

A decade before, Memon (1989) expressed a similar view. Using Personal Construct Psychology as a theoretical base, Memon adopted a multi-method data collection strategy which included individual and group interviews, repertory grids, observation and teachers' diaries.

Memon (1989: i) was concerned with curriculum change mechanisms in Pakistan which he suggested were 'based on a bureaucratic model in which teachers are "humble servants" of the system'. He was interested in the teacher's and student's perspectives on innovations which were developed (externally to the schools) in the area of teaching and learning English as an Additional Compulsory Language (TEACL). Memon's findings indicated that teachers were faced with the conflict of demands between the desired goals of innovations proposed by the Pakistani education authorities (largely imported from the West) and the current examination system. Teachers found that they lacked any support mechanisms to guide their classroom actions in relation to the innovations required. The main sources of practical problems he identified were what he called governing factors (teachers' personal theories), frame factors (instructional milieu) and social factors (learning milieu).

Memon argued that there was a lack of due consideration being given to teachers' personal and professional values and theories and a lack of recognition of their professional autonomy. He used a conversational and interactive approach when developing the repertory grids and the conversation with each teacher was audio-recorded. During the conversations each participant was encouraged to elaborate on their reasons for choosing particular constructs. Two grids were elicited, one reflecting the teachers' perceptions of teaching methods and the other on their perceptions of the teachers' role. Prior to the individual elicitation, an orientation session was used with the whole group of teachers which allowed Memon to describe the purpose and the theoretical basis of the grids and to negotiate a common set of elements for the repertory grids. The elements used for the teaching methods were: *grammar translation, direct method, audio-visual, audio-lingual, situational, communicative, natural, structural, silent way.*

When Memon inspected the clustering of these elements in the individual teachers grids he often found that the officially recommended *audio-lingual* appeared to be quite isolated in the element tree, showing their dislike for this new method. Some teachers were of the opinion that the audio-lingual method did not suit the learning context because it demanded more use of the target language in the classroom, where students were unable to speak English spontaneously all the time. Each of Memon's teachers provided their personal constructs in relation to the common element set and, therefore, Memon was able to get rich data regarding their construing of the various teaching methods used for TEACL.

The second grid represented the teachers perceptions of their role. The consensus elements used are shown below:

- to motivate the students for learning English;
- to encourage the students to converse in English;
- to make lesson planning interesting;
- to maintain friendly relationship with the students;
- to teach for understanding through various methods;
- to provide feedback when marking the students' work;
- to convey enthusiasm for English;
- to develop students' creative thinking;
- to develop students' confidence.

We present below some extracts from one teacher in Memon's study in order to gain an insight into her views on the teaching of English and her views on the teaching profession. We hope it will give you a sense of the value of using grid methodology combined with a range of more flexible conversational tools. We have indicated in brackets after each quotation the source technique.

First consider her view on the teaching of English:

> It has been the practice that the teaching of English has been restricted to only the development of students reading and writing skills and the rest of the skills are ignored. We need to adopt a rational approach for teaching English to develop all skills and competence ... (interview)

Next the teacher reflects on the clustering of her elements on the teacher's role grid. She had two main clusters. Here she is reflecting on the cluster containing elements related to providing feedback, maintenance of friendly relationships with students, the development of students confidence, the encouragement of students to converse in English and her role in conveying enthusiasm for English which was more loosely linked with the other elements in that cluster:

> Teaching is a social activity. I consider school as a society and the classroom as a community in which a group has a common interest ... Each individual by nature is different, therefore, we must organise common activities in a way that every student can take an interest ... we have to create a sense of responsibility amongst them. The teacher's job is to stimulate and provoke her students thoughts and feelings and help them in learning ... (grid conversation)
>
> So far as the facilitator role is concerned I think it will enable both the teacher and taught to decide what activities to be included and how these activities be organised and managed for the students for meaningful learning. The teachers and students should negotiate ... accomplish their tasks jointly. (interview)
>
> I have just seen the school curricula emphasising the completion of the examination syllabus. It also further mentions that so and so lessons are deleted from the examination syllabus. The interesting thing is that these are lessons I already taught and they seem to be interesting for the students who really enjoyed them ... (teacher's daily diary)

On the basis of his evidence, Memon suggested that improvement can only be brought about through a true dialogue and partnership between teachers, students and outside developers. Teachers need to be considered as active agents in the practical affairs of the curriculum and curriculum planners must respect and acknowledge the complexity of the contextual reality of the classroom. Memon argued that improvements cannot come about by way of externally imposed prescriptions and suggestions which make no real allowance for the experience and personal meanings of the teachers.

In contrast to Memon's study, which used a multi-method approach, Nelson (1993) adopted the storytelling metaphor to investigate what it means to be a teacher from the perspective of practising teachers. She used narrative enquiry which we discussed in Chapter 5. Nelson argued that, in many investigations into teacher thinking, teachers' voices are neutered. She sent letters to the entire teaching staff of one school district asking them to share their stories about meaningful moments in their teaching careers. Fifty-five teachers eventually contributed stories, those who agreed to participate audio-taping their stories. In this way Nelson felt that the investigator was unobtrusive. She subsequently transcribed the tapes verbatim and, with the help of three independent readers, was able to categorize the stories into eight themes. The 55 participating teachers contributed a total of 146 stories. Nelson emphasized that, even though the stories were self-selected in response to an open invitation, patterns within them revealed some commonality of perspectives and values. The themes were not imposed on the stories but evoked from them. We know from our own experiences as researchers using narrative enquiry that it is often difficult to convey in print the richness and diversity of the teachers' stories. Nevertheless we hope in the following extracts to give you a sense of the teachers' voice for just two of Nelson's categories.

The first extracts refer to the category 'job description' which relates to stories that highlight the challenges, responsibilities or rewards of teaching:

> My philosophy about kids is that generally they'll live up to your expectations. If you expect nothing that is what you will get, on the other hand, if you believe in them and you have very high expectations, with some support and some help and guidance they are going to get there.
>
> On a day to day basis, I found that I am learning from the children all the time, as well as my being able to give them new ways of thinking about themselves and the world they live in ... I want to instil in them my love for learning and the fact that I feel that I can always improve myself and there's always so much out there for me to learn ... (Nelson, 1993: 157)

The most frequently occurring category was labelled the 'student perspective'. Nelson (1993: 160) wrote as follows:

> the most beautiful example of student perspective was evoked when a teacher declined to answer the question, 'why are we here and who made us?' because she felt it was a religious question. However another student said, 'don't worry Mrs C., I'll take care of this one', and proceeded with his rendition of creation.
>
> Well it was like this. One day God was sitting around doing nothing, so he decided that he wanted to colour. So he got the biggest paper he could find ... and the biggest box of crayons he could find ... when he was all finished he looked over the paper and really liked it. He decided that he would just make it real. You see, it is simple and that is why we are here.

Many poignant examples of the teachers' stories provided powerful stimulus material for considering the challenges and rewards of the teaching profession. Nelson's readers who collaborated in categorizing the stories found them of great value. She quotes one of her readers who said 'I realised how much value this would have for anyone interested in teaching ... these stories are wonderful' (Nelson, 1993: 164).

Continuing our theme of presenting different techniques for understanding teachers' own perceptions of teaching we now turn to the work of Martin and Kompf (1996) who used journals and concept mapping techniques to determine teacher concepts of effective teaching and practice in inclusive classroom settings. We discussed concept mapping in Chapter 5. In Canada the trend over the past decade has been the merger of special and mainstream pupils within the same classrooms. Some schools have good support from special education teachers, who provide tremendous resource and support, while others depend heavily on the teachers rising to the challenge of dealing effectively with the task of meeting the needs of all pupils within their classes. Inclusive initiatives have caused much debate among educational researchers and practising teachers regarding the merits of this educational practice.

Martin and Kompf's interest lay in helping to develop strategies for helping teachers face the challenge. As constructivists, Martin and Kompf recognized that the challenge may require a reconstruction of existing concepts. The change in teachers' construing could be minor or, if dramatic changes were required then the radical shift might potentially challenge core constructs. As Martin and Kompf (1996: 96) put it:

> Teachers have a negative bias towards the behaviourally disordered student in the context of the regular education classroom which can be seen to be related to teacher self efficacy as well as a conceptual misperception of the disorder. Unless these two aspects are radically reconstructed, many behaviourally disordered students will find that the legislative and economic forces driving school boards and districts to an inclusive model of educational service delivery, will serve to facilitate their exclusion for an equitable educational opportunity, or at worst, an educational opportunity. Concept mapping and reflective practice along with cognitive rehearsal are identified as powerful heuristics that may well serve this purpose.

Martin and Kompf described cognitive rehearsal as a process by which participants share their recollections and interpretations of experience with another. This allows the participant to reflect on the learning experience and to make sense of what has been experienced. They engaged with their participants over a period of time. Initially they met as a group to discuss the process which had five components. The first component involved a group concept mapping exercise where members of the group brainstormed concepts to be included regarding 'effective teaching' and they decided to create a collaborative concept map that represented the groups perspective. Then each teacher was introduced to a notion of reflective journalling, where they were asked to identify a positive experience involving a 'behaviourally difficult student' and to visualize and recall the incident and make notes of their thoughts and feelings that they could recall regarding the incident. They were also asked to consider a negative experience with the same type of student and follow the same pattern. At the end of the journalling process they were asked to identify a metaphor which captured how the experience (positive or negative) made them feel. The teachers were interviewed at frequent and regular intervals for cognitive rehearsal where the teachers expressed their feelings about the journalling exercise and how they perceived it impinging on their thinking and their practice in the classroom. Towards the end of the period the group met together again to share experiences and to produce a second concept map in a similar way to the construction of the first concept map. Follow-up sessions took place with the group to reflect on the overall findings.

In the first concept map Martin and Kompf found that the teachers' perceived conceptualization of effective teaching practice in the inclusive classroom was very structured. Effective teaching was conceptualized by two superordinate concepts: *program* and *practice*. The program was linked to resources, documents, curriculum guidelines and learning outcomes. It was cross-linked to practice through academic expectations and students. The other overarching or superordinate concept of practice contained items such as students' expectations, skills, methods and training. There were further cross linkages and a superordinate teacher response which represented teachers' efficacy. Teaching effectiveness was seen to be a function of program and practice.

Martin and Kompf report a dramatically different concept map produced on the second occasion. The two key superordinate concepts were no longer *practice* and *program*. These were replaced by the *interaction between teacher and students*. Concepts of documents and guidelines and curriculum were replaced with student input and student outcomes based on abilities and special needs. There were numerous and complex interlinkages with areas related to communication. In the first map, top-down conceptualization reflected a perceived need for control. On the second map this was reversed and the teachers now suggested that, to be effective, they had to relinquish some of that control in order to involve the students in the program as well as in the practice. This inevitably involved some risk. Effective teaching practice was now identified as residing in the relationships between the teachers, the students, parents, support staff and resources. As Martin and Kompf (1996: 100) commented, 'it is a network of team players with much consultation, collaboration and negotiation involved'. They suggested that the methodology of concept mapping (combined with reflecting through journalling and interview) is a powerful tool to illuminate teachers' stories. They point to the utility of sharing the experience with other teachers of inclusive classrooms. In this way some of the frustrations and feelings of being overwhelmed could perhaps be alleviated. Martin and Kompf's study suggests one possible way of assisting teachers to improve practice and to increase meaningful learning for both teachers and students who face the challenge of inclusive classrooms.

From time to time throughout this book we have alluded to some shared assumptions between notions expressed in George Kelly's work and those of other theorists. Watts and Vaz (1997) provided an interesting discussion of some of the shared assumptions between George Kelly and Paolo Freire, particularly with respect to generating themes to capture personal meaning. In comparing personal constructs (Kelly) and 'meaningful thematics' (Freire) Watts and Vaz noted that they both conceive culture as constructed. Kelly assumed people construed their experience in a similar way because they belong to the same cultural group and have come to a common construction of their experience. Freire emphasized the notion that it is people's constructions that consolidate to become a culture. Watts and Vaz suggest that there are a number of parallels between the repertory grid technique and the criteria of Freire's 'thematic investigation'. Watts and Vaz (1997: 334) described the thematic investigation strategy as follows: such a research strategy should:

- probe teachers' theories and practices in equal proportions
- allow investigations to be focussed without the investigator being the one to define the focus
- be dialectic, that is, begin to find within volunteers the concept that they have of themselves and their praxis
- exploit the role frustrations and difficulties in their thinking.

Watts and Vaz (1997: 334) drew on both Freire and Kelly since they both proposed 'forward-looking theories, the former at the level of the culture of the group and the latter at the psychological level of the individual'. Their research centred on the themes which emerged during conversations with primary teachers of science. These were those seen as emotionally significant for them. After the themes were identified these were re-presented to the teachers for further dialogue. They, Watts and Vaz, then designed what they referred to as a 'problematizing' program for teachers' professional development, which drew on the elicited themes for its broad content. They met with the teachers on three different occasions over a period of about four weeks for one hour sessions. In the first session, Watts and Vaz presented the teachers with 22 questions, each written on a card, and teachers were asked to write responses in a designated space. They were also given blank cards to provide any extra elements for discussion. Teachers were asked to recall events marked by a particular emotion to which there was an explicit reference in the question. Some cards prompted positive feelings and others prompted episodes associated with negative feelings.

The teachers were asked to select nine from their set of cards which became the elements in a repertory grid. Personal constructs were elicited using the traditional triadic elicitation method and the repertory grid was analysed using the FOCUS program (Shaw, 1993). The second and third meetings were devoted to conversations with the teachers about their experience and their beliefs and assumptions about the teaching of science. These discussions began with a reflection on the focused grid and according to Watts and Vaz (1997: 336), 'a dialogue with a clearly problematising tone emerges'. The repertory grid techniques allowed the researchers to discuss very specific elements of the teachers' professional knowledge and experience while they were encouraged to justify their personal constructs. Reflection on the grids produced a rich source of generative themes. Watts and Vaz report an example of the many themes which emerged during the course of the conversations. This concerned the teachers' need to exercise 'didactic restraint', to organize their class-rooms for what became known as 'hands-off teaching for hands-off learning'. This theme reflected the teachers' dilemma of hoping to encourage pupils to find out about science for themselves while resisting telling children what to do and conveying the 'received' view of science. We give one example below:

> I think it is better if the activity comes from them because they feel they achieve it on their own. When it comes from them, they can see the value – because they own that work. They have a sense of ownership. If it comes from me I own it ... the challenge for me is to hold back. There is obviously frustration when they go off at a very different tangent and I want to get them back over here. (Watts and Vaz, 1997: 336)

The teachers in Watts and Vaz's study showed a recognition of the impor-tance of the child constructing their knowledge. This is in line with the constructivist principles we discussed in Chapter 2 and which we elabo-rated further in the examples given in Chapter 7. Watts and Vaz (1997: 337) supported this constructivist position when they suggested:

> problematising the notion of 'hands on learning' is just one facet of the teachers' themes arising from the conversations: in this case the criticising of the appropriateness of curriculum wisdom. The act of problematisation provides an opportunity for teachers to free themselves from habitual ways of thinking, to perceive what governs their world and workplace. This is a process of placing learning and thinking into a wider context so that aspects of one's problems are connected to broader social forces. Problematisation helps people to locate their personal problems within a social context; to explore the often contradictory and ambiguous nexus where private troubles meet public issues.

Many of the stories we have considered so far in this chapter have addressed these contradictory and ambiguous situations where the personal meanings of teachers need to be considered alongside other frames of reference. The final study in this section considers this interplay in relation to the lived experiences of change in Swedish language teachers' pedagogical knowledge during their careers. The participants teach English as a foreign language. In the course of her study, Apelgren (work in progress) has analysed the similarities between phenomenology, phenomenography and Personal Construct Psychology. Apelgren noted that phenomenology is seen by her as her 'philosophical tree of knowledge', whereas phenomenography and personal constructivism have provided her with *tools* for data collection and analysis. She used questionnaires combined with career-rivers and interviews which elicited personal narratives from the teachers. Apelgren preferred to call the technique a career-river rather than a snake because 'they showed the flow of the teachers' experiences over time'.

Apelgren asked each teacher to think back on his or her career in terms of a winding river in which each bend represented an experience that had influenced his or her direction. The teacher was then asked to draw this river and write a few words about these critical incidents. The teaching stories that evolved as each teacher discussed the rivers, after they had spent a period alone drawing up their own river were tape-recorded. The rivers became the agenda for the interview and the content of the stories differed depending on the participants, choice of focus.

Despite the individual focus, Apelgren was able to draw out some commonalities in the way her participants had experienced change and development. She identified four major themes, described as 'gaining inspiration from external sources', 'adapting to new directives', 'interacting with colleagues' and 'adopting perspectives from more experienced teachers'. The external sources were in-service training and other courses which provided initiation for individual change and development in teaching. The new directives were the official directives from Swedish education authorities. Interacting with colleagues was one of the most important features for initiating changes for the teachers in Apelgren's study. Teachers welcomed the daily interaction as being essential for development work and fostering change. Adopting the perspective of a more experienced teacher was a specific form of interaction. Apelgren spoke of stories of teachers being 'moulded' and inspired with help from older and more experienced teachers who provided a guide to the profession.

Apelgren also found qualitatively different ways of experiencing language teaching based on the participants' self-perception of the teacher's role and their personal theories of English as a Foreign Language teaching. She has identified four categories with particular metaphors: 'teaching as a mutual affair', 'teaching as guiding with an invisible hand', 'teaching as a social activity' and 'teaching as being a captain of a ship'.

In Chapter 1 we discussed four potential perspectives on teaching and warned about the dangers of stereotyping individuals as falling within one category for all of their engagement with teaching. Apelgren called her categories *orientations* to imply potential fluidity in the teachers' perspectives. The use of narratives and career rivers provided Apelgren with a thick description of the complexity of her participants' personal theories on teaching and their views on their own professional development. She also wished to capture what she referred to as 'voices on participating'. She recognized that the constructivist techniques used in the research required the participants to 'relive certain parts of one's life, also those parts that can be regarded as belonging to one's professional life can be emotional in several ways'. Many of the teachers mentioned how taking part in the study had encouraged them to reflect on their teaching. Some found it traumatic, others found the process enlightening and empowering. Apelgren noted that the opportunity to sit down and recollect past experiences with someone else listening is regarded 'stimulating' and 'satisfying'. This is especially true for those who are near the ends of their careers and have experienced many changes in their professional lives. Further, those in their mid careers described how telling about and structuring their own teaching have made them more aware of their professional role:

> It was interesting and helpful to focus on my own career this way. Life-story perspectives adds to how I see myself as a professional person.

In addition it has made them aware of their everyday teaching:

> It also makes me 'clear my mind' and I have to decide what teaching is about, what goals I have and why I do certain things. Everyday life is so hectic so there is little time to evaluate what you do, what you have done and if you have achieved the goals you set up.

The expression 'clear my mind' indicates a possibility for the teacher to stop and move behind the actual practice, to reflect and recollect. Gaining a perspective means allowing the present to encounter the past, as well as realizing how the past influences one's thinking. Apelgren cited examples of participants who showed 'a strong sense of gratitude in the comments on experiences of taking part in the study'. She noted that 'the process of reflection and recollection of lived experiences can come close to the concepts of *empowering* and *emancipation*'. Part of this is the positive feeling that teachers experience of 'someone listening to their voices'. She gave several examples, one of which we will provide below.

It is satisfying that somebody is interested in your career. Most people like talking about themselves, and so do I. It has made me structure my recollections of the years at school in a way I have found stimulating.

In our view, Apelgren's work represents the spirit of work underpinned by Personal Construct Psychology in that it allows the researcher to gain insights into a phenomena in a way that leaves participants feeling that they have also benefited from the process.

However, before we leave this section on school teachers' thinking we present a contribution from one of our colleagues Carolyn Boulter, whose work with primary school teachers also represents the true spirit of constructivist collaborative enquiry.

Enabling and analysing the construction of scientific knowledge

In science teaching and learning over the last twenty years a major movement has been that of establishing the nature of pupils' existing conceptions about scientific phenomena and the building of curricula which use constructivist principles to progress these understandings. Foremost in England in the field of primary school science has been the work of the Science Process and Concept Exploration (SPACE) group working at Liverpool University (e.g. Russell et al., 1998) charting children's existing conceptions in most of the areas of the science curriculum. From this, a scheme of work for science (e.g. Nuffield Primary Science: The Earth in Space (1995) which involved tasks that teachers could use to elicit pupils understandings and then expand, challenge and test them, was developed. This approach acknowledged that knowledge is personally and socially constructed.

The roots of this approach lay in the personal constructivism and stage theory of Piaget which had informed the Nuffield 5–13 primary science course (Schools Council, 1980) that preceded it. However, it had taken on board the work of social constructivists and theorists such as Vygotsky. Learners were seen as actively constructing their own meanings through intelligent adaptive problem-solving in the company of the teacher, as the interaction between their existing conceptions and new experiences provided by the teacher led to conceptual change. The teacher's role was seen as one of diagnosing the personal knowledge of the pupil and of providing interactional space for ideas and phenomena where that meaning could be mediated towards a more scientifically acceptable understanding.

The reconstruction in pupils' thinking was seen as happening at the personal level within the mind of the individual, and at the group level as the class of learners in group dialogue tried to reach a shared understanding. The research findings influenced the levels at which the content in the new National Curriculum was placed. Sadly, the market-driven performance ethos of the new curriculum and regime of assessing with external tests has reduced the place for the very interactivity which is essential to a constructivist methodology and it has taken a back seat as science classes have reverted to an instructional format.

It is within this context that the work of two projects are discussed here. The first is the work of a small group of primary school teachers who have met for nearly five years to support each other as they carry out research into children's understandings in science in their own classrooms. Because of the commitment of the coordinator Carolyn Boulter, to constructivist and collaborative principles (Boulter, 1992) this group was set up from the start with the following parameters:

The group was committed to researching their own practice and to investigating questions which arose from their own classrooms.

The group decided the limits of the frame of ideas within which they would research and this frame was "understandings of scale" in science.

The coordinator's role was to provide clarification and a firm management structure of meetings and minutes, so that everyone's voice could be heard.

The coordinator's role was to enable the research to take place and to help teachers to reflect on their own ideas and the research of other people, and to bring it to publication for other teachers to read.

Teachers were encouraged to make their mental models explicit and the coordinator did not evaluate these but was available to supply access to previous research when asked.

In this way the teachers themselves were in control of what was being investigated and how it was to be done. They came to agreement through their participation in collaborative discussion. The result is that the knowledge that they built related directly to their own context and was constructed as they argued, tried out their own understandings of the nature of the science learning, discussed how to investigate it and what the results meant. Models were built through this process of individual and social interaction. The continued functioning of the group supports the assumption that it is only when collaborative control and participation in the language of the group are enabled by an appropriate leader, action research project in which constructivist learning can take place. The group has published a book of findings (Boulter, 1997) and several articles for teachers journals (Marsh et al., 1997; 1998; 1999).

The second project (Boulter et al., 1999) started from the same assumptions about the individual and about social construction of knowledge only being possible in collaborative settings, but it is concerned with the learning of ecological principles by teachers in training. This project structured a ten-week course along constructivist lines. Students were taken each week into a different habitat where they raised questions to investigate in small groups. Each week, time was allowed for whole class collaborative discussion of the findings and for the raising of questions for the next week. The group interactions in the field and in the lab were noted, the whole class sessions were recorded and students' poster representations of the environments were collected. The verbal interactions are being analysed to show the patterns of participation and persuasive argument in model building. The poster representations are being analysed for the models they show as the end product of the group reflection. These are then compared with the most complete explanatory model that the lecturers can produce for that habitat. This has required the development of an analysis system that looks at the structure, behaviour and mechanism of the models at various different levels (Buckley and Boulter, 1998). First attempts at the analysis are revealing that the collaborative pedagogy has allowed for complex model building (Gilbert and Boulter, 1998) and a deep involvement in the process of conceptualizing, something which has not been present in previous years.

Both these projects take an integrated individual and social constructivist approach to research and to learning, while they use collaborative principles to enable this construction to take place (Pope *et al.*, 1999).

In this chapter we have chosen examples which adopt this perspective. We have explored the fledgling personal theories of student teacher and recounted some stories from experienced teachers. Most of the students and teachers we have considered so far have been located in the school context. In the next two sections we journey beyond the school and enter the experiential climate of teachers in universities and other professions.

Appraisal, staff development and transforming practice

In many countries the appraisal of teaching competence is commonplace for decisions on tenure or promotion. Although teachers are the ultimate key to educational change and improvement, respect for teacher thinking and teachers' work were not the inspiration for educational reform in England. We discussed system constraints and the work of the teacher in Pope *et al.* (1999). Increasingly teaching in schools and teacher training establishments are being inspected by the Office for Standards in Education (OFSTED). Fuller (1997) argued that the government seems to want to reconstruct teacher professionalism by deconstructing existing arrangements and making teachers more responsible to the demands of the State and the 'market'.

Within Higher Education there are regular subject reviews by the Quality Assurance Agency who undertake teaching quality assessments. While we recognize the importance of 'accountability' in education we suggest that the appraisal of teaching used only as a summative measure neglects an important dimension.

Our constructivist philosophy suggests that what is needed are appraisal procedures that are transformative and lead to increased teacher autonomy. Thus the individual teacher is enabled to take control over his/her development while at the same time achieving increased professional effectiveness. There are echoes of this in Barnett's (1997) thought and in other contemporary texts. Richart (1997) suggested that teacher educators themselves need to research their practice so that a reflective and enquiring stance is conveyed by example to their students. Constructivist techniques have been used to further this aim.

Barnett (1997) presented a challenge to all of those engaged in higher education, academics and students alike. Among the wealth of reforms to thinking and practice which he advocated, one salient to this book is that professionals should evaluate critically their own practice. He recognized that engagement between teaching, learning and research may not be a simple task since educational settings are complex:

> Pedagogical roles and relationships become uncertain, and necessarily invite risk into the proceedings. If students are to be given the space genuinely to form their own critical evaluations, and to engage in critical acts, the educational process has to become uncertain. (Barnett, 1997: 110)

Denicolo (1997) described an action research study in which students and tutors collaborated in exploration of how students' ideas about the role of the teacher evolved during their training. The study afforded Denicolo, her colleagues and their students the opportunity to reflect on various constructs students have regarding the role of the teacher at different stages on the course. The study challenged and amplified the course team's espoused theory, which was intended to develop not just reflective practitioners but practitioners who could evaluate critically their own and each other's practice. Denicolo and her colleagues agreed with Loughran (1997: 654) who noted:

> If teacher educators do not take risks with their own practice, if they do not overtly model the need to extend margins of understanding and experience for their own pedagogy, it makes it difficult for student teachers to believe that the value of taking risks would be worth the discomfort they would experience in practice!

The students on Denicolo's course were involved in a one year PGCEA (Post Graduate Course in the Education of Adults). She utilized repertory grids to encourage the students and tutors on the course to consider the role of the teacher and to evaluate the extent to which the students had changed hopefully throughout the course. Participants were assured that this was not part of the course assessment procedures nor a test for measuring their performance but was a way of evaluating the course. It was conveyed to the students that since it would provide them with feedback on how their ideas were developing, it might prove a useful tool in later stages of their careers for reviewing their own practice and ideas. During the first data collection session each student teacher was provided with a blank grid form on which there were nine labels to represent particular teachers who had taught them in the past, such as in 'teacher who really helped me learn', 'I consider "expert" teacher', 'teacher who put me off learning'.

For each of the elements the participants had to identify a real teacher from their experience, using each person only once, annotating the element label with initials or nicknames that only they would recognize. Denicolo and the group then worked through the traditional repertory grid process that we discussed in Chapter 4. After they had elicited a number of constructs about other teachers they were asked to put their own initials in the last, up to then empty, box at the top of the last column to rate themselves as teachers against the dimensions they had devised for the other teachers. As Denicolo noted, there were a great deal of 'oohs' and 'aahs' and laughs at that point especially from her fellow tutors who also completed grids at the same time.

Student teachers and tutors were then asked to write on the back of the grid a self-characterization sketch or vignette describing themselves in the third person as teachers from the viewpoint of a friend who knew them well in that role and would give an honest description. This material was collected and copied and returned to them, this time with the ratings deleted, part way through the course. They were asked to review the constructs used, deleting any which they felt were no longer appropriate, re-rating those that remained and then adding any new attributes they now felt were important and rating those. These were again copied and returned with similar deletions towards the end of the year and the process repeated. Denicolo (1997) stressed that the main value of the work lay in the discussions that students had with each other and with their tutors regarding their developing views on effective teaching. Further, the course team found value in reviewing the patterns that emerged from the data. Denicolo noted these were a mix of interesting, sometimes rewarding, occasionally challenging and frequently thought-provoking.

From the list of constructs obtained from all the students, Denicolo was able to identify the quantity and what kinds of constructs students came to the course with and how they changed over time. The course team was able to gauge the effects of the first short period of teaching practice and the longer more intensive period of practice in the second half of the year. They were able to consider the extent to which the principles that they had hoped to convey to the students were taken on board by the students or did not seem to have an impact on the students. The team was also able to identify those ideas that they had, as a group, overemphasized.

It was noted that the first category of constructs listed by students at the beginning of the course consisted mainly of the personal descriptive kind such as 'intelligent' as opposed to 'can't go beyond their notes', or 'has a sense of humour' as opposed to 'boring'. An emphasis on 'taking into account student need' increased over the year. Attributes related to teaching methods were very general at first, e.g. *teaches well/badly*. By the second grid a large number of students added constructs related to the ability to maintain control in the classroom while by the third, and final, grid aspects such as 'flexibility in method and style' became a valued dimension. Having acknowledged the value of the exercise Denicolo (1997: 12) warned, though, that it was not a gentle course evaluation process:

> This was not, of course, totally without pain in the process ... some discussions had been warm if not heated, a few feathers were ruffled and so on. Some [staff] were not as eager as others to be themselves part of the exploratory process but had gone along with the idea in principle ... perhaps the most salutary aspect of the experience, and yet one which is difficult to measure, was the increased collegiality between students and staff which tutors reported.

Researching one's own practice, especially with all one's colleagues involved, was a risky business. However, it is a very necessary process in team building and course evaluation.

Bond (personal communication) is concerned to help lecturers of education to reflect on their teaching experiences and to consider how their concepts of their professional self are perceived and change over time. He has noted how experiences early in lecturers' careers appear to set the basis for ongoing development of their professional self-definition, with one area of particular interest being the relationships they develop with their students.

Bond is using repertory grids and reflective interviews in research and development work. Below he describes one strategy he has employed to capture lecturers' views of their professional selves:

> Each lecturer was given a copy of a repertory grid sheet and 11 blank cards. They were asked to number the cards 1 through 10 in the upper right hand corner and the mark the 11th card "self". The lecturers were then asked to designate former primary or secondary school students to the roles indicated on the grid. Choosing different individuals with whom they had been familiar and who had had an impact on themselves as teachers. The 10 roles or elements of the grid were:
>
> - most congenial student
> - least congenial student
> - most successful student
> - least successful student
> - most cooperative student (with teacher agenda)

- least cooperative student (with teacher agenda)
- most supportive student (of teacher)
- least supportive student (of teacher)
- most articulate student
- least articulate student.

The student's name was entered in the appropriate area on the grid and on the card with the corresponding number. The next step was that of construct elicitation, during which respondents were asked to consider selected role figures in triads (with "self" as a constant) and determine a way in which two of them are similar and one is different. For example, the first triad was "self, most congenial student, least congenial student". So cards marked "self" and 1 and 2 were selected from the stack of 11 and arranged on the table. It is preferable that the distinguishing factors (or constructs) pertain to philosophical or psychological dimensions (e.g. passive/active, likes people/loner rather than physical, e.g. tall/short, female/male). A three-point rating scale was used to assign each student and "self" along the construct dimensions, so that each lecturer's view of self was compared with their view of the various students included within the grid. The degree of match with each student was then identified. Information obtained was used to determine the impact of these roles and concepts on their professional self-concepts.

Drawing from the repertory grid and the series of open-ended questions, it was seen that participants identified strongly with students they perceived as possessing qualities which enhance the professional image of the teacher (hard-working, responsible, honest, doing things right, wanting to achieve, focused) as well as desirable personal qualities (musical, caring, outgoing, positive). Student attitudes towards them affected the lecturers' concepts of professional self which they perceived as changing over time. It seems socially significant that the experiences that they related were, spontaneously, drawn from their earliest teaching experiences.

Even in the simple form the Kelly RepGrid is laborious to construct, administer and score. Bond did not use a FOCUS program, however, the process yielded information which was spontaneously generated by the lecturers. Further, the responses obtained have provided a range of insights into personality construction which cannot be obtained from forced-choice category responses, so often used to investigate lecturers' personal meaning.

Professional development and professional training

Increasingly, staff in institutions of Further and Higher Education are collaborating with colleagues in industry and in the public sector to develop approaches to education and training which will help transform practice. Indeed, we have been involved in developing such approaches and have found this work stimulating and rewarding. We have transformed our own practice as a result. In the final section we continue to provide examples of implementation in practice.

Nurse education now falls within Higher Education. Preparing health professionals for practice through education and training also involves professionals with different role remits. Mazhindu (1995) (see also Mazhindu and Pope, 1996) advanced the case for interprofessional education by examining the personal constructs employed by nurse lecturers, practice nurse tutors in universities, in the community and hospitals and students in three discipline areas of nursing – Adult General, Mental Health and Learning Disability (who divide their time between university and practice). Repertory grids explored what for them constituted an 'ideal' nursing student, using as elements particular examples of achieving students, from high to low, and the worst student in their experience as well as their notion of an 'ideal' student. Themes derived from the constructs included attitudes, abilities, personality, academic and behavioural factors. Similarities and differences in the frequency of use of themes, as well as in particular constructs used by each group of participants, were compared. The analysis of the data led to the devising of a Staff and Student Development Strategy.

Mazhindu's staff and student development strategy took the form of a Reflective Workshop which aimed to enable nurse lecturers, nurse practitioners and student nurses to examine their perceptions of student nurses' professional achievements. This provided a means of raising the personal and professional awareness of all parties and a way of sharing understanding regarding the assessment of student nurses' professional achievements. Mazhindu adopted a participatory approach. The completion of repertory grids, feedback on grid content and dialogue among participants was used to further the following aims:

* raise perceptual awareness and identify constructs used;
* examine the similarities and differences noted in the type and nature of constructs used;
* examine, debate and share views about the meaning of the constructs used;
* examine, debate and share views about the level of importance assigned to constructs used;
* empower student nurses not only to debate educational assessment issues on a equal basis with nurse lecturers and nurse practitioners, but also to challenge the assumptions held and decisions made about their professional performances and achievements;
* provide a platform for dialogue, debate, collaboration, cooperation and sharing of ideas between nurse lecturers, nurse practitioners and student nurses as a basis for mutual personal professional development (Mazhindu, 1995: 243–7).

A participant presented an evaluation of the reflective workshop. He found that:

> the debate between the nurse lecturers, nurse practitioners and student nurses was thought to be extremely useful on all sides, as a way of developing an understanding of others' views, sharing perceptions, challenging the opinions held and assumptions made, the examining definitions, terms and labels used to describe student nurses' professional achievements. It was also thought that discussions of this nature might create circumstances whereby theoretical achievements and the development and acquisition of practical skills are seen to be of equal importance, when assessing student nurses from a holistic perspective, instead of seeing theory as more important than practice. Another benefit was thought to be the potential to promote a constructive, collaborative approach to improving personal awareness and professional development – as one person pointed out: 'It is extremely useful to participate and evaluate students *with* the students present, and not imposing on them.' (Nurse lecturer – general nursing)

Earlier we mentioned the work of Tjok-a-Tam. In her thesis (1994), she explored the variety of pressures impinging on colleges of Further and Higher Education which demanded a review of their provision of management education. She then employed an action research approach, using personal construct approaches including Personal Development Journals, critical incident snakes and grids, to illuminate the perspectives of the managers on programmes of study and their teachers about their experiences and needs. Tjok-a-Tam argued that, to enable transformative learning by manager-learners through a process of emancipatory education, a complementary, parallel process of critical, active reflection must be established for the teaching staff-as-learners within innovative educational programmes.

In a contemporaneous study, Denicolo worked with novice teachers from the same education sector, again using an action research approach, to help them reflect on their own learning development as they engaged in their first year of probation. This study incorporated professional self-characterization sketches, completed every three months and used to review the recent months and then the year as a whole. The following is a compilation of some excerpts from one teacher, let us call her Naomie:

In the beginning ...
Naomie started with her new classes feeling very motivated and enthusiastic, but also very worried about whether she could remember all the things she would need to tell her classes. She is very approachable and enjoys the interaction with the students but has a niggling concern about her credibility to them ...

Later in the year ...
Naomie is still enjoying the practical experience and remains enthusiastic but
the lesson preparation takes a long time. She must keep up with her reading as
well as the marking and she is very nervous about experimenting with new
teaching methods. She has discovered that she is a better time manager than
she thought she would be but she does not always remember to project her
voice clearly in larger classes. This is not a problem with small groups but does
lead to repetition and embarrassment in larger ones ...

Near the end of the year ...
A visit by her mentor has boosted her confidence; her teaching voice is coming
more naturally now and she had the opportunity to teach a very large group in
a lecture theatre. Although it was scary, everyone seemed to be able to hear her,
looked interested and asked good questions at the end. Has tried a few new
methods which worked well and the lecture session has encouraged her to let
the students ask more questions and take a more active part in lessons. Still a
lot to learn though ... letting go is hard when she is not yet confident of being in
total control of the situation.

Naomie produced each sketch for a discussion about her progress and
about what aspects of her role she could develop further, and how. These
he left behind and they were only reviewed in toto at the end of the year.
Since she usually declared that she could not remember what she had
written the last time, she was surprised at the threads and themes which
e-occurred but delighted at the progress that was demonstrated in her
thinking about her practice as well as in the practice itself. She had
become used to standing back in a critical stance from the rush and
umble of her professional life, unearthing and confronting her 'niggling
oncerns', and devising steps to address them. Naomie planned to implement the process of 'reflective sketching' as she proceeds with her career
nd declared herself as transforming into her own mentor.

Harwood and Denicolo (1994) were also concerned to listen to
people's voices, and to encourage them to listen to their own, in the realm
of personal and professional development. Their method was the by-now
raditional grid technique but the topic and results are significant here.
The participants were a group of people from a variety of professional
backgrounds working within one large organization; the purpose was to
earn from their experience of participating in any activities which might
conceivably contribute to their learning and development as profes-
ionals. The elements of the grid were derived from a group elicitation of
those activities viewed as developmental. These were then negotiated into
a manageable set to include a range of activities, from individual and
nformal to group and formal. The first point of interest is that, though
hey were given the opportunity to complete separate grids for personal

and for professional development, the majority chose to combine the two, indicating that they saw them as interconnected. All the detail of the analysis cannot be provided here but some points are worthy of note in this context.

More than two-thirds of the participants rated as very similar in-house activities provided by a presenter from the same organization or provided by a specialist from outside. From a purely practical aspect this might be interpreted as representing support for the use of expertise within an organization for staff development activities although a more detailed analysis demonstrated that several caveats are relevant. Proper time away from the temptation or pressing needs of daily activities needs to be guarded and a trusting, confidential atmosphere is needed. Staff development activities should 'widen horizons', 'improve performance' and be 'demonstrably relevant', to name but a few of the positive constructs, while they should not leave a participant feeling 'de-skilled and inadequate' or 'highly isolated' and instructors should 'take individuals seriously'.

It has been claimed (Moses, 1985, for example) that people participating in staff development and training activities want practical advice, prescriptive guidelines, do's and don'ts. The studies we have presented in this section did not support that view. Taken together, the constructs tell a story of the desire by staff for a developmental environment which offers the provocation of, and opportunities for, stretching and extending the individual in dimensions in which he/she is interested while providing the means by which there is time to reflect on what is being achieved. In common with Moses's participants, we have found that individuals did want a supportive climate, but they particularly valued a challenging, interactive learning situation in which views could be shared and discussed in a co-operative manner. They seemed to agree with Pope (1990: 5) that:

> Staff development strategies which do not invite challenge of a person's implicit theories may be seen as comfortable but will not lead to any reappraisal of current theory and practice.

Having been given insights, if only brief ones, into the diversity of contexts in which other professionals have found particular methods illuminative, we hope that readers will by now see the potential relevance for personal construct approaches and methods for their own personal and professional development – a topic we will pursue in the next, and final, chapter.

CHAPTER 9

Anticipation and transformation

Tis with our judgements as our watches, none go just alike, yet each believes his own.

Alexander Pope, *Essay on Criticism*

New things are made familiar, and familiar things are made new.

Samuel Johnson, *The Lives of the English Poets* (on Pope, 1757)

Engaging with change

We began this book by noting that the world in which we live is changing rapidly. Developments in knowledge, technology and modes of delivery of education in response to client demand have produced consequent pressures on teachers for continuous learning beyond that which was previously assumed in more stable eras i.e. the accretion of knowledge and the honing of skills derived from additional experience. Fullan (1991: xiii) raised a salutary question in the preface to his book about educational change, and this was:

> how to get good at change – that is, how to increase the *capacity* of individuals and organisations to know when to reject certain change possibilities, to know when and how to pursue and implement others, and to know how to cope with policies and programs that are imposed on them.

Each of these possible responses to change, that is to resist, engage in or accommodate to it, are improved if they are based on an evaluative stance. Such evaluation requires as a precursor that current purposes and values are rendered explicit to allow for adequate comparisons to be made with proposed modifications and developments. This provides a cognitive framework of justification for responses rather than allowing them to be simple, automatic reactions to perceived threat.

Fullan went on to suggest that even well-intentioned change can cause havoc unless individuals develop a healthy respect for change and ways of adapting to it.

Adapting to change can be problematic. Jones (1994: 302) alluded to the difficulties which may arise if we are unaware of the goggles we wear to view the world. He recognized that 'seeing the world through our own theoretical lenses' is not in itself a problem, however, it can become one when this interpretative process, based on implicit theories and beliefs, remains completely unconscious. Implicit theories that were 'once tools for thoughtful interpretation' become constraints or 'boundaries or frames around what we see and how we interpret experience ... However, once identified, currently held views maybe addressed in a critical way.' A similar view was expressed by Beattie (1995: 143) who argued that:

> to change the way in which we think requires that we make new forms, new relations and connections, and transform what we know by building a reconstructed personal world within which we live out a new and transformed story of ourselves. The personal and the professional are linked in an extricable ways ... In our decisions to become teachers and educational researchers we create situations in which the necessity for continuous learning and professional growth, and the telling and retelling of our stories, is a fundamental aspect of that professionalism.

All of these authors eschew a passive response to change and appear to advocate transformative practice for those involved in education. Their views have some commonality at least with the way in which we described transformatory practice in our prologue, i.e. the development of alternative ways of looking at practice in education which can result in productive change. The essence of these ideas is optimism – the notion derived from Kelly's work that we need not find ourselves painted into a corner – well laced with a commitment to finding ways of actively getting out of the corner. In this final chapter we draw together for the reader some of the innovative ideas that we have proposed in the book, hoping that by now they feel more familiar. We also suggest that the new ways of perceiving the familiar, advocated in the book, present possible ways of facilitating transformative practice.

Connecting threads

As this book draws to a close we felt that it would be helpful to us and, hopefully to our readers, if we were to review and 'lift out the connecting threads' (Dilthey) that have been woven in preceding pages.

In analysing, in Chapter 1, the philosophical approaches which underpin education we drew attention to the diversity of perspectives and the interconnection between views of knowledge, views on learner and the learner, and the practice of education. We recognized these as alternative viewpoints that had powerful implications. Often these beliefs go unchallenged and remain tacit. Drawing on published and current work of our own, our colleagues and our research students, we gave a flavour of the possibilities inherent in a range of diverse educational contexts.

In focusing on the learner as a personal scientist, we described explorations carried out by teachers and researchers designed to reveal, and encourage, meaningful learning at school. Several of these studies addressed the pupils' implicit theories regarding scientific concepts while others revealed the development of understanding in other areas of the curriculum. Challenges inherent in understanding adolescents' 'anti-social behaviour' were identified. So too, were the challenges of providing an effective education for able children. Many of the examples we explored are consistent with the direction suggested by Rudduck *et al.* (1996: 3) who argued: 'we need to involve pupils in talking about what makes learning difficult for them, what diminishes motivation, and engagement, what makes some give up or settle for minimum effort'. These authors suggested that 'learning is much more powerful when it involves partnerships and mutual learning amongst pupils, teachers and parents'.

Throughout this book we have stressed the importance of the teacher engaging with the pupil's perspective. We have also acknowledged the pressures of today's complex educational environment and the relentless, and often contradictory, exhortations to change demanded of teachers in our schools. Teachers, in a range of educational contexts, are vital in the pursuit of change and development. It is for this reason we have provided examples of ways in which the teachers implicit beliefs about education have been revealed. We have suggested that it is helpful to begin with student teachers' epistemology and beliefs regarding teaching. The experienced teachers personal and practical knowledge has been considered in a number of studies. We have also recognized that teaching and learning in Higher Education and the interface between Higher Education and the Professions are also areas of interest that benefit from adopting a Personal Construct Psychology approach.

We suggested that education as defined within Personal Construct Psychology approaches to education, described in detail in Chapter 2, had more to offer in that it encourages the engagement of the individual with their own learning in contexts which make that learning not only relevant but necessary and sometimes urgent.

These approaches, we proposed, involved activities that:

- encouraged the examining of ideas afresh, both those derived from received wisdom and those composed of personal theories and assumptions;

- involved self-consciously assessing personal and professional relevance;
- stimulated the re-interpretation of knowledge instead of the taking for granted of that which is presented;

This seems to us an appropriate and transformative way for students and teachers to engage in learning. Many professionals that we have encountered in the course of our work recognize this description in the sense that it aligns with their espoused theories about how their own development should proceed. On the other hand, they have, and continue to do so, reported that they frequently find difficulty in changing habitual methods and 'theories in use' in work contexts fraught with work overload and staff shortages. They also reported that the constraining effects of theories imposed from without, often from government policy, sometimes left a feeling of powerlessness. Other authors have noted the erosion of professional autonomy at a general level and the diminishing of a personal sense of efficacy at the individual level. For instance, Handy (1985), in his report of working within organizations which were in danger of fading away because they were unable to change, described staff as 'beavering away' at what they did best, working harder and more efficiently at diminishing tasks. They may, of course, be preserving current values but this analogy conveys an unreasoned response to imposed pressure.

A picturesque example of a similar notion was provided by Cuthbert (1988). He saw the staff symbolically as captive GERBILS (an acronym for the Great Education Reform Bill), condemned to run endlessly on a tread-mill, dissipating energy, perhaps becoming leaner and fitter, but without making any progress in the sense of conserving what is good and making use of opportunity for productive change. There is further evidence of the human cost to staff of failure to recognize the implication of imposed change. Castling (1983) spoke of the intolerable levels of stress experienced by individuals during times of rapid change within their organizations. Change can be energy-draining, time-consuming and personal costs include the feelings of insecurity when expertise seems threatened, the associated loss of self-esteem, the fear of failure and demotivation. These can be profound and far-reaching.

In such circumstances it is important that tools are found which empower people by allowing them to own changes to be made to their practice. Such ownership derives from change chosen as having *personal* relevance that results from research and explorations that are salient to the context and to fellow, respected professionals. Thus their behaviour can be deemed *professional* in the proper sense of the word since it incorporates the autonomy and informed, balanced judgement that society expects of its professionals. Consideration of what kinds of research might appropriately inform such judgements was given in Chapter 3, in which we noted the limitations of research:

- which neglects the importance of understanding the view of the world held by the actors in any situation;
- which misguidedly assumes objectivity;
- and which adheres to well-practised processes with traditional tools which barely skim the surface of an interaction.

We described a contrasting, more imaginative and, we argued, more scientific approach which encourages the exploration of alternative perspectives and understandings. In the three chapters which followed we then presented a range of tools, starting with the well-known repertory grid in Chapter 4 but then expanding, in Chapter 5, the principles which underpin that structured technique to a plethora of mechanisms which provide a framework for in-depth exploration of human construing. In Chapter 6 we amplified on ways to successfully implement these techniques, providing in Chapters 7 and 8 examples of their application in teaching and learning.

Often the ideas of educational theorists are firmly focused on the learner as the main actor in the process. Teaching is generally understood to be a process that involves finding ways to help others engage with learning. We have suggested that this only a partial account. The very engagement suggested by educational theorists inevitably means that teachers too must be continually engaged in learning – for instance what resources might be available, what might be viewed differently, when to act and when to leave well alone, to name but a few possibilities. To eschew the notion of a passive learner means that teachers cannot afford to be passive teachers. We often use the titles 'teacher' and 'learner' for administrative convenience to denote, perhaps length and range of experience and to ensure that support is supplied more in one direction than another, rather than to represent the kind of *processes engaged in.* We have suggested a more symbiotic relationship. The activities of teaching and learning are best intimately combined, each gaining from the other. We would hope that this symbiotic relationship could exist in all educational contexts from the school, through initial teacher training, in the practice of the experienced teacher in schools, further and higher education and in the practice of professional education.

These connecting threads are not intended to be a comprehensive but we trust that they serve to highlight the potential of a range of techniques that promote understanding and transformation. One vital dimension is the sharing of individual and group perspectives, through dialogue.

Implementing a dialogue

In the course of these chapters we have emphasized the value of liberating the mind from past habits by rigorous examination of current thinking. Although we have acknowledged that we cannot entirely escape our perspectives derived from previous experience, and that our current ways of knowing and ways of being may have many forms of value, we have challenged the notion that we are hostage to past involvements. In effect, we recognize the worth of role models etc. but urge that they do not become role corsets! We suggested dialogue as the starting point, but we reiterate here that the first dialogue should be with one's own self, recognizing that current hypotheses are open to gradual challenge or dramatic invalidation and that learning is a personal, creative act. Only then can we effectively engage with others in their personal journeys of learning. In that activity the process of stimulating the articulation of ideas and perspectives is paramount for, unless and until they are articulated, they cannot be challenged, nor can we, our colleagues and our students in negotiation with participants, be experimental in devising strategies to put them to the test. We have, in our examples, indicated that the techniques we and others have devised provide powerful means of clarifying thoughts and of promoting consideration of self-managed change.

This latter point serves to remind us that any intervention should be a co-operative venture, though there may be an educative intent to transform the practice of others to help them to make it more effective. The dynamic evolution of a profession in response to the needs of the culture in which it is embedded is generally perceived as positive, not just expedient but desirable. However, although at the macroscopic level general movement may be identified as forward in direction, at the microscopic level, from the individual teacher or student's perspective, it may seem more like apparently random motion. They may feel buffeted, like particles in the smoke rising from a chimney, by innumerable, and sometimes invisible, external pressures. It is proposed here that PCP, in providing processes which allow teachers to share their constructions of their roles and remits, to identify activities they feel impelled to engage in and the paths they choose to take and why, would both raise their consciousness about the direction of their learning and allow them to hone the contribution they can make to transforming the experiences of their students.

Throughout this book we have focused on the *individual* as he/she develops as a person and as a professional but recognize that construing

ncludes a *social* dimension. Kelly recognized this himself and hence the
ommonality and sociality corollaries are important aspects of the theory.
Iowever, as psychologists we have an abiding concern with the individual
nd seek to redress the prevalent social emphasis on social determinism in
nuch of the literature on education and training. Society through the
rocesses of socialization certainly influences individuals in their develop-
nent, personal or professional, but we take the view that these processes
re mediated through the individual as they chose to be influenced by
hem, to a greater or lesser extent, or to choose which of competing
iscourses to heed or resist and which to validate themselves or their
ractice by.

Thus, we contend that PCP processes and techniques have an impor-
int contribution to make to education because they have the potential for
romoting *real* development of teacher and students rather than
nposing 'pseudo-development' through the re-packaging of 'old and
me-weary products' based on traditional education and training
echniques (Gleeson and Mardle, 1980: 149). Developing staff, or rather
nstigating self-development, is not about merely providing new tools but
bout helping people to choose their own and to learn the skills to use
nem and their own abilities to the full.

Interventions which will succeed in this aim will result from careful
onsideration of the paradigm in which they are based and its appropriate-
ess for professional transformation. Their design demands careful
lanning, with methods chosen which fit comfortably with the aims of the
roject, the context in which it is embedded and the ability and needs of
ne participants. Attention needs to be paid to time factors in terms of
nanageability of the task, how much the participants are willing to commit
nd when it might be feasible to ask that commitment of them. Preparation
me is also paramount. We have indicated throughout the sections dealing
vith techniques that some of them need a degree of practice for successful
nplementation, though they are extremely powerful when used well.
qually, time beyond that required for the implementation of some of these
owerful techniques may be required so that participants can draw on
upport, having confronted previously submerged ideas or challenged
trongly held ones. A final demand is that for flexibility, a willingness to
nonitor and review the process continuously, on the part of the investi-
ator or researcher. Although some adjustments might be relatively trivial,
erhaps a subtle change of emphasis to incorporate additional needs
dentified during the process, others may be more swingeing. Some possi-
ilities are that a change in technique might be required when the planned
ne proves less fruitful or it may be that a need for a follow-up becomes
bvious as the exploration develops. Even the best laid plans ...!

A choice: to join the dance or remain a spectator

In workshops which we run as part of the Centre for Personal Construct Psychology in Education to introduce the philosophy and approaches to novices we are similarly at pains, as we have been above, to provide caveats and warnings to potential users, yet each year new members join the group. Equally, each year we are able to provide reports not only of successful and innovative research and satisfied customers of our consultancy, but also of the enthusiastic reception of the ideas and techniques by those who participated in constructivist activities, interventions and research with us and our students. Sometimes colleagues jokingly accuse us of casting a spell over student participants in such workshops. Sadly this metaphor of weaving magic belies the hard work and dedication required of proponents and users of PCP, so we invite you now to reflect on what you have learnt during your reading of this book.

We recognize that within this wealth of ideas that we have presented there may be some which resonate with yours while others may be more provocative. If there is sufficient resonance then you may be tempted to adopt a PCP approach within your working practice. Our own experience suggests that this will be a challenging task to undertake. Our empathy with your plight is demonstrated from the following summary provided in a recent paper (Denicolo, 1996b: 56):

> One of the frustrating things about espousing a personal construct philosophy, or indeed any of a range of phenomenological approaches to research, is that it behoves one to take into account an astonishing variety of possible interpretations or alternative constructions of reality. Holding to the tenets of these approaches does not compel one to agree with all the options or to rate them equally, but it does present an *embarras de choix* on which to base personal selection to inform decision making. How much easier it would be to return to a childlike belief that there is an answer to every problem as long as one conforms to a simple set of rules and obtains the relevant information from experts and books.
>
> Few of us are very old before we discover that the rules are not simple, nor is there only one set, and that experts frequently disagree and sometimes 'don't know'.

A declaration in that paper was that we increasingly find ourselves having to make choices in a field of uncertainty and in the face of contradictory evidence.

Our choices may imply transformations or to use George Kelly's term 'transitions'. Kelly (1955: 486) recognized that having to consider change can engender emotional experiences which maybe liberating or may result in the denial of the need for change, i.e. hostility. He noted that 'construct&

enable a person to hear recurrent themes in the onrushing sound and fury of life'. The construct system generally remains 'relatively serene and secure'; however, at times 'constructs themselves undergo change. And it is in the transitions from theme to theme that most of life's puzzling problems arise.' Our serene and secure constructs provide us with a frame for anticipating events. These personal theories are useful for prediction. However, if our predictions do not allow us to embrace future experiences, transitions or transformations of our construct system need to occur. Choices must be made. Progress will occur if we are courageous in the choices we make when faced with complex dilemmas.

Since we cannot rely on conventional wisdom that implores us to look before we leap knowing that s/he who hesitates is lost, we take heart from Nussbaum (1985: 260) who declared:

> The experience of conflict can also be a time of learning and development ... a progress that comes from an increase in self knowledge and knowledge of the world.

Miller (1994) also provided consolation drawn from his work exploring the value of introducing the consideration of dilemmic situations into the school curriculum. This led him to suggest that by helping others to recognize the existence of dilemmas and by the encouragement of debate on their resolution, active learning can be assisted, which includes relativistic reasoning, dialectical thinking and reflective moral judgement. From another viewpoint, Goodlad (1984: 297) provided this additional salutary reminder:

> education for a profession is the product of several competing interests which act as checks and balances on one another. If any one agency comes to dominate at the expense of the others, then the rich, pluralistic (and therefore potentially democratic) texture of education will be diminished.

We implore you to take advantage of a 'still point', having reached the end of this book, to consider the implications for your views of the world, and those of others with whom you might engage, if you decide to try out and experiment with the approach and techniques. We may have raised your awareness simply and sufficiently that you give pause occasionally to consider whether your constructs might be constraining you unnecessarily, or you may like to create opportunities for sharing views and perspectives with others, or you may choose to implement some of the techniques and ideas in the process of your work or even to engage in formal research about it. For our part, we will continue to stretch the notions embedded here to their limits, to experiment creatively with alternative techniques, yet adhering to the founding philosophy of the approach – to value and to try to understand and to learn from other ways of being. We would be delighted if, after due reflection, you joined us in the dance, sometimes following our footsteps, sometimes improvising your own.

References

Adams-Webber JR (1970) Elicitated versus provided constructs in Repertory Grid Technique: A Review. Br. J. Med. Psychol. 43: 349–53.7.

Adelman C, Walker R (1975) Developing pictures for other frames; action research and case study. In Chanan G and Delmont S (eds) Frontiers of Classroom Research. Slough: NFER.

Aguirre JM, Haggerty FM, Linder CJ (1990) Student teachers' conception of science teaching and learning: a case study in pre-service science education. International Journal of Science Education 12(4): 381–90.

Albanese M (1999) Feeding the needs of the dual mind: application and implications of a dual creative and analytical thinking mode approach to academic writing instruction. Unpublished PhD. University of Reading, UK.

Allport GW (1955) Becoming. New Haven: Yale University Press.

Apelgren B (work in progress).

Ashwin P (2000) An Anatomy of Peer Learning: An examination of the implementation operation and significance of Peer Support at Newham College of Further Education. Unpublished PhD. University College, London, UK.

Ausubel DP (1968) Educational Psychology: a Cognitive View, 2nd edn. New York: Holt, Rinehart & Winston.

Bakan D (1967) On Method: Towards a Reconstruction of Psychological Investigation. San Francisco: Jossey-Bass Inc.

Bannister D, Fransella F (1971) Inquiring Man. London: Penguin.

Bannister D, Mair JMM (1968) The Evaluation of Personal Constructs. London: Academic Press.

Barnett R (1997) Higher Education: a critical business. Buckingham: Society for Research into Higher Education, Open University Press.

Bateson G (1972) Steps to an Ecology of Mind: Collected essays. Anthology; Psychiatry, Evolution and Epistemology. San Francisco: Chandler Pub. Co.

Beail N (ed.) (1985) Repertory Grid Techniques and Personal Constructs: Applications in Clinical and Educational Settings. Cambridge Mass: Brookline Books.

Beattie M (1995) Constructing Professional Knowledge in Teaching: A Narrative of Change and Development. Toronto: OISE Press.

Bell B, Gilbert J (1996) Teacher Development: A model from Science Education. London: Falmer Press.

Ben-Peretz M (1984) Kelly's theory of personal constructs as a paradigm for investigating teacher thinking. In Halkes R, Olson JK (eds) Teacher Thinking: A New Perspective on Persisting Problems in Education. Lisse: Swets & Zeitlinger, 103–12.

Bentley D, Watts DM (1992) Communicating in School Science. London: Falmer Press.

Berger PL, Luckmann T (1967) The Social Construction of Reality. London: Allen Lane.

Berman LM, Roderick JA (1973) The relationship between curriculum development and research methodology. J.Res.Devel.Educ. 6(3): 30–13.

Biggs JB (1976) Educology! the theory of educational practice. Contemp. Educ Psychol. 1: 274–84.

Blase JJ (1986) A qualitative analysis of sources of teacher stress: consequences for performance. American Journal of Educational Research 22: 13–40.

Bloom BS (1953) Thought processes in lectures and discussions. Journal of General Education 7: 160–9.

Blumer H (1966) Psychological implications of the thought of George Herbert Mead. AM. J.Soc. 71: 535–48.

Blumer H (1978) Methodological principles of empirical science. In Denzin N (ed.) Sociological Methods: A source book. NY: McGraw-Hill.

Boei F, Corporaal A, Wim H (1989) Describing teacher cognitions with the rep grid. In Lowyck J, Clark CM (eds), Teacher Thinking and Professional Action. Leuven: Leuven University Press.

Bond (personal communication).

Boulter C (1992) Collaborating to Investigate Questions: A Model for Primary Science. Unpublished PhD Thesis. University of Reading, UK.

Boulter C (ed.) (1997). Aspects of Primary Children's Understandings of Scale: Work by the Teacher/Researchers within the MISTRE Primary Classroom Reseach Group. Reading: The New Bulmershe Papers.

Boulter C, France B, Buckley B (1999) Understanding decay: models in biology and biotechnology. Presented at NARST Annual Meeting, Boston, MA, 28-31 March 1999.

Britton J (1976) Bread and Water. J.Educ.Thought 10: 3–4.

Bruner JS (1966) Towards a Theory of Instruction. New York: Norton.

Bruner JS (1990) Acts of Meaning. Cambridge, Mass: Harvard Univ Press.

Buber M (1965) Between Man and Man. New York and London: Macmillan.

Buckley B, Boulter C (1998) Analysis of representations in model-based teaching and learning in science. Presented at the VRI '98 Conference, University of Liverpool, UK. 22–23 September 1998.

Burnard P (1999) Into different worlds: children's experience of musical improvisation and composition. Unpublished PhD. University of Reading, UK.

Burr V, Butt T (1992) Invitation to Personal Construct Psychology. London: Whurr.

Cabaroglu N (1999) Development of student teachers' beliefs about learning and teaching in the context of a one-year postgraduate Certificate of Education programme in modern foriegn languages. Unpublished PhD. University of Reading, UK.

Candy P (1990) Repertory grids: playing verbal chess. In Mezirow J et al. (eds), Fostering Critical Reflection in Adulthood: A Guide to Transformative and Emancipatory Learning. Jossey-Bass: San Francisco.

Carlgren I (1996) Professionalism and teachers as designers. In Kompf M, Bond WR, Dworet D, Boak TR (eds) Changing Research and Practice: Teachers' Professionalism, Identities and Knowledge. London: Falmer Press.

Carr W, Kemmis S (1986) Becoming Critical: Education, Knowledge and Action. London: Falmer Press.

Castling A (1983) Staff development: a case study on stress. In Squires (ed.), Innovation through Recession. SRHE Conference: Society for Research in Higher Education.

Chin P (1997) Teaching and Learning in teacher education: who is carrying the ball? In Loughran J, Russell T (eds), Teaching about Teaching: Purpose, Passion and Pedagogy in Teacher Education. London: Falmer Press.

Clandinin DJ (1986) Classroom Practice: Teacher Images in Action. London: Falmer Press.

Clark CM (1986) Ten years of conceptual development in research on teacher thinking. In Ben-Peretz M, Bromme R, Halkes R (eds), Advances in Research on Teacher Thinking. Lisse, Netherlands: Swets and Zeitlinger.

Clark CM (1995) Thoughtful Teaching. London: Cassell.

Cohen L, Manion L (1989) Research Methods in Education. London: Routledge.

Colinvaux D (1992) Theories and conceptions of change: a study in science education. Unpublished PhD. University of Reading, UK.

Connelly FM, Clandinin DJ (1984) Personal Knowledge at Bay St. School: Ritual, Personal Philosophy and Image. In Halkes R, Olsen JK (eds), Teacher Thinking: A New Perspective on Persisting Problems in Education. Lisse, Netherlands: Swets & Zeitlinger.

Connelly FM, Clandinin DJ (1990) C and C stories of experience and narrative inquiry. Educational Researcher 19(5): 2–14.

Cooley CH (1964) Human Nature and the Social Order. New York: Schoken.

Cormack DFS (1996) The critical incident technique. In Cormack DFS (ed.), The Research Process in Nursing, 3rd edn. Oxford: Blackwell Sciences.

Cortazzi M (1993) Narrative Analysis. London: Falmer Press.

Cortazzi D and Roote S (1975) Illuminative Incident Analysis. London: McGraw-Hill.

Cox CB and Dyson AE (1969) The Fight for Education; and The Crisis in Education. Black Papers 1 and 2, Critical Quarterly Society.

Crotty M (1998) The Foundations of Social Research: Meaning and Perspective in the Research Process. London: Sage.

Cuthbert R (ed.) (1988) Going Corporate. Occasional Paper. Further Education Staff College: Blagdon.

Dalton P, Dunnett G (1992) A Psychology for Living. Chichester: Wiley and Sons.

Davies T (personal communication)

Deforges C, McNamara D (1979) Theory and practice: methodological procedures for the objectification of craft knowledge. British Journal of Teacher Education 2: 145–52.

Denicolo PM (1996a) Explorations of constructivist approaches in continuing professional education: staff development for changing contexts. In Kalekin-Fishman D, Walker B (eds), The Construction of Group Realities. Malabar, Florida: Krieger Publishing Company, 267–82.

Denicolo PM (1996b) Productively confronting dilemmas in educational practice and research. In Kompf M, Bond R, Dworet D, Boak RT (eds), Changing Research and Practice: Teachers' Professionalism, Identities and Knowledge. London: Falmer Press.

Denicolo PM, Entwistle N, Hounsell D (1992) What is Active Learning. Sheffield: CVCP/SDTU.

Denicolo PM (1997) Developmental evaluation of teacher training courses: an example of student/teacher partnership. A paper presented at the International Study Association on Teacher Thinking. 8th Biennial Conference, Kiel, October.

Denicolo PM, Pope ML (1990) Adults Learning – Teachers Thinking. In Day C, Pope ML, Denicolo PM (eds), Insight into Teachers' Thinking and Practice. London: Falmer Press.

Denicolo PM, Pope ML (1994) The postgraduate's journey – an interplay of roles. In Zuber-Skerritt O, Ryan Y (eds), Quality in Postgraduate Education. London: Kogan Page.

Denzin NK, Lincoln YS (eds) (1984) Handbook of Qualitative Research. London: Sage.

Dewey J (1916) Democracy and Education: An Introduction to the Philosophy of Education. New York: Free Press.

Dewey J (1938) Experience and Education. New York: Macmillan.

Dewey J, Dewey E (1915) Schools of Tomorrow. New York: Dutton and Co.

Dewey J, McLellan (1895) Early Works 1882–98, Vol. 5. S Illinois, Carbondale; London: London University Press; New York: Schaffer and Simon (1972).

Diamond CPT (1985) Fixed role treatment: enacting alternative scenarios. Australian Journal of Education 29(2): 161–73.

Diamond CPT, Mullen CA (1999) Post Modern Educator: Arts-Based Inquiries and Teacher Development. New York: Peter Lang Pub. Inc.

Dilthey W (1976) W Dilthey -Selected Writings. Ed. and transl. Rickman HP Cambridge: Cambridge University Press.

Dolk M, Korthagen P, Wubbels T (1999) Instruments to investigate knowledge in teaching situations. Paper presented to ISATT Conference Dublin July 1999.

Douglas B, Moustakas C (1984) Heuristic Inquiry: the Internal Search to Know. Detroit: Center for Humanistic Studies.

Driver R (1982) Children's Learning in Science. Educational Analysis 4(2): 69–79.

Driver R, Guesne P, Tiberghien A (1985) Children's Ideas in Science. Milton Keynes: Open University Press.

Driver R, Oldham B (1986) A constructivist approach to curriculum development in science. Studies in Science Education 13: 105–22.

Driver R, Squires A, Rushworth P, Wood-Robinson V (1992) Making Sense of Secondary Science: Support Materials for Teachers. Leeds: Routledge.

Egan G (1975) The Skilled Helper. California: Wadsworth.

Eisner EW (1985) (ed.) Learning and Teaching the Ways of Knowing. Chicago: University of Chicago Press.

Eisner EW (1988) The primary experience and the politics of method. Educational Researcher 17(5): 15–20.

Eisner EW (1993) Forms of understanding and the future of educational research. Educational Researcher 22(7): 5–11.

Ekman P (1969) Body position, facial expression, and verbal behaviour during interviews. Journal of Abnormal and Social Psychology 68: 295–301.

Elbaz F (1990) Knowledge and discourse: the evolution of research on teacher thinking. In Day C, Pope ML, Denicolo PM (eds), Insights into Teachers' Thinking and Practice. London: Falmer Press.

Elliott J (1995) What is good action research? some criteria. Action Researcher 2: 10–11.

Elliott J, Whitehead D (eds) (1980) Action Research for Professional Development and Improvement in Schooling. Cambridge: CARN Publications.

Ely M, Vinz R, Downing M, Anzul M (1997) On Writing Qualitative Research – Living by Words. London: The Falmer Press.

Esland GM (1971) Teaching and learning as organisation of knowledge. In Young MFD (ed.), Knowledge and Control. London: Collier Macmillan.

Fals-Borda O, Rachman MA (1991) Action and knowledge: breaking the monopoly with participatory action research. New York: Apex.

Fox D (1983) Personal theories of teaching. Studies in Higher Education 8(2). |

Fransella F (1983) What sort of scientist is the person-as-scientist. In Adams-Webber J, Mancuso JC (eds) Applications of Personal Construct Theory. Toronto: Academic Press.

Fransella F, Bannister D (1977) A Manual for Repertory Grid Technique. London: Academic Press.

Freire P (1973) By learning they can teach. Convergence 6(1).

Frensham P, White R, Gunstone R (1994) The Content of Science: a Constructivist Approach to its Teaching and Learning. London: Falmer Press.

Freud S (1913) The claims of psycho-analysis to the scientific interest – the educational interest. In Strachey J (ed.) (1953) The Complete Psychological Works of Sigmund Freud, Vol. 13. London: Hogarth Press.

Fullan MG (1991) The New Meaning of Educational Change. London: Cassell Education Ltd.

Fuller M (1997) Partnership between schools and higher education. A paper presented as the International Study Association on Teacher Thinking. 8th Biennial Conference, Kiel, October.

Garfinkel H (1967) Studies in Ethnomethodology. New Jersey: Prentice Hall.

Gilbert J, Boulter C (1998) Learning science through models and modelling. In Fraser B and Tobin K (eds), International Handbook of Science Education, Vol. 2, section 1.4.

Gilbert JK, Pope ML (1982) School children discussing energy. Unpublished manuscript. Guildford: Institute of Educational Development, University of Surrey, UK.

Gilbert JK, Pope ML (1984) Making Use of Research into Teaching and Learning. Institute of Educational Development, Guildford: University of Surrey.

Gleeson D, Mardle G (1980) Further Education or Training; A Case in the Theory and Practice of Day-Release Education. London: Routledge & Kegan Paul.

Goodlad S (ed.) (1984) Education for the Professions, Quis custodiet? Guildford: SRHE | and NFER-Nelson, 297–302.

Goodman N (1984) Of Mind and Other Matters. Cambridge, Mass: Harvard University Press.

Goodman P (1972) Compulsory Miseducation. London: Penguin.

Goodson I (1996) Representing teachers: Bringing teachers back in. In Kompf M et al. Changing Research and Practice. London: Falmer Press.

Goodson I, Hargreaves A (eds) (1996) Teachers' Professional Lives. London: Falmer | | Press.

Guba EG, Lincoln YS (1989) Fourth Generation Evaluation. Newby Park, Ca: Sage.

Guba EG, Lincoln YS (1994) Competing paradigms in qualitative research. In Denzin NK, Lincoln YS (eds), Handbook of Qualitative Research. Thousand Oaks, Ca: Sage.

Habermas J (1971) Knowledge and Human Interest. Boston: Beacon Press.

Halkes R, Olson JK (eds) (1984) Teacher Thinking: A New Perspective on Persisting Problems in Education. Lisse, Netherlands: Swets and Zeitlinger.

Hamilton D, Delamont S (1974) Classroom research: a cautionary tale. Res Educ 11: 1–15.

Handy C (1985) Understanding Organisations, 3rd edn. Harmondsworth: Penguin.

Hargreaves A (1994) Changing Teachers, Changing Times. London: Cassell.

Harwood AG, Denicolo PM (1994) Views on personal and professional development: listening to people's voices. In Scheer J and Catina A (eds), Empirical Constructivism in Europe. Giessen: Psychosozial-Verlag, 220–8.

Henessey F (1993) Situated cognition and cognitive apprenticeship: implications for classroom learning. Studies in Science Education 22: 1–41.

Holt J (1966) How Children Fail. London: Pitman.

Howard GS (1988) Kelly's thoughts at age 33: suggestions for conceptual methodological refinements. International Journal of Personal Construct Psychology 1: 263–72.

Huberman M (1989) The Lives of Teachers. London: Cassell.

Hudson L (1968) Frames of Mind. London: Methuen.

Hull C (1943) Principles of Behaviour. New York: Appleton Century Croft.

Hutchins RM (1936) The Higher Learning in America. New Haven, Conn: Yale University Press.

Iantaffi A (1997) Chorus and solos: sharing educational rivers, winding interviews and biting snakes. Paper presented at the British Educational Research Association Research Students Conference, University of York.

Iantaffi A (1999) Lost tales? The academic experiences of some disabled women students in higher education in England. Unpublished PhD. University of Reading, UK.

Illich I (1971) De-Schooling Society. New York: Harper & Row.

Jones B (1989) In conversations with myself: becoming an action researcher. In Lomax P (ed.), The Management of Change. BERA Dialogue No 1 Multilingual Matters Ltd.

Jones BL (1994) Qualitative enquiry into aspects of school-based tutoring in secondary schools in the context of initial teacher education. Unpublished PhD, University of Reading, UK.

Jordon DC (1973) ANISA: A new comprehensive early education model for developing human potential. J. Res. Dev.Educ. 6(3): 83–93.

Joyce B (1972) Curriculum and humanistic education. In Weinberg C (ed.), Humanistic Foundations of Education. New Jersey: Prentice Hall.

Kalekin-Fishman D, Walker B (eds) (1996) The Construction of Group Realities. Florida: Krieger.

Kelly GA (1955) The Psychology of Personal Constructs, Vols 1 & 2. New York: WW Norton and Co. Inc. Republished (1991) London: Routledge.

Kelly GA (1966) Fixed role therapy. MS prepared as a chapter in Jurjuvich M (ed.) Handbook of Direct and Behaviour Therapies. Unpublished.

Kelly GA (1969a) Ontological acceleration. In Maher B (ed.), The Collected Papers of George Kelly: Clinical Psychology and Personality. New York: John Wiley.

Kelly GA (1969b) The strategy of psychological research. In Maher B (ed.), The Collected Papers of George Kelly: Clinical Psychology and Personality. New York: John Wiley.

Kelly GA (1969c) The language of hypothesis: man's psychological instrument. In Maher B (ed.), The Collected Papers of George Kelly: Clinical Psychology and Personality. New York: Wiley, 147–62.

Kelly GA (1970a) A brief introduction to personal construct theory. In Bannister D (ed.), Perspectives on Personal Construct Theory. London: Academic Press.

Kelly GA (1970b) Behaviour as an experiment. In Bannister D (ed.), Perspectives on Personal Construct Theory. London: Academic Press.

Kemmis S, McTaggart R (1982) The Action Research Planner. Victoria: Deacon University Press.

Knowles M (1978) The Adult Learner – A Neglected Species, 2nd edn. Houston: Gulf Publishing Co.

Koestler A (1976) The vision that links the poet, the painter and the scientist. The Times, 25 Aug.

Kolb D, Fry F (1975) Towards an Applied Theory of Experiential Learning. London: Wiley.

Kompf M (1999) There is more to me than my story – examination of what narrative researchers leave behind. Paper presented at the 9th Biennial meeting of the International Study Association on Teachers and Teaching, St Patrick's College, Dublin, 25–31 July.

Kuhn TS (1970) Logic of discovery or psychology of research. In Lakatos I, Musgrave A (eds), Criticism and the Growth of Knowledge. Cambridge: Cambridge University Press.

Laing RD (1967) The Politics of Experience. London: Penguin.

Lakatos I (1970) Falsification and the methodology of scientific research programmes In Lakatos I, Musgrave A (eds), Criticism and the Growth of Knowledge. Cambridge: Cambridge University Press.

Lakoff G, Johnson M (1980) Metaphors We Live By. Chicago: University of Chicago Press.

Lawless C, Smee P, O'Shea T (1998) Using concept sorting and concept mapping in business and public administration, and in education: an overview. Educational Research 40(2): 219–35.

Lee-Corbin H (1996) Portraits of the able child: factors associated with achievement and under-achievement. Unpublished PhD thesis. University of Reading, UK.

Lee-Corbin H, Denicolo P (1998) Recognising and Supporting Able Children in Primary Schools. London: David Fulton Publishers Ltd.

Lincoln YS (1992) Sympathetic connections between qualitative methods and health research. Qualitative Health Research 2: 375–92.

Lincoln YS, Guba EG (1985) Naturalistic Enquiry. Beverley Hills, Ca: Sage.

Loughran J (1997) An introduction to purpose, passion and pedagogy. In Loughran J, Russell T (eds), Teaching about Teaching: Purpose, Passion and Pedagogy in Teacher Education. London: Falmer Press.

Loughran J (1997) Teaching about teaching: principles in practice. In Loughran J, Russell T (eds), Teaching about Teaching: Purpose, Passion and Pedagogy in Teacher Education. London: Falmer Press.

Lynch PA (1996) Alternative constructs of adolescent smoking – an enquiry into health education practice. Unpublished PhD Thesis, The University of Reading.

McEwan H, Egan K (eds) (1995) Narrative in Teaching, Learning and Research. New York: Teachers College Press.

Magee B (1973) Popper. London: Fontana.

Mahoney M (1988) Constructive metatheory. International Journal of Personal Construct Psychology 1: 1–36.

Mair JMM (1970) Psychologists are human too. In Bannister D (ed.), Perspectives in Personal Construct Theory. London and New York: Academic Press.

Mair JMM (1977) The community of self. In Bannister D (ed.), New Perspectives in Personal Construct Theory. London: Academic Press.

Mair JMM (1988) Psychology as story-telling, International Journal of Personal Construct Psychology 1(1): 125–37.

Mair JMM (1989) Kelly, Bannister and story telling psychology. International Journal of Personal Construct Psychology 2: 1–14.

Marsh G, Boulter C (1997) What do you mean, what scale is it?: three teacher/researchers investigate children's ideas of scale. Primary Science Review 50:12–14.

Marsh G, Boulter C (1998) What size is it really? three teacher/researchers investigate how children deal with representations of scale. Primary Science Review 53:11–14.

Marsh G, Willimont G, Boulter C (1999) Modelling the solar system. Primary Science Review 59: 24–6.

Martin JM, Kompf M (1996) Teaching in inclusive classroom settings: the use of journals and concept mapping techniques. In Kompf M, Bond WR, Dworet D, Boak RT (eds), Changing Research And Practice: Teachers' Professionalism, Identities and Knowledge. London: Falmer Press.

Mason J (1996) Qualitative Researching. London: Sage.

Mazhindu G (1995) Professional achievement in nurse education. Unpublished PhD thesis. University of Reading, UK.

Mazhindu G, Pope ML (1996) Interprofessional education in nursing. In Scheer, Catina (eds) Empirical Constructivism in Europe. Giessen: Psychosozial-Verlag, 260–7.

Mead GH (1934) Mind, Self and Society. Chicago: University of Chicago Press.

Memon M (1989) An illuminative study of curriculum changes in English language teaching and learning in Pakistan. Unpublished PhD thesis. University of Surrey, UK.

Merleau-Ponty M (1962) Phenomenology of Perception, London: Routledge & Kegan Paul.

Mezirow J (1981) A critical theory of adult learning and education. Adult Education 32(1).

Mezirow J (1990) Fostering Critical Reflection in Adulthood: a Guide to Transformative and Emancipatory Learning. San Francisco: Vassey Bass.

Miller P (1994) Perspectives on the recognition and resolution of dilemma within an educational framework. Unpublished PhD thesis: University of Surrey.

Morrison A, MacIntyre D (1973) Teachers and Teaching. London: Penguin.

Moses I (1985) Academic development units and the improvement of teaching. Higher Education 14: 75–100.

Neill AS (1964) Summerhill: A Radical Approach to Child-Rearing. New York: Holt, Rinehart & Winston.

Nelson MH (1993) Teachers' stories: an analysis of the themes. In Day C, Calderhead J, Denicolo P (eds), Research on Teacher Thinking: Understanding Professional Development. London: Falmer Press.

Novak J (1983) Personal construct theory and other perceptual pedagogies. In Adams-Webber J, Mancuso JC (eds), Applications of Personal Construct Theory. London: Academic Press.

Novak JD (1995) The use of metacognitive tools to facilitate meaningful learning and the construction of knowledge. Paper presented at the 11th International Conference on Personal Construct Psychology, Barcelona, July.

Novak JD (1998) Learning, Creating and Using Knowledge – Concept Maps as Facilitative Tools in Schools and Corporations. Mahwah, New Jersey: Lawrence Erlbaum Associates.

Novak JD (ed.) (1987) Proceedings of the 2nd International Seminar: Misconceptions and Educational Strategies in Science and Mathematics. Ithaca, NY: Cornell University Press.

Novak JD, Gowin DB (1984) Learning How to Learn. New York: Cambridge University Press.

Nuffield Primary Science (1995) The Earth in Space: 7–12. Teachers Guide. London: Collins.

Nussbaum M (1985) Aeschylus and practical conflict. Ethics 95: 233-67.

Nystedt L, Magnusson D (1982) Construction of experience. In Mancuso J, Adams Webber J (eds), The Construing Person. New York: Praeger Publishers.

Oberg AA (1989) The ground of professional practice. In Lowyck J, Clark CM (eds), Teacher Thinking and Professional Action. Leuven: Leuven University Press.

Olson JK (1992) Understanding Teaching. Milton Keynes: Open University Press.

Osborne R, Gilbert J (1980) A Technique for exploring students' views of the world. Physics Education 15(6): 376–9.

Parla-Petrou E (personal communication)

Patton MQ (1990) Qualitative Evaluation and Research Methods, 2nd edn. London: Sage.

Pfundt H, Duit R (1994).Bibliography: Student Alternative Frameworks and Science Education. Kiel: Institute of Education, University of Kiel.

Piaget J (1954) The Construction of Reality in Children. Trans Cook M. New York: Basic Books.

Polanyi M (1958) Personal Knowledge. Chicago: University of Chicago Press.

Pope ML (1978) Monitoring and reflecting in teacher training. In Fransella F (ed.), Personal Construct Psychology 1977. London: Academic Press.

Pope ML (1981) In true spirit: constructive alternativism in educational research. Paper presented at Fourth International Congress on Personal Construct Psychology, Brock University, St Catherine's, Canada.

Pope ML (1990) Academic staff development: a constructivist perspective and research-on-action. Address to the Finnish National Higher Education Symposium, Finland.

Pope ML, Denicolo PM (1986) Intuitive theories – a researcher's dilemma: some practical methodological implications. British Educational Research Journal 12: 153–65.

Pope ML, Denicolo PM (1991) Developing constructive action: personal construct psychology research and professional development. In Zuber-Skerritt O (ed.), Action Research for Change and Development. Aldershot: Avebury.

Pope ML, Denicolo PM (1993) The art and science of constructivist research in teacher thinking. Teacher and Teacher Education 9(5–6): 529–44.

Pope ML, Denicolo PM (1997) Student career decision making: a constructivist approach. Paper presented at British Education Association conference, York, September 1997.

Pope ML, Gilbert JK (1985) Constructive science education. In Epting F, Landfield A (eds), Anticipating Personal Construct Psychology. University of Nebraska Press, 111–27.

Pope ML, Fuller M, Boulter C, Denicolo P, Wells P (1999) Partnership and Colloration in Education. In Lang M, Olson J, Buendger W (eds), Teachers Professional Development: Changes in Teachers' Practice and Working Environment. London: Falmer Press.

Pope ML, Keen TR (1981) Personal Construct Psychology and Education, London: Academic Press.

Pope ML, Saka RC (1997) The learning of English as a foreign language: a personal constructivist approach. In Denicolo P, Pope ML (eds) Sharing, Understanding and Practice. Farnborough: EPCA Publications.

Pope ML, Scott EM (1984) Teachers' epistemology and practice. In Halkes R, Olson JK (eds), Teacher Thinking: New Perspectives on Persisting Problems in Education. Lisse: Swets Zeitlinger.

Pope ML, Watts DM (1988) Constructivist goggles: implications for process in teaching and learning physics. Eur. J. Physics 9: 101–9.

Pope ML, Yeung KW (1996) Thinking about stress: the student teachers' viewpoint. In Kompf M, Bond WR, Dworet D, Boak RT (eds), Changing Research and Practice, Teachers' Professionalism, Identities and Knowledge. London: Falmer Press.

Popper K (1963) Conjectures and Reputations: The Growth of Scientific Knowledge. London: Routledge & Kegan Paul.

Popper K (1970) Normal science and its dangers. In Lakatos I, Musgrave A (eds), Criticisms and the Growth of Knowledge. Cambridge: Cambridge University Press.

Postman N, Weingartner L (1971) Teaching as a Subversive Activity. London: Penguin.

Priestley P, McQuire J, Flegg D, Hemsley V, Welham D (1978) Social Skills and Personal Problem Solving. London: Tavistock.

Quinn A (1999) The use of experiential learning to help social work students assess their attitudes towards practice with older people. Social Work Education 18(2): 171–82.

Quinn A (personal communication).

Ravenette AT (1997) Tom Ravenette: Selected Papers, PCP and the Practice of an Educational Psychologist. Farnborough: EPCA.

Reason P, Rowan J (eds) (1981) Human Inquiry: A Source Book of New Paradigm Research. Chichester: John Wiley & Son.

Reidford P (1972) Educational Research. In Weinberg C (ed.), Humanistic Foundations of Education. New Jersey: Prentice Hall Inc.

Reimer E (1971) School is Dead. London: Penguin.

Richart A (1997) Teaching teachers for the challenge of change. In Loughran J, Russell T (eds), Teaching about Teaching: Purpose, Passion and Pedagogy in Teacher Education. London: Falmer Press.

Rickman HP (ed. and transl.) (1976) W. Dilthey-Selected Writings. Cambridge: Cambridge University Press.

Roberts J (personal communication).

Rogers C (1961) On Becoming a Person. London: Constable and Co.

Rogers C (1965) Client-Centred Therapy. Boston: Houghton-Mifflin.

Rogers C (1969) Freedom to Learn: A View of What Education Might Become. Columbus, Ohio: Charles E. Merril.

Rogers C (1983) Freedom to Learn for the 80s. Columbus Ohio: Charles E. Merril.

Rose P (1983) Parallel Lives. New York: Vintage Books.

Ruddock J (1992) Practitioner research and programs of initial teacher education. In Russell T, Munby H (eds) Teachers and Teaching. London: Falmer Press.

Rudduck J, Chaplain R, Wallace G (1996) School Improvement: What Can Pupils Tell Us. London: David Fulton.

Russell T, McGuigan L, Hughes A (1998) Primary Space Project Research Report: Forces. Liverpool: Liverpool University Press.

Saka R (1995) The teaching and learning of English as a foreign language: a constructivist approach. Unpublished PhD thesis. University of Reading, UK.

Salmon P (1984) Classroom Collaboration. London: Routledge & Kegan Paul.

Salmon P, Bannister D (1974) Education in the light of personal construct theory. Education for Teaching 94: 25–38.

Sartre J-P (1947) Existentialism. New York: Philosophica Library.

Schon DA (1983) The Reflective Practitioner: How Professionals Think in Action. New York: Basic Books.

Schon DA (1987) Educating the Reflective Practitioner: Towards a New Design for Teaching and Learning in the Professions. San Francisco: Jossey-Bass.

Schools Council (1980) Learning Through Science: Science 5/13. London: Macdonald Educational.

Schutz A (1967) The Phenomenology of the Social World. Evanston: North Western University Press.

Schwandt TA (1994) Constructivist, interpretavist approaches to human inquiry. In Denzin N, Lincoln YS (eds), Handbook of Qualitative Research. London: Sage.

Sendan FC (1995) Patterns of Development in EFL student teachers' personal theories: a constructivist approach. Unpublished PhD. University of Reading, UK.

Sexton R, Denicolo PM (1997) Formative critical incidents in early professional life – a stimulated recall approach. In Denicolo PM, Pope ML (eds), Sharing, Understanding and Practice. Farnborough: EPCA.

Shaw MLG (1980) On Becoming a Personal Scientist. London: Academic Press.

Shaw MLG (1993) RepGrid 2. Calgary: Centre for Personal Computer Studies.

Silberman CE (1971) Crisis in the Classroom: Remaking of American Education. New York: Vintage Press.

Skinner BF (1968) The Technology of Teaching. New York: Appleton-Century-Crofts.

Skinner BF (1971) Beyond Freedom and Dignity. London: Jonathan Cape.

Slater P (Ed) (1977) The Measurement of Intrapersonal Space by Grid Technique: Dimensions of Intrapersonal Space. Chichester: Wiley.

Smith D, Neale D (1989) The construction of subject matter knowledge in primary science teaching. Teaching and Teacher Education 5(1): 1–20.

Smyth J (ed.) 1995 Critical Discourses on Teacher Development. London: Cassell.

Snow RE (1974) Representative and quasi-representative designs for research on teaching. Rev Educ Res. 44: 265–91.

Stenhouse L (1975) An Introduction to Curriculum Research. London: Heinemann Educational.

Stewart J (1980) Techniques for assessing representing information in cognitive structure, Science Education 63(3): 223–33.

Stewart V, Stewart A (1981) Business Applications of the Repertory Grid. London: McGraw Hill Book Co. Ltd.

Stringer P, Bannister D (eds) (1979) Constructs of Sociality in Individuality. London: Academic Press.

Sullivan HS (1953) In Perry HS, Gawel ML (eds), The Interpersonal Theory of Psychiatry. New York: Norton.

Sutton C (1981) Making sense of new ideas. In Sutton C (ed.), Communication in Classroom. London: Hodder & Stoughton.

Sutton CR (1981) Metaphorical imagery: a means of coping with complex and unfamiliar information in Science. Durham and Newcastle Research Review 9 (46).

Swift DJ (1987) Curricula philosophy and students' personal epistemologies of science. Unpublished PhD thesis. University of Surrey, UK.

Taylor SJ, Bogdan R (1998) An Introduction to Qualitative Research Methods. New York: John Wiley and Sons.

Thomas L (1995) The Medusa and the Snail: More Notes for Biology Watchers. Viking Penguin.

Thomas LF and Harri-Augstein S (1985) Self Organised Learning: Foundations of a Conversational Science of Psychology. London: Routledge & Kegan Paul.

Thomaz M (1986) Towards a constructivist model for science teacher education. Unpublished PhD. Guildford, University of Surrey, UK.

Tjok-a-Tam S (1994) Learning-in-action in management development: the facilitation of self-created learning opportunities. Unpublished PhD thesis, the University of Surrey.

Turner S (1992) Teaching and Learning about Food: A Study of Curriculum Change in Nutrition Education on Primary Schools. London: Institute of Education, University of London.

Von Glaserfeld E (1984) An introduction to Radical Constructivism. In Watzlawick P. (ed.), The Invented Reality. New York: Norton, 18–40.

Watts DM (1983) A study of alternative frameworks in school science. Unpublished PhD thesis. Guildford, University of Surrey, UK.

Watts DM, Pope M (1989) Thinking about thinking, learning about learning: constructivism in physics education. Physics Education 24(3/6): 331.

Watts M, Vaz A (1997) Freire meets Kelly: using constructs to generate themes in education. In Denicolo P, Pope M (eds), Sharing, Understanding and Practice. Farnborough: EPCA Publications.

Whyte WF (1991) Participatory Action Research. London: Sage.

Woods P (1985) Conversations with teachers: some aspects of life-history method. British Educational Research Journal 11: 13–25.

Wragg GC (1974) Teaching Teaching. Newton Abbott: David & Charles.

Yeung KW (1992) The use of repertory grid technique to study student teacher stress. Unpublished MA thesis, the University of Reading, UK.

Zeichner KM (1981) Reflective teaching and field-based experiences in teacher education. Interchange 12: 1–22.

Zylbersztajn A (1983) A conceptual framework for science education: investigating curricula materials and classroom interaction in secondary school physics. Unpublished PhD thesis, University of Surrey, UK.

Index

accommodation, 10
accounts, use of, 100
accumulative fragmentalism (Kelly), 29, 58
action research, 43, 63, 64, 86, 189
  models, 62
  spiral, 62–3
  see also teacher/teaching
adult learners, 47; *see also* student nurses; student teachers
agency, 33
alienation, school as reinforcer of, 15
alternative frameworks, 134–5
analysis, 82–90
  cluster analysis, 83–4
  cluster diagram, 160
  factor analysis, 82, 83
  FOCUS, 83, 86
  illuminative incident analysis, 108–10, 136
  INGRID, 83
  principal component analysis, 83–4
  SOCIOGRID, 87
  and see repertory grid
anecdotes, use of, 104–5
anticipation, 35, 95, chapter 9 passim;
  see also prediction
anxiety, 34
assimilation, 10
associationism, 5
Ausubel, D.P., 11
authenticity, 60–1
autobiography, 104–5; *see also* self-characterization

behaviourism, 4, 5–6, 25
  behaviour modification, 4, 24
'Black Box' approach *see* behaviourism
body/mind dualism, 28
Bruner, J., 10–11
Buber, M., 14

career snakes, 111, 112, 113
categorization, 10
  relativity of (Kelly), 31
change, 197–8
  regulated, 37
  resistance to *see* hostility
choice corollary (Kelly), 59
Clandinin, D.J., 26
cognitions, 10
  proactive, 43
cognitive conflict, 9
cognitive development, 5
cognitive rehearsal, 180
cognitive structure, 5
  hierarchical, 11
collaborative enquiry, 61
commonality corollary (Kelly), 26, 134
communication, 12
  failure of, 14, 15
computer programs *see* FOCUS; INGRID; NUDIST*4; RepGrid 2
concept maps, mapping (Novak), 115–18, 137–40
conceptual change, development, 34–9
conceptualization, 10, 11
confidentiality, 126
connecting threads, 111, 112–13,

198–202
consciousness raising, 100
construal, construing, 28
constructs, 36, 66–7, 96–7
    cluster, 37
    core, 40
    definition of, 66
    elicitation, 73–9, 97; triadic method
        (minimum context form), 74, 75,
        154, 167, 182
    incompatible, 39
    naïve, 134
    organization of, 67
    permeability of, 37, 38
    personal, 35
    splitting, 74
Constructive Alternativism, 28–9, 43,
    55–64
constructivism, 24, 31–4, 43, 61
contingency theory, 5
contracts, 67–71, 125
    contract learning, 8
control, 47
    bilateral, 61
conversation
    'conversational model' (Mair), 50
    repertory grid interview as, 67, 75
critical reflection, 18; and see also under
    reflection
culture
    constructed, 182
    cultural transmission, 4–6
curriculum
    change, 176
    development, 31–2

Dartington Hall, as 'school without
    walls', 13; and see de-schooling
de-schooling, 13–15
determinism, 5
    environmental, 10
development
    conceptual, 38
    emotional, 6
    professional, 192–6
Dewey, J., 9, 10, 12, 15
dialogue, 202–3
diaries, 103–4

Dilthey, W., 22, 104, 112
discipline, self-directed, 17
dogmatism, 18–19, 55–64
drawings, use of 109; see also stimulated
    recall; visual/pictorial stimuli

education
    for domestication (Freire), 17
    emancipatory, 17
    ideologies, theories of, 3
    negative (Rousseau), 6
    personal   construct   psychology
        approaches in, chapter 2 passim
    research, 50–1, chapter 3 passim
    sociology of, 31
    structural analysis of, 26
    see also de-schooling
elements, homogeneity of, 73–9 and see
    repertory grid
emergent pole see repertory grid analysis
empiricism, British, 10
empowerment, 17, 63, 185
'Empty Organism' approach see behav-
    iourism
epistemology, 55, 164–5, 166
ethics, ethical framework, 125–7
existentialism, 14, 28
experience, 129–30

facilitation, 47
feedback, 89, 152, 154
Fight for Education (Black Paper), 5
fixation, 7
Fixed Role Therapy (Kelly), 40, 44
    Fixed Role Methods, 40, 41
Flanders Interaction Categories, 48–9
FOCUS (computer program), 83, 86,
    158, 167, 171, 182
folklore, 8
fragmentation corollary (Kelly), 37, 38–9
free will, 5
Freire, P., 17, 182
Freud, S., 7, 8

generalization, 59
    context-free, 63
goodness, 6
growing theory, 99

Habermas, J., 17, 62
Heidegger, M., 16
holism and qualitative research, 61
hostility, 34, 38, 44
humanism, 6, 15, 16–18, 54
hypothesis
    testing, 39, 49, 57, 63
    working, 59

idealism, 7
Illich, I., 13, 15
images (Clandinin), 26
implicit pole *see* repertory grid analysis
inconsistency, 38
individuality corollary (Kelly), 26, 30, 36
INGRID (computer program), 83
INSET *see* professional development and
    training
instrumentalism, 4–6
interpretativism, 60
interview
    focus group, 143
    interviews about instances, 110–11,
        133–6
'invitational mood' (Kelly), 91

James, W., 10
journals, reflective, 103–4, 179

Kant, I., 7
Kelly, G., 2
    career of, 23–4
    meta-theory, 18
    and see passim and under accumula-
        tive fragmentalism, categorization;
        commonality corollary; construc-
        tive alternativism; 'invitational
        mood'; man: the scientist; modu-
        lation corollary; organization
        corollary; personal construct psy-
        chology, personal construct
        theory; repertory grid analysis;
        sociality corollary; universe of dis-
        course
Kierkegaard, S., 15
knowledge
    as construction of reality, 56
    impersonal, 14

objective, 5
phenomenological, 14
private, personal, 16, 27, 53
professional, 175
public, 16, 27
relativity of, 28–33
sociology of, 31
stock of, 31
subjective, 52
theories of, passivist vs activist
    (Lakatos), 58
transmission of, 14
true, 7
Kuhn, T., 30

labels, 71–2
laddering, 80, 124, 167
Laing, R.D., 16
learner
    -learner interaction, 10
    as scientist, chapter 7 passim
learning
    active, 103
    cycle (Kolb and Fry), 62
    by doing, 15
    emancipatory (Habermas) 17
    guided, 5
    to learn, 10
    learner-based, 16
    lifelong, 2, 13, 18–21
    as personal exploration, 27
    reflective, 154
    self-directed, self-discovered, 8, 16,
        49
    teacher-based, 16
Lebensfelt, 31
life history, 104
listening, 121–3
Locke, J., 5
logs, 100, 101–2

man as machine, 5, 56; *see also* metaphor
man the scientist (Kelly), 25, 29, 35, 41,
    57
maturation
    biological, 10
    maturational theory, 7
'McFalls Mystical Monitor', 130

Mead, G.H., 12
meaning-making, 26
meaning-seeking, 56
Merleau-Ponty, M., 16, 111
metaphor
  psychological, 25
  story-telling, 64–5
  uses of, 98–100, 114, 180
Mezirow, J., 17–18, 127
micro-teaching, 49, 52
modulation corollary (Kelly), 37
morphogenic nuclear structure, 43
motivation, 9
  theories of, 25

narrative
  professional, 95
  techniques, 93–106
  see also story telling
naturalism, 58–9
NUDIST*4 (computer program), 141
nurse education, 193

operant reinforcement, 5; and see behaviourism
organism-environment interaction, 10
organization corollary (Kelly), 35–6, 67

participation, collaborative, 64
perception, 10, 11
permeability, 41
person as machine, 56
person as scientist, 199
person-as-storyteller, 64
personal, the, 25
  perspective of, 24–7, 51
personal construct psychology in education, chapter 2 passim
Personal Construct Theory, 2, 23; see also analysis; constructive alternativism; construal/construing; constructs; Kelly; narrative; repertory grid
Personal Construction Knowledge Group, 133
phenomenology, 14, 50, 140
philosophy of science, 30

Piaget, J., 10
Plato, 7
Popper, K., 30, 128
positivism, 50
Postman, N., 13, 15, 27
pragmatism, 10, 29
praxis, 63
  emancipatory, 59
prediction, 35, 111
problem-solving, experiential, 9
process description, 100
professional development, continuing, 18–21, 192–6
progressivism, 7, 8, 9–13, 18, 26
psychoanalytic theory, 7
psychology, hard vs. soft, 54
psychometry, 51, 59
purpose, 67–71
pyramiding, 80; cf. laddering

radical constructivism (Von Glaserfeld), 58
range of convenience, 38, 41
realism, 5, 29
reality, 10
  constructions of, 25, 29, 56
  external, 33, 34
  spiritual, 7
reflection, 127
  reflection-in-action, 95
  reflection-on-action, 95
  reflective learning, 154
  reflective practitioner, 43
regard, 17
reinforcement, scheduled, 5–6
relevance, 27–8
reliability, 60
repertory grid, 36, 40
  analysis 82–90
  application extractive mode, 71
  application, reflective mode, 71
  case studies: English as a Foreign Language, 146–7, 168–9, 184–6; health education, 148–50; music improvisation, 143–4; nurse education, 194; reflective learning, 154–5; science education, 137–40,

140–2; teacher effectiveness, 180–3; TEACL, 176–8; tertiary education, 175–6; under-achievers, 150–1
conversation, 74–5
elements, 68, 72; choice of, 71–3
element trees (examples), 160, 161
elicitation, 67, 70, 72; flow diagram,79; group, 81; postal, 82
interview as conversation, 68
purpose, 67–71
ranked, 76–7
rating scales, 77
techniques, chapter 4 passim
RepGrid 2 (computer program), 70, 145, 167, 171
representation, 25, 93
research
  action, 43, 62–3, 64, 86, 189
  aims of, 50
  co-operative, 54
  diary, 101
  educational, 22, 48
  qualitative, 55–64
  spiral (Kemmis and McTaggart), 63
  systematic, 48
resistance, 44
responsibility, 27–8
river of experience, 111, 144–5, 155, 184
Rogers, C., 16–17, 27
role construct, 66
role play, 149
role theory, 12
Romanticism, 6–8
Rousseau, J.-J., 6, 8, 13, 15

Sartre, J.-P., 14, 16
Schon, D.A., 17, 62
'school without walls', 13
science education, 39–43, 133–42, 165–6, 186–8
scientist-subject distinction, 50
self-characterization, 53, 105–6, 149, 152, 190
self-organization, 33
  self-organizing development, 43
sense impressions, 7

shaping theory, 99
signs, non-verbal, 122
Silberman, C.E., 13
Skinner, B.F., 5–6
snake technique, 111, 112, 113–14, 168, 169, 175
social development, 12
social phenomenology (Schutz), 31
social power, 41
social science, new paradigm research approach, 61
sociality corollary (Kelly), 28, 36–7
SOCIOGRID analysis, 87, 171
staff development, 188
Stanley-Hall, G.S., 7, 13
stimulated recall, 107–8, 143
stimulus-response psychology, 5, 25
story telling, 178
  psychology as (Mair), 64, 96
'strategies for survival', 15
student teachers, 158–73
  stress, 169–73
  subjective theories of, 162
  teaching behaviour, 162
subjectivity, 162
Summerhill, as 'school without walls', 13; and see de-schooling
survival strategies, 32
symbolic interactionism, 12
systematic observation schedules, 48–9

transfer theory, 99
teacher
  appraisal, 188–92
  as constructivist, 43–5
  demands on, 19–20
  education, 1, 20–1
  effectiveness, assessment of, 48, 84–6
  as facilitator, 35
  as guide, 9, 11
  -learner interaction, 10
  perceptive, chapter 8 passim
  professional development, 182,192–6
  as researcher, 20
  role of, 14–15, 33–4, 37
teaching
  beliefs about, 168

conceptual change in, 39
theory testing, 35
transfer theory, 99
transformation, chapter 9 passim
travelling theory, 99
triangulation, 126
truth, 4, 125
    absolute, 5, 31
    coherentist theory of, 64
    cultural, 4
    nuggets of, 18, 29

universe of discourse (Kelly), 68
utility, 59

validity, 60
Verstehen, 60, 92
visual/pictorial stimuli, 107–18
vocabulary, and construct system, 123–4

Weingartner, C., 13, 14, 27
whole person system, 38
world view, 57
    construction of, 35
    invalidation of, 34
    and language use, 8, 17